Wise Women

INVEST IN
REAL
ESTATE

Achieve Financial
Independence and Live the
Lifestyle of Your Dreams

Lisa Moren Bromma

McGraw-Hill

New York   Chicago   San Francisco   Lisbon   London
Madrid   Mexico City   Milan   New Delhi   San Juan
Seoul   Singapore   Sydney   Toronto

1 2 3 4 5 6 7 8 9 0   FGR/FGR   0 9 8 7 6

ISBN-13: 978-0-0-07-147684-3
ISBN-10: 0-07-147684-9

Contents

Acknowledgments   vii

Introduction   ix

Chapter 1   Why Women *Inherently* Make
Great Real Estate Investors   1

Chapter 2   Preparing to Succeed: Getting
Your Financials in Order   25

Chapter 3   What Type of Property Do You Want to Invest In?
Determining Your Investing Strategy   47

Chapter 4   Research Your Target Market   75

Chapter 5   Rehabbing and Other Short-Term
Investing Strategies   93

Chapter 6   Working with Real Estate Agents: A Professioal
Source to Help You Find Property   115

Chapter 7   Winning Negotiation Strategies for Women   131

Chapter 8   Rental Property Management:
What Every Investor Must Know   163

Chapter 9   Mortgage Financing and Tax Strategies   203

Chapter 10   When and How to Sell and How to
Stage a Property for Resale   239

Contents

Chapter 11   Buying Properties in a Down Market   259

Chapter 12   For Realtors Only: You Can Be Both
an Agent and an Investor   283

Chapter 13   Final Words of Wisdom: How to Be a
Successful Real Estate Investor   301

Appendix A   Recommended Resources   321

Appendix B   Background on the Women
Interviewed for This Book   327

Index   331

Acknowledgments

This book would not have been possible without the wonderful women who agreed to be interviewed, to share their stories and experiences and to give this book a voice. Many thanks to Barbara O'Connell; Tami Spaulding; Anna Mills; Renee Falgout; Tracy Rewey; Jennifer Dizmang; Dorliss Ware; Magi Bird, Jamie Raskulinecz and Rebecca McLean.

I especially want to acknowledge my husband Hubert Bromma; without his support and guidance this book would not have been possible.

And finally, to you my reader. This book is for you and was made possible by the many women who have sat through my presentations and seminars. You asked that I write this to help those who wish to use the tools and roadmaps in this book so you too can accomplish dreams you never thought possible through having a portfolio of real estate that you know, understand and can control.

Please e-mail me and let me know how you are doing with your new venture! I would love to hear from you.

All the best,
Lisa Moren Bromma
mailto:lbromma@theentrustgroup.com

Introduction

There has never been a better time to invest in real estate: although as I write this, interest rates are somewhat unstable, we are at an interest rate of around 7 percent, and everyone is concerned about the economy, real estate still makes sense as a part of every woman's portfolio. We need to be in a position to take control of our investments, plan for our retirement, and accumulate wealth. We need to not only manage our financial future but live our dreams. Real estate is an excellent vehicle to help us achieve our dreams.

When the stock market crashed in 1929, those who continued to have wealth were invested in real estate. No matter what sort of cycle real estate goes through, if you hold property for the long term, it will eventually come back and appreciate even more. Yes, volatility in the economy makes a difference for a short-term strategy. But over time, real estate has been the most stable asset you can have in your portfolio.

According to the *Economist*, 23 percent of all property bought in 2004 was for investment purposes, and another 13 percent was second homes, which can also be considered investment property. Real estate investments are consistent. You can see, feel, and touch property, unlike a stock. You have control over whether you want to buy and sell it, buy and hold it, or fix it up for resale. The opportunities are enormous for those who take advantage of them.

Many investors buy a few properties, hold them for the long term, and collect monthly checks from their tenants. Some successful investors may decide to trade up to nicer-quality properties. Others become so passionate about real estate that they actually develop a business around it.

Introduction

As a real estate investor for almost 30 years, I have learned the value of real estate and have made it work for my portfolio. I've taught more than 1,000 workshops and seminars on the subject. Over the years, I have met thousands of women Realtors through my association with NAR (the National Association of Realtors), women who have property management businesses through NAA (the National Apartment Association), and women investors through NREIA (the National Real Estate Investors Association). In addition, there are millions of women business owners who would love to learn more about real estate as an investment for compounding their wealth. I believe that women make great real estate investors.

I've always wanted to write a book that would help more women learn how to invest and grow rich in real estate. Real estate is a perfect vehicle for women: with a little education and the right road map, you can master some simple techniques that will allow you to take control of this part of your portfolio by acquiring investments that you already know, understand, and have control over. Yes, this is more hands-on than investing in the stock market, but real estate can be a great opportunity to put your children through college, build your own nest egg, start a business, develop a retirement vehicle, save on taxes, and be successful in what was, at one time, a predominantly male-oriented field.

My main goal for this book is to teach women the techniques for finding, financing, holding, and selling property; earning cash flow and income along the way; and gaining the financial freedom you, the reader, need to pursue so you can move forward with financial freedom to set the path necessary for you to accomplish the important dreams you have for yourself, your family, and your future. I think of real estate as the guaranteed income portion of my earnings. Jobs can come and go, the stock market can take dramatic swings, but in real estate, even if the market goes down (which for me spells opportunity), my income can rise if I raise rents.

Although this book is intended to be "for women only," the information and advice contained in the following pages are applicable to both men and women. All of the success stories are from women who have been successful in all aspects of real estate investing:

- Buying and selling single-family residential properties, apartment buildings, and commercial property
- Rehabbing and renovating
- Holding for the long term and renting to tenants
- Buying mortgage notes
- Staging property for maximum resale value
- Doing property management, either for their own properties or for others as a business

I wrote this book because I believe that if I could be successful, so can anybody else. When I bought my first piece of property, I didn't have a clue as to what I was doing. I learned as I went, with no "how-to" book or guidance or mentor. Today, close to 30 years later, I have bought, held, and sold single-family homes, town homes, land, mobile-home parks, small commercial buildings, and multifamily units. I have traded a van for a private mortgage loan; bartered and exchanged for other property; done lease options, flips, wrap-arounds, and tax lien sales; and bought at auction. It has been a wild ride, one that was filled with excitement, and at times it felt as if I was on a roller coaster. I have learned a lot, and I hope to be able to share these ideas with you so that you too can enjoy the flexibility and freedom that real estate can bring, thanks to your own efforts.

If I Can Do It, You Can, Too

In 1978, I was in my twenties and single, with two young kids, and I moved to Florida. I had never owned property before, but I decided that we would be better off owning instead of renting. I found a home in an area that was affordable for me at the time. I negotiated the price with the broker, who was also the owner of the property. This was back in the days when interest rates were very high, and I felt that I had negotiated a great deal for myself: only a $1,000 down payment, with $39,000 financed by the owner, at 12½ percent interest, for 30 years. I had no credit; I was new to Florida and had just started a job. The real estate broker took a chance on me.

My children and I lived in that property for five years, until 1983, when I sold that property for $43,900. That was my introduction to investing in real estate. With no experience, I had been able to buy a piece of real estate with only $1,000 and to convince the owner to finance the sale for me so that I didn't have to get a mortgage from a bank (which I probably wouldn't have been able to do at that stage, because I had no credit). When I sold the property for a profit five years later, I took that profit and bought another piece of real estate.

And that's how my real estate career started. At first, I bought and sold several properties for my family to live in, but after only a few years, I bought my first rental property. With close to 30 years' experience, I have had the opportunity to do dozens of transactions in different regions of the United States and abroad. My goal has always been to retire and live off the income and cash flow that these properties could generate.

How this Book Can Help *You* Invest in Real Estate Successfully

You don't need to be a rocket scientist or even have an education to be successful in real estate. Yes, you need to learn the basics, which this book provides, and more. After reading *Wise Women Invest in Real Estate*, you will know

- Why women have the right natural talents and skills to be great real estate investors (see Chapter 1)
- How to prepare yourself financially before you start investing (see Chapter 2)
- What type of property you want to invest in (see Chapter 3)
- How to research the market that interests you before you buy (see Chapter 4)
- What you need to know about rehabbing and other short-term investment strategies (see Chapter 5)
- How to work effectively with a real estate agent to help you find good properties (see Chapter 6)
- How to negotiate like a pro—and why women are especially good at this (see Chapter 7)
- Whether you want to be a landlord or to hire a property manager to handle your rental properties (see Chapter 8)
- What you need to know about mortgages, other financing strategies, and how to defer taxes on real estate (see Chapter 9)

- When and how to sell to get the best price for your property (see Chapter 10)
- What to do when the real estate market is volatile: how investors can use lease options, "subject-to" arrangements, short sales, and foreclosures (see Chapter 11)
- How to move into investing if you're currently a real estate agent (and how to be both; see Chapter 12)
- How to be really successful in real estate investing (see Chapter 13)

The book includes a number of checklists giving valuable information that you should keep in mind on each of these topics. And it features countless stories of women who have been successful at buying, renting out, and selling different types of properties. You'll read about women—of all ages; who are single, married, divorced, or widowed; of all races and income backgrounds (from privileged to middle class to downright poor)—and how they made money in real estate. You will read stories of successful women investors from rehabbers in California to wholesalers in Michigan; every real estate strategy has a story and a lesson behind it. And I've included a few horror stories along the way, so you'll know what pitfalls to avoid so that you don't end up broke. I also interviewed many experienced women working in various aspects of the real estate industry—Realtors, investors, property managers, and more—all of whom have used numerous and diverse strategies to make money in real estate. You'll read their ideas throughout the book (and detailed bios of these women are provided at the end of the book).

Finally, this book can help you even if you've never owned property, not even the home you're currently living in. For example, Jill is a successful real estate investor in Sarasota, Florida. She rents the home she lives in and has been there for the last 25 years—yet she owns 20 investment properties around the country. She leases her personal residence because it's on the water in a magnificent area. The rent on the property hasn't kept up with the price of houses in the area, and she would never pay what it's really worth today. And because her rent is so much less than what a mortgage on a comparable house would be, she's been able to invest successfully in other properties all over the United States.

Similarly, there are other people living in regions where it makes more sense to rent than to buy their primary residence—for example, in New York City or Santa Monica, California, where there's rent control and properties are so expensive that many people can't afford to buy. Or in Marin County, California, where the median price is almost $1 million—and that's for a 1,700-square-foot small square box. So when you look at those areas, many people would prefer to rent because the mortgage payment on a house like that is going to be more than $5,000 a month. So if you rent your residence in such areas, that may enable you to buy in an area of the country where property costs less, if it makes financial sense to do that.

In short, *Wise Women Invest in Real Estate* is a guide to help you assess what makes the most financial sense as a way for you to build wealth. Real estate should be one facet of your investing portfolio. So let's get started and find out how to do it well.

1

Why Women *Inherently* Make Great Real Estate Investors

During almost 30 years of investing in real estate, I have rarely run into women who have been successful as real estate investors. I've never understood why there were not more women in the field. Most of the successful investors I've met share similar qualities—qualities that come naturally to women. This chapter takes a look at why women make great real estate investors—and then looks at why there aren't more. I will also offer some suggestions for how you can become empowered and knowledgeable about real estate investing.

Reason 1: Women Are Good Listeners

People love to talk. I don't mean to sound sexist, but when you get together with a group of people and listen to them talking, you'll see that women tend to be better listeners than men. We can devote our full attention to an individual and to getting a person's story. We make great negotiators because of our listening skills. People tend to open up more to women, and this gives us an advantage when we're looking for potential real estate investments. By being a better listener and not saying a lot, you allow the other party to open up and give you information that could be critical in your buying of real estate.

For example, a couple of years ago, I bought a property in California that was a great investment. The sellers sold it to me even though they met with two other potential investors on the same day. The other investors were men, and neither one of them got anywhere with the sellers because they didn't take the time to listen to the sellers' needs. Here's what happened.

There was a property for sale in one of the neighborhoods that I had targeted as potential areas for buying real estate. I went to see it. I happened to be out looking at properties with two other investors, and I suggested that we all go and take a look. The property had been on the market about a month, and the seller had a fair asking price.

We arrived at the house and met the owners, who were a couple in their late forties to mid-fifties. The investors I was with just walked in, looked around, and said, "When do you need to move? When do you need to close? How much money do you need?" It was obvious to me that the woman felt bombarded and somewhat intimidated.

The couple had a very small house, with nice livable space. The wife was a very quiet person. I wanted to find out her motivation for selling and make her feel comfortable with me. I noticed that she had a massage table, so I asked her if she was a massage therapist, and she said, yes, she did that on the side, and that her husband was an accountant. She told me that she loved doing massage and that she was into yoga and Zen and Feng Shui. I had also noticed that a lot of her art and furnishings were Asian. She had mirrors in every single room, so I asked her why, and she explained that mirrors were a principle of Feng Shui. She sat down and became more relaxed, so I sat down on the couch and continued talking to her.

Then I said, "Well, you have a lovely home; why do you want to sell it?" And she started telling me that she and her husband wanted to relocate to the wine country. She told me about the peace that the move would bring, the escape from the hectic pace of the city, and the fun of rehabbing an old Victorian home that would be theirs. She said that she and her husband were ready to retire, and her husband wasn't in the best of health; they wanted to live in a warmer and drier climate. An old Victorian home in the perfect location had come on the market. They couldn't buy this property until they sold their existing home. Look at how much information she'd already given me about her motivation to sell!

I was interested in finding out more about the house and exploring possibilities to help the seller and to buy the property for the right price. I sat there while my friends went outside to wait until I was through with my discussions.

People tend to open up more to women,
and this gives us an advantage when we're looking
for potential real estate investments.

In the end, I was there about 45 minutes. I didn't make an offer; I didn't even ask her how much she needed (which was the first question my fellow investors had asked her when they walked into the house!). I just let her chat and tell me all the reasons why she wanted to move away from where she was, and what she didn't like about the neighborhood. The latter is very important if you're a real estate investor, because you may be able to glean information from the seller that tells you why you might not want to buy the property. Information like this can be valuable, as is information about any problems with the property. The more you let the seller talk, the more you can find out what you need to know to assess the property and make the right offer. I believe women overall do a much better job than men do of visiting with the seller and making that person feel comfortable. We seem to have this built into our genetic makeup.

I did buy the property. The seller never followed up with the other two investors, but I followed up with her. She did leave the property listed, so other people were looking at it, but I didn't feel like, "Oh my God, I have to hurry up and make an offer today or I'm going to lose this deal"—I never feel that way. Instead, I walk in, and I simply try to make conversation with the seller—*I listen* to what the seller has to say. It may take two or three visits with somebody to be able to do this.

In this case, I went back two more times. We discussed the couple's needs and what the timeline for relocation was. I learned what would make the couple happy and was able to decide that this was something that would be profitable and fit my needs. By spending the time and developing rapport, I was able to purchase the property and have a "win" for all parties. I met the sellers' financial and emotional needs.

I found out when their contract on the new property in the wine country would expire, so that I could meet their financial need. I ended up buying the property at a price that allowed me to make a profit.

I succeeded in buying this property because I listened to the seller talk about her and her husband's situation. This was a couple whose need was not really financial; instead, the two of them had an *emotional* need to relocate to a more peaceful place. I wanted to hear their story, because by listening to their story and understanding emotionally where the sellers were coming from, I was able to assimilate the facts and make my offer based on all their needs, not just their financial needs. It seems to me that women do a much better job of paying attention to what the other party really needs and developing the rapport to move forward and have a positive outcome.

Reason 2: Women Pay Close Attention to Details and Are Good Researchers

In addition to having great listening skills, women pay attention to details. Women will research until the cows come home if they are passionate about what they are trying to accomplish. Items like looking up comparables (also called comps) on sold properties (researching what other properties actually sold for), searching the Internet for properties (which I'll discuss in Chapter 4), and even doing the final touches in staging a property for sale are skills that women are especially strong in. But before we get to those chapters, let's look in general at how women pay attention to detail.

As illustrated in the example of the California property I just described, getting the details on the property itself is not the most important thing in terms of what you're trying to accomplish. The attention to detail needs to be part of your preparation.

Develop a checklist or a "to-do" list. Successful investors know what they are trying to accomplish from the beginning, have goals and objectives, stick to their own agenda, and always follow up.

For example, for some investors, the goal is to buy property, then turn around and sell it within a few months, or even sooner. Other investors' intentions may be to buy property for the long term and capitalize on income and appreciation. And still other investors need the tax advantages of owning property. You need to have *your own objectives* in place before you can spend any time developing your real estate investment portfolio.

Having the attention to detail that we women have, developing a checklist or road map to get where you want to go, and solving problems along the way gives you the ability to achieve a positive outcome. Your game plan will help you to be more successful than if you just think off the top of your head and try to get the deal without thinking about and checking off the items that are most important. I know many real estate investors who've been burned by reacting emotionally to a property and a situation. Instead, you should research a property, and women are good at researching and finding solutions.

Successful investors know what they are trying to accomplish from the beginning, have goals and objectives, stick to their own agenda, and always follow up.

Here are examples of research that can help you in your investing career.

- *Learn the ropes at your courthouse.* Go to the register of deeds, the tax assessor's office, or city government offices to gather information on a particular property. Items like the owner's name, property taxes, zoning, and other such information are available. In some parts of the country, this information is online, so you will not even have to visit the courthouse.
- *Get MLS (multiple listing service) information.* When a Realtor lists a property for sale, he or she will enter the information about that property on an MLS so that other Realtors can view it online. All of the information about the property is included in the MLS listing.
- *If you are trying to research what is for sale, contact a local Realtor and get up-to-date comps for the area where you are trying to buy.* There are a couple of different Web sites where you can see what property has been sold by Zip code. If you want objective research on sold properties, you can do this yourself. If you feel confident and you trust the Realtor you've found, have the Realtor do it for you. Find out

what sells, what rents, what is available, and what is realistic. Look at the square footage as well as the price and then calculate the cost per square foot (which makes it easier to compare different properties of different sizes).

- *Research what's for sale and how long it's been on the market.*
- *Find out what has sold and how quickly it sold.*
- *Check out what was the original asking price vs. the sold price.*

All of this information will help you gauge a potential investment and help you make an intelligent offer.

Here's an example. In 1997, I was in Colorado, and I had an opportunity through a Realtor to look at a property that was being sold through a relocation company. The relocation company was working with the largest employer in that area at the time, which was transferring an individual from this particular city to California, and the company could not sell the house. It was an enormous home with three levels, but the bottom level was completely unfinished; the whole house was open, and there were no doors separating the bottom level from the other two levels.

I did extensive research to see what the market in that particular neighborhood and found that the asking price was way over what buyers were spending on homes in that neighborhood. I determined that this property was overpriced because the lower level was completely unfinished and therefore had no value. The finished space was on the main and upper levels, so we based our price on the square footage on those two levels and made an offer to the relocation company. I got the deal, bought the property, lived in the house, fixed up the lower level, and turned around and sold it six years later—for close to double the price I paid. *That's* a real estate investment success story.

If you *don't* do the necessary research before investing in a property, though, you might have a horror story instead. For example, I met one investor recently who bought property on a travel tour. He lives in New England. He went to a real estate presentation that was being held in his city at which people were offering investment opportunities in Florida. He went to Florida with the group to look at specific properties and the area in general. He ended up buying a property on the spot, without researching the local economy, what inventory was out there, and what the expected profit potential would be. What he bought was a spec home that he thought was going to be built in six months. Unfortunately, he had no idea what the value of the property was, and he believed the salesman's story.

A year and a half later, that home has still not been completed. The investor did not foresee a bad hurricane season, overbuilding in the local economy, and slashing of local real estate prices. He didn't do any research. As of this writing, the value of the property has gone down 10 percent. This person has lost money, and the property is still not ready for occupancy.

What *should* he have done? He should have asked all of the following questions:

- How long does it take to get a permit?
- How long does it take to be able to break ground?
- How busy are the local contractors?
- Who's going to build this property?
- What's the background of the builder? Has the builder ever had any bankruptcies or does the company have mechanic's liens on the property or development?
- Is the property in a condition where it's ready for a certificate of occupancy (CO)?

Women are, in general, more empathetic than men, and we're usually perceived as less threatening. This quality also helps others open up to us.

In short, when you're investing in new construction, there are a lot of pieces that have to be put together, and they all need to be on your checklist. This investor bought this property and put up the construction money, so, essentially, the builder had borrowed money to build these houses. Now, the market in Florida is flat, the area is flooded with new inventory, sellers are slashing their prices, and this investor is stuck. By the time he closes on his new property, the value of the house will be less. He could be in financial trouble because he didn't do any research before he bought.

Reason 3: Women Are Generally Seen as Nonthreatening

A characteristic that's related to listening well is the fact that women are, in general, more empathetic than men, and we're usually perceived as less threatening. This quality also helps others open up to us. When you're talking to sellers, keep in mind that *nobody* sells a property at a discount unless that person has an immediate need to do so. And sometimes that need may be emotional rather than or as well as financial (as illustrated in the first example in this chapter).

Here's an example that illustrates how women can benefit from being perceived as nonthreatening. I found a property that I thought would make a good investment. This was a 45-year-old home owned by a woman who had recently been widowed. She was working with a real estate broker who wanted her to buy a condo to live in and another condo as an investment. I went and looked at the home she was selling. I started talking to the woman and asking her the questions necessary to help explore solutions.

She needed to downsize to a much smaller property than this five-bedroom home where she had raised her children and lived for the last 40 years. She also told me that because this was where she had raised her family, she needed to make sure that whoever bought the property would take good care of it. She felt that she could relate to me because, as a woman, I would probably better understand the emotional ties she had to her house. This is the nonthreatening aspect that I think women have that many men don't.

Imagine her sitting there talking to some guy who just views her as a little old lady, a widow whose house he can buy at a very large discount. She probably wouldn't have shared this personal, emotional information with a "stranger," someone that she did not feel comfortable with. "I raised my children here; my husband died in our bedroom. I need to live in a smaller home where everything is taken care of for me because I'm getting older. My real estate broker wants to sell me another condo, and I'm not sure that's the right thing to do. Maybe I'm better off with the cash." She probably wouldn't have told any of her story to someone she was not comfortable with.

But she told me *all* of this. I wouldn't have gotten that far if I hadn't seemed to her to be nonthreatening, empathetic to her situation, and understanding of where she was coming from. She didn't want to drive by her house after she sold it and see weeds on the front lawn. She wanted the property to be well taken care of, and I had to assure her that if I bought this property, I would make sure that it was picture perfect. I was able to find out what her true *emotional* need was in selling the house, and I was able to do that by being nonthreatening to her.

Reason 4: Real Estate Does Not Need to Be a Male-Dominated Industry

An increasing number of women are discovering their niche in real estate. My intention is to help those who want to learn to be successful real estate investors, to develop the creative strategies and the mindset to be successful from a woman's perspective. Real estate investing has primarily been a male-dominated field. Throughout this book, however, are success stories from women, with the message that if you're properly prepared, you, too, can do this.

Women look at this industry as being a man's world because it's finance-driven. For example, when you talk to a banker, you may not feel all that confident and you might be somewhat intimidated. Some bankers—men and women both—do not take female real estate investors as seriously as they would male investors. It's just perception, because men are accustomed to working in finance. Believe it or not, many people still think that men have mathematical brains and women are "Susie Homemakers." (Even the former dean of Harvard thought so—and said so, which is why he's the *former* dean.)

Years ago, when I first moved to Colorado, I was active in the private mortgage business. This is where the seller of a property finances the sale for the buyer instead of the buyer making payments to a bank. This income stream can be sold to an investor. Many times, the investor will buy the income stream at a discount. There was another longtime investor living in the same community that I had just moved to, and I was introduced to him by a mutual friend.

This investor's attitude was, "What do *you* know about notes?" He immediately assumed that because I was female, I had no credibility when it came to investing in this product. It took years and evidence of my credibility to others before he accepted the idea that I knew what I was doing. My partner at the time was also male; the old-timer had no problem with him.

Right now, I am working on purchasing a small commercial property. I am working with a bank where the management is female. I chose this bank because I'll be working with someone who identifies with me and my objective. This is somebody I can look up to, and someone with whom I can share what I'm trying to accomplish as a result of purchasing this property. In contrast, if I go to a bank and meet with a man, I'll have the same financial information, but a man is more likely to ask me a lot of questions to assess my abilities. The conversation's going to start from more of a defense posture.

Women look at this industry as being a man's world because it's finance-driven. . . . Many people still think that men have mathematical brains and women are "Susie Homemakers."

Reason 5: Most Real Estate *Agents* Are Women, so Why Not *Investors*, Too?

If you look at the real estate industry as a whole, you'll find that most real estate agents are women: in The National Association of Realtors (NAR), more than 70 percent of the membership base is female. In addition, within the NAR, there's a Women's Council of Realtors (WCR), which is a separate organization just for women.

So women do understand real estate—and they're typically very good at brokering deals. The successful agents are friendly and persistent, and they follow up with their prospects. But more women need to make the transition from real estate broker or real estate agent to real estate *investor*. Most people who get into real estate are interested in one thing: earning commissions on sales of property; they may or may not think about real estate as an investment.

If you can be a real estate agent, you can be a real estate investor. And even if you're not an agent but are friendly, are persistent, and do follow up, you would make a great real estate investor.

And although there aren't any statistics on how many women real estate agents become investors, the NAR has realized that there are enough people who are interested in investing to warrant assessing the need to be teaching real estate investor courses.

Another benefit for women Realtors who want to become investors is that when sellers are getting ready to sell their property, they contact a real estate agent. When they do that, if they go through a real estate agent and sign a listing agreement, that property is going to be listed on multiple listing services (MLSs). Before the property is listed, however, that Realtor has an opportunity to buy that piece of real estate herself and get it off the market (or to allow someone in her sphere of influence to do so). Real estate agents therefore get a built-in opportunity to look at property at a discount before other real estate investors see it. Imagine having this opportunity to acquire real estate because you are in the business already. Right now, the mentality of most real estate professionals is to sell as much property as they can through conventional means and move on to the next deal.

Yet some realtors do become investors—for example, Anna Mills, who has been a Realtor with Century 21 in Ohio and Michigan for more than 30 years. After only a year as a Realtor, Anna became an investor because "I realized if I kept telling people, 'Housing is the most important purchase of your life,' I should be doing it myself." So she started acquiring properties with no money down, and later building properties, and she currently manages dozens of single-family properties that she rents out.

Anna has become so successful as a real estate investor that she's currently serving her tenth term as local president of the Toledo (Ohio) Real Estate Investors Association; she's also a past president of the National Real Estate Investors Association (NREIA) and past president of the Ohio Real Estate Investors Association (ORIEA).

When sellers are getting ready to sell their property, they contact a real estate agent. . . . Real estate agents therefore get a built-in opportunity to look at property at a discount before other real estate investors see it.

Reason 6: More Women Are Starting Their Own Businesses

According to the Small Business Administration, more than 50 percent of new start-up businesses are owned by women. More important, most small businesses that are still successful after three years are owned by women. We are gaining confidence and spreading our wings. It is time we take hold and do the same with our investments. There's a correlation between being successful as a real estate investor and being successful in owning and operating a business.

Real Estate Investing Offers Balance to Your Financial Portfolio

Investing in real estate has many benefits for your portfolio:

- It provides slow and steady growth.
- It generates a regular income stream.
- It appreciates over time.
- It provides diversification with your other investments.

These are just a few of the reasons why real estate investments should be a part of every woman's portfolio. Once you master the basics, the returns on real estate can exceed 100 percent.

For example, with respect to diversification, every investor knows about stocks, bonds, and mutual funds. But a lot of people are not aware that real estate investments would make sense. You don't need to limit yourself to investing in physical property; you can also make loans, invest in REITs, invest in private mortgages, or make loans to individuals that are secured by real estate. Some people don't want to *buy* real estate; they look at real estate as a job, but they would be happy to know how to make a loan secured by real estate to someone else.

What's the worst that can happen to the investor when he or she makes such a loan? If you make a loan to somebody that's secured by a piece of real estate, and if that person doesn't pay off the loan, you can foreclose and take the property. Now you've got the property and you can resell it; you got the down payment and monthly payments for some period of time, and you have the opportunity for additional profit. So, if you look at your goals, and you are interested in investments that offer slow and steady growth, income, and appreciation potential, investing in real estate makes sense. But there are other things that individuals can do to get the returns in real estate that can exceed 100 percent, and lending is just one of them.

Last year, I made a loan to a friend so that she could make an investment: the terms were 12½ percent interest over one year, with no payments, with a balloon payment at the end of the first year. I took a $57,000 investment and turned it into $68,000. What was my profit? Enough. Plus, I did this through my IRA, so the profit was tax deferred (more on this subject in Chapter 9). This is the kind of investing we need to learn. Real estate investing includes more options than just owning a building with tenants and toilets. Of course, you can buy buildings, but there are also other real estate–related investments, including loans, leases, and more.

> *If you look at your goals, and you are interested in investments that offer slow and steady growth, income, and appreciation potential, investing in real estate makes sense.*

Why So Few Women Invest in Real Estate

So why is it that so few women have made real estate investing part of their financial portfolios? I think it's because we are afraid. Many would-be investors are afraid of not knowing how to invest, what makes a good investment, when to buy, and when to sell. They're afraid to negotiate with banks, private lenders, contractors, and others who may or may not intimidate them or at least think they can. Many women are afraid of taking a perceived financial risk. And many are afraid that they don't have the know-how to manage and control their financial futures firsthand.

Moreover, many other women in the industry agree with me on this point; when I asked them, "What do you think is the biggest reason more women are not comfortable as investors?" here are some of the answers I got:

They don't know how. They're afraid to do it on their own, and they don't have a good coach.
— Tami Spaulding, a Realtor for 26 years.

The commercial real estate industry is still dominated by men, and they seem to get the most publicity. There are no public or recognizable role models for women to emulate or turn to for information.
— Jaime Raskulinecz, a real estate broker
and founder and principal of a third-party
property management firm since 1994.

The thing that holds most women back as investors is fear. Fear of the unknown, fear of failure, fear of making the wrong decision. In general, women are not taught to trust their gut when it comes to large financial decisions. Many times they trust it in other areas of life, such as relationships, but not in investing.
— Jennifer Dizmang, an entrepreneur, speaker,
and financial advisor for 12 years and
a real estate investor since 1992.

One of the biggest [reasons] *is all the myths and horror stories that abound about dealing with rental properties. Many of these are true, but they are often due to lack of knowledge or lack of involvement. Misinformation is the biggest barrier.*
I think the second cause is that women haven't been encouraged to understand their finances. Many of them were not taught that they need to think independently about their own long-term financial security. I was lucky in that way. My grandmother was widowed very early in life and became a savvy investor to support

her three young children on her own. She was a true inspiration and a great source of education."

—Rebecca McLean, executive director of the National Real Estate Investors Association.

I believe the reason we don't see more women as investors is because women are not confident in their abilities to care for a property. They certainly have the financial abilities to build strong real estate portfolios. What they don't realize is that many investors aren't all "hands on." While it can shave cost off maintenance to do repairs yourself, most investors are too busy and instead hire good "handymen" or "handyman companies" to attend to problems when they arise. . . .

Another reason we don't see more women as investors is because women are more lenient when renters start falling behind on rental payments. The best way to handle this is to make sure your potential renter is a good risk before they move in.

—Renee Falgout, seven years' experience as operations manager of a mortgage company. (Renee offers advice on how to address these problems in Chapters 13 and 8, respectively.)

[I think the reason is] *the worry of losing money they have invested and not being able to provide for the family. You can't rely on the income to pay the mortgage, insurance, and taxes on the house; you need to have a reserve of three months' worth of mortgage, taxes, and insurance. I have found also, from several women I've spoken to, that they will allow a tenant, especially, if she is a single mother, to skip a month's rent, because of the children. Most women are too soft-hearted, therefore getting themselves into trouble with their mortgage on the house. An investment home is a business and should be treated as a business.*

—Dorrliss Cisy Ware, a broker and residential property manager working in real estate since 1997.

Fear causes paralysis. Women often feel the need to be perfect, so they delay either from a fear of failure or the desire to have everything "just right" before taking action. Fortunately, fear can be banished with knowledge and practice. At some point, we have to take the plunge.

—Tracy Rewey, a real estate note and
owner-financing expert since 1985.

Our money education comes from our parents, who received their money education from their parents, who were children of the Depression era. Most of us never received any financial education but simply gleaned attitudes that came to us 60 to 80 years out of date. . . . Most women essentially have no grounding in finances, and would be reluctant to ask questions. . . . Most women today still carry the belief system of their grandmothers, that handling the money is a man's job, while hers is hearth and home. It is very human to fear the unknown, and to bear the consequences of making a mistake, a responsibility that most women are reluctant to accept.

—Magi Bird, a broker and founder of an
educational/training company that teaches
Realtors portfolio development and other financial
skills on wealth building, preservation, and diversification.

Personally, I do not believe it is a gender issue. My experience is that when it comes to buying the family home, women almost always are the decision makers. . . . Even single women do not seem to have a problem making a decision on buying a home and then living in it themselves, if they can afford to do so.

Where both genders seem to fall down is taking the next step by actually strategically investing in real estate as an investment. More men are involved in the real estate construction industry than women. Therefore they have an automatic advantage in that they are less intimidated by the maintenance aspect of owning real estate. Usually, they either have the skills to fix it them-

selves or they have a buddy who has the knowledge to help. Since many women take care of the family finances, or they are single and have to take care of their own finances, they tend to be more comfortable with the financing aspect of real estate. . . .

Most people of both genders have precious little experience and knowledge in strategically investing in anything, whether it is in stocks, bonds, real estate . . . or any other type of investments. . . . Typically, people have a 401(k) or IRA, and their company or some investment advisor makes suggestions as to what to do with their money. . . . Most people don't have a clue how to weigh the various choices in any investment. As a result, they end up choosing from a short list of potential investments that may not actually be the best investment for them at all.

Real estate is not typically an investment that companies and advisors have much experience in themselves. As a result, only a small percentage of people, prior to the most recent real estate boom, have owned any real estate other than the primary family home. Recently, that has changed, however, . . . [leading] to a phenomenon I call the "accidental real estate investor." Typically, . . . a person or family has bought a family home and then some years later purchased a second home. The primary original intention was not to invest wisely in real estate for profits, but it was to merely own either a recreation property for pleasure or to plan for retirement. Coincidentally, at the same time . . . real estate prices started to rise dramatically. . . . Most of these people are not real estate investors . . . many of us just got lucky. . . .

I think most people, both women and men, are uncomfortable doing something they have no background in or real experience at doing. Unfortunately, this business really is a trial-and-error kind of business. It definitely is one of those businesses where each deal is a life lesson in itself.

—Barbara O'Connell, an investor, developer,
real estate agent, project manager, property manager,
and consultant and seminar leader in commercial
and residential real estate since the mid-1980s.

Wise Women Invest in Real Estate

Finally, one response defended women unequivocally:

Women are excellent investors! Women who quit listening to preconceived notions or what they have learned growing up become investors quicker. Many women are detail oriented, great as multitaskers, willing to get educated and quite often have people person skills. The only puzzle part missing may be learning to treat investing as a "business."
—Anna Mills, a Century 21 Realtor for 30 years.

Women have traditionally depended on others for financial advice (as Barbara O'Connell also mentioned). But financial professionals usually won't recommend real estate as part of a portfolio, because they don't receive commissions for suggesting real estate as an investment. A financial planner won't get a commission on investing in a piece of real estate, nor will a stockbroker. Even fee-based financial planners, who get 1 or 1½ percent of a client's portfolio no matter what the portfolio is invested in, don't benefit financially from the client's investing in real estate, because once a client (i.e., *you*) invests in a property, that takes money *out* of your financial portfolio (though, of course, you still have the asset).

Investing in real estate is a skill you have to learn. If a financial planner or broker doesn't understand how to invest in real estate, he or she will tend not to recommend it. For example, I know a woman who wanted to buy some real estate in New Jersey, so she went to her financial planner (who was a fee-only planner), and he tried to sell her an insurance annuity instead. She asked me to call this fee-only planner, and I said to him, "Why would you not want her to invest in this property, where she can get 12 percent return on her investment, instead of your annuity?"

He defended his suggestion by saying, "Well, we don't know if the property's going to go up or down [in terms of value], and she can't afford to lose her money." My response to that was, "Shouldn't *she* be the one to make that decision instead of you making it for her?" As you can see, unfortunately, there's still a general perception that when you work with a financial planner, he or she is going to take care of you, and that's a major problem if you're trying to get ahead, because financial planners don't have a crystal ball. There is nothing wrong with getting financial advice. Financial planners and advisors are a great source of information for many types of investments. However, the most successful people I know take control of their future destiny. Financial advisors are knowledgeable in their field of expertise and offer guidance to assist you in making the right decision. In the end, however, it is up to us to decide what we want to achieve and how to grow our portfolios.

Many would-be investors are afraid of not knowing how to invest, what makes a good investment, when to buy, and when to sell.

There are, of course, some financial professionals who are knowledgeable about real estate; they typically have taken extra courses to learn about alternative investments, As real estate investing has become more popular, more financial professionals have become accustomed to discussing real estate as an option.

If you're looking for one-on-one financial guidance, check out the following organizations:

- The Financial Planning Association, whose members are commission-based planners.
- NAFA, the National Association of Fee-Only Planners. These planners are fee-based, meaning that they get a fee that is based on a percentage of the entire portfolio.

Financial planners will also be aware of and may recommend investments in private REITs (real estate investment trusts). They may also recommend what is known as a *tenancy in common* (TIC), which is a fractional share or interest in a commercial building, such as a strip center or apartment complex. In general, though, financial planners aren't keen on their clients buying real estate as an investment on their own, because it takes away from the money that the planner is managing for those clients.

One of the reasons I have written this book is to provide information on this one type of financial investment that most financial professionals won't provide. I'm not saying that you shouldn't use financial planners. You definitely *should* work with financial planners if you feel that you want and need investment advice from a professional. On the other hand (as my colleague Jim Napier used to say in seminars he taught), no one will take as good care of your money as you. It's *your* money. If you want to give it to somebody else to manage, that's your prerogative, and certainly you might give your "mattress money" to that person. But if you're trying to get ahead financially or trying to diversify your financial portfolio into other investments, there are a lot of different investments you can make to get ahead. These aren't limited to real estate, of course, but that's the focus of this book. So let's look at what you need to do to get started.

Get Empowered and Knowledgeable to Become a Savvy and Successful Investor

If real estate investing is exciting to you, keep reading. I want to encourage everyone to learn the basics of real estate investing—the terminology, the types of real estate you may wish to acquire, the rental market if you decide to hold property for the long term, and other necessary information that will help you build a base of understanding. This will be important in helping to develop your investment philosophy.

There are many Web sites and books on the subject of real estate investing that you can study. I do want to put in a comment here. Throughout this book, I recommend books and authors that can help to educate you, but I recommend only those that I feel are credible—i.e., those where I know that the author has direct experience doing what he or she writes about. I can't recommend books if I don't know that the author has experience in that particular aspect of the business. Please also study your local marketplace as it relates to the type of investing you wish to do.

If you're thinking about getting started in real estate investing, the first thing you should do is identify what your financial goals are and what amount of time you have to devote to meeting them. Then do a little research and gain information before you invest: join a real estate investors' association; subscribe to real estate investing newsletters and other publications so that you can learn the lingo and feel comfortable with what you'll be doing. Start looking at properties once you've determined what type of investment you want to buy—e.g., single-family homes, duplexes, rehabs or fixer-uppers, and so on.

For example, I know a woman we'll call Naomi. She was 34 years old, and she had an MBA and significant work experience in the information technology sector. She was working full-time and making a halfway decent income, but she was also a working mother of a preschooler, and she wanted to have another child. Naomi's number one need was to reduce her working hours so that she could spend more time with her growing family. However, she also needed monthly income. How could she do this?

Naomi spent weeks developing a plan. Her investment strategy was to buy one property a year. She started looking around her community, took a couple of different courses, and subscribed to a couple of different newsletters. She joined a local real estate investors' club that met only once a month in the evening. (The National Real Estate Investors Association can assist you in locating a local real estate investors' club where you live.) Her husband stayed home with their child while Naomi attended the monthly meetings. She empowered herself by gaining the knowledge she needed to decide what she wanted to do and develop an investment philosophy. Six years ago, she bought her first property.

When Naomi had her second child, she did not return to work. The 10 properties she has purchased over the last six years generate enough cash flow to allow Naomi to be home with her children. Naomi is now living the life she wants and spending her time with her children. She does her own property management and has developed a time-efficient process for managing her property (which I'll discuss in more detail in Chapter 8). Naomi is totally devoted to real estate.

Look at the skill sets this 34-year-old woman learned. If she hadn't taken the initiative in the first place, she wouldn't be successful today. And along the way in her real estate investing, she also developed other skill sets that had the added benefit of making her feel better about herself. She developed more self-confidence because she was negotiating with bankers, with lenders, with contractors, and with other individuals.

Eight Traits of Successful Investors

So what does it take to be a successful investor? I believe it requires the following traits:

1. *You need imagination.* You need to be able to visualize what will happen with the property and the future of the property. You need to know in advance what you're trying to accomplish.

2. *You need to be resourceful.* You need to have a problem-solver mentality. When you see an opportunity in a situation, you're going to have different strategies in your mind that you can use to help the seller and to close the deal.

3. *You need to be persistent.* You need to continually look for the right opportunity and be persistent in following up on potential opportunities.

4. *You need self-confidence.* You need to believe that you can be successful in real estate investing, because self-confidence does come across when you're talking with others. And the lack of self-confidence also comes across. As previously mentioned, you need to empower yourself to become knowledgeable so that you will feel confident.

5. *You need to accept risk.* You need to be able to analyze the risk of what you're getting yourself into with each individual property; to learn ways to reduce that risk; and then, if you are willing, to be able to accept that risk. For example, let's say you're looking at a piece of real estate that you want to buy, and you're not going to make any monthly income off that real estate; you're buying it solely for appreciation. In today's market, you could be taking a risk because the market is so volatile right now. However, if you really believe in the deal, and you think that five or ten years down the road (if you decide to hold it for that long), the property may be worth 20 or 30 percent more than what it is worth today, then you've accepted that risk, and you're going forward in your mind. If you take the risk, you shouldn't look back and say, "I would have, should have, could have done things differently." You need to truly *accept* the risk and not lose sleep over it.

6. *You need to be very organized.* The successful investors I know are organized. They understand the type of property they wish to acquire, how long they want to hold the property, what the seller's motivation

is, and where the property is located. They determine whether or not that property falls within their guidelines. When you are organized, you don't waste valuable time looking at deals that aren't going to work. You should have an idea of the outcome in advance, before you go to look at the investment; this increases your profit potential and gives you time to find the next deal.

You need to be able to visualize what will happen with the property and the future of the property. You need to know in advance what you're trying to accomplish.

---

7. *You need to be willing to make financial decisions on the spot.* Have a cash reserve or financing in place. In some cases, you may need a little bit more cash to consummate some of your transactions. If you can sacrifice something else in order to have cash and/or financing available, you will be able to invest in those properties at below market value and profit.

8. *You need to have courage—and to be willing to accept rejection.* You have to realize that you're going to lose some deals, and that those losses aren't personal. Not every seller will want to sell to you. You will win some deals, and you will lose some. If you can accept this reality, you will be able to enjoy investing in real estate.

Conclusion

Now you know why women are naturally suited to being good real estate investors and how *you* can get started. By gaining knowledge about opportunities in real estate investing, you too can become empowered. You will develop the basic skill sets that will help you prepare to identify opportunity. And as we move forward in this book, you will learn how to invest with confidence.

Wise women who are successful real estate investors know that *personal* traits such as being honest, following up, and following the Golden Rule will help you achieve success. Now, let's go a step further and look at your *strategy* for identifying the right real estate properties for you.

2

Preparing to Succeed: Getting Your Financials in Order

The goal of this chapter is to help you get your financials in order, so that you'll be in a position to go out and identify real estate investing opportunities. To prepare you to take on real estate investing, this chapter gives you the tools to assess your current financial situation, determine your financial goals, look at your credit history (and improve it, if you need to), identify where you can get additional financing, and find your financial comfort level so that you can focus on the right type of property that will meet your goals.

Checklist 2-1 explores a few key questions that you need to answer to assist you in your preparation. This chapter answers all of the questions in the checklist—and more—so that you can prepare yourself both financially and emotionally before you even start looking at properties that may be investment opportunities. These questions are also important to prevent you from being taken advantage of or from making mistakes that you could have avoided. If you are prepared, and if you know exactly what you're trying to accomplish, you'll find that real estate investing will be easier in the long run.

Checklist 2-1   Financial Questions You Should Ask Yourself Before You Invest

❑   Do you have savings stored away, including emergency savings?

❑   Do you know where you are going to get the cash for down payments on property?

❑   What is your goal in buying real estate in the first place? Different investors buy for different reasons—for example:

  ❑   Is your goal *appreciation*—do you want to buy property in a gentrifying neighborhood and sell it for a profit?

  ❑   Is your goal *income*—do you want to rent out property and generate monthly cash flow?

  ❑   Is your goal to have *tax benefits*—do you want to be able to depreciate the property and write off expenses from the property on your income taxes?

❑   Do you need to leverage your real estate investments (i.e., do you need to borrow on every deal you do), or are you planning on paying cash for your investment properties?

❑   In other words, have you outlined your financial goals and objectives from both a financial and an emotional perspective, so that you can start identifying investments for your portfolio?

Ann is an administrative assistant in Wyoming. She and her husband wanted to move to California because they enjoyed the climate. Before they started researching the market, Ann spent some time making a list of financial goals that they wished to achieve. She outlined their financial situation, and she developed a plan.

Having taken the time to develop a plan and to gather the documentation they needed to prequalify for a loan, Ann and her husband knew exactly what they could afford and wasted no time finding the perfect home. They even brought a letter from the lender to show that they had been prequalified, which made them look stronger to potential sellers. Ann got exactly what she wanted, and so can you!

*Prepare yourself financially and emotionally
before you even start looking at properties that
may be investment opportunities.*

Identify Your Financial Goals and Objectives

In order to identify what your objectives in buying real estate are (in general, before you even invest in a property), you need to know what your goals are. You need to assess where you currently are in life. Checklist 2-2 can help you think through some of the key issues.

Checklist 2-2   Determining Your Financial Goals and Objectives

❏ Are you working?

❏ How much money do you need to earn every year?

❏ What do you do in your current profession that could assist you as a real estate investor? You want to utilize your skill sets from the start. Are you a salesperson or a legal professional? No matter whether you are employed or working at home, you have skills that you can use to help you achieve success as an investor.

❏ If you're going to buy property and hold it for the long term, how many properties will it take for you to be able to achieve your financial goal?

❏ Do you have the resources to go out and buy property on your own? For instance, do you have equity in your existing residence so that you could refinance your property and use the proceeds to buy investment property? A lot of people invest this way.

❏ Is your objective to buy and sell, or to buy and hold? There's a big difference in terms of strategy here (which I'll cover in more detail later in this chapter).

Answering the questions in this checklist will help you assess where you are currently, in financial terms. Shelly had spent the last seven years as an office manager for a law firm in Seattle. She was ready for a change, and she wanted to be her own boss. At a party, she met Linda, who had been successfully rehabbing properties since she was 22. Linda's enthusiasm for rehabbing got Shelly's attention. Shelly decided to try investing because she had security in her employment. She wrote a financial plan, and she found her first property through a local contractor friend.

Today, Shelly rehabs three properties a year and lives off the profit. She has a small crew of handymen who remodel the properties she buys. Shelly is earning more income from rehabbing properties than she did as an office manager. "Meeting Linda changed my life and gave me confidence in my ability to succeed and grow," she says. She started with a plan.

Unfortunately, it's not really possible to put a ballpark figure on these financial issues. No one can really tell you that "you need at least X amount of money before you can start investing in real estate," because so many factors vary in different regions around the country. For example, the median price of a home in California is obviously going to be different from the median price of a home in Florida. And each investor's needs are different as well. You need to know the exact dollar figure that *you're* accustomed to living on per month so that you can determine your financial goals regarding real estate investments.

Suppose you need $10,000 per month to live. Calculate how many properties you need to buy in order to eventually pay off the investment property and have free and clear income of $10,000 per month.

Without considering the local or national economy, you cannot successfully plan to invest in real estate. The economy is a factor, as is the volatility in your local marketplace. There is not a minimum capital of money required, because the amount of money you need will depend on your investing strategy. For instance, some investors buy options on real estate; they may be able to purchase an option to buy the real estate for as little as $1,000. An option gives the investor the right to purchase the property for a fixed price during a specified period of time. If the market goes down during that period, the worst that can happen is that the investor is out $1,000. If the market goes up, the investor can assign the option for a fee—

let's say $2,000, thereby doubling her investment—or she can purchase the property for the fixed price, knowing that it has gone up in value. The investor is in control of the property. (More on this subject in Chapter 11.)

Are you a risk taker? Or is security the
most important value to you?

Some investors borrow every dime when they buy real estate: They get help from their family or a private lender, or they get a line of credit that allows them to capitalize on a property. By determining your success formula, you gain a competitive advantage and can quickly identify bargain-priced investments.

- Are you looking to buy real estate for appreciation?
- Are you investing in real estate to generate cash flow?
- Are you trying to reduce your income taxes?
- Are you looking for current monthly income?

In other words, you need to set up a game plan first. If you know the answers to these questions, you can develop your road map to get you where you want to go.

Know Your Financial Comfort Level

Are you a risk taker? Or is security the most important value to you? Are you comfortable with income projections, being direct with your financial situation, and looking to diversify beyond the traditional stocks, bonds, and mutual funds? Knowing your comfort level on investing will take you a long way toward becoming successful if you eliminate the obstacles. If you are not comfortable with risk, you may not want to invest in real estate. You may feel more comfortable with investments that others participate in or identify with.

Decrease Your Risk by Investing
in Multiple Residential Properties

If you buy five houses, take out five loans, and have five tenants paying you, you can spread your risk over five properties. In contrast, suppose you buy one commercial office building with only one tenant. If the tenant doesn't pay, and that is the only tenant for the property, you could be in trouble. In the other scenario, if one tenant out of five doesn't pay, you still have four who are paying. If you're comfortable with only one tenant, great—but you need to identify your comfort level up front, *before* you buy.

How is your credit? Are you a good credit risk?
Do you know what your credit score is?

Some people are very interested in having security. If security is important to you, it's important that you know exactly what type of property you want to look at. When you're evaluating property, you're going to be evaluating it on price, on the financing, and on the terms of that financing because sometimes it isn't the price that you're paying that'll be the deal breaker—it may be the terms. Do the terms of the loan make sense (the time period of the loan, the interest rate, and the amount you end up financing make up the terms)?

You will want to know beforehand what this property is going to generate in cash flow so that you're not blindsided later on. In commercial property, you tend to have a longer-term tenant with a lease that has built-in inflationary clauses. This might be a better strategy for somebody who is looking for a continuing income.

Find Out What Your Credit Says about You: Get Your Credit History and Your FICO Score

If you're going to finance a property, you need to have your sources of capital lined up. Some people use conventional methods of financing (Chapter 9 covers that in more detail), and others will use private financing. Which way are *you* going to go? How is your credit? Are you a good credit risk? Do you know what your credit score is?

Renee Falgout, operations manager for a mortgage company, confirms this:

Credit is so important in determining what mortgage programs are available to a buyer and how much risk a lender is willing to carry.

Buyers with high credit scores can get 100 percent financing with very competitive rates. With high credit scores, income no longer becomes the major factor, nor even the property value. . . .

After credit considerations, lenders also want to see good debt-to-income ratios, but that can be mitigated with substantial assets. Lenders like to see the buyer having cash equaling at least six months' worth of bills in the bank in case of emergencies. And they want to see that it's been there for at least two months. It can't just appear overnight. Liquid assets are viewed as a compensating factor. The more, the better!

In order to be able to line up outside financial resources (i.e., to get a loan), you need to know your FICO score. This is a compilation of your credit history, and lenders need to know it before they'll agree to lend you any money (for real estate or for any other type of investment). FICO stands for the Fair Isaac Corporation, which created the credit reporting score. Your FICO score can range from 300 to 850. If your credit score is over 700, you're usually an excellent credit risk for a lender. Mortgage company operations manager Renee Falgout says that "lenders like to see at least a 620 middle credit score, two years of steady employment, and at least 12 months' of rental payment history, with no late payments."

To find out what your FICO score is, contact the three largest credit-reporting agencies that produce credit reports that will include your FICO score:

- Equifax: www.eqifax.com
- TransUnion: www.transunion.com
- Experian: www.experian.com

You can order your reports from these individual credit agencies. (You're entitled to a free credit report once a year. Also, the more your credit report is requested, the lower your score goes. And you need to ensure that there has been no fraudulent activity on your credit report.) You might wonder, "Why do I need a credit report from all three of these agencies?" You should get your credit report from *all* of these agencies because, believe it or not, you may see a little bit of divergence in your credit rating and your

FICO score. The FICO score is really a composite of *all* your credit; the higher your number, the better your score, and the more money you'll be able to borrow.

> *Paying cash may help you manage your spending (and saving) better, but it doesn't help you invest in real estate, because if you pay cash for everything, you're not establishing any credit history.*

Your credit report lists how much credit you have available on your credit cards and other credit lines, how much debt you owe, and whether you've met your payment obligations in the past. Your credit report and a good credit history are vitally important: I know lenders firsthand who make loans based only on credit scores. So, if you recognize that your credit report is your financial history, you will understand that you need to create a history if you don't have one already.

Establishing a good credit history is critical if you want to invest in real estate. It's helpful to show that you're a good financial risk in case you need to borrow money for any reason at all, perhaps because of some calamity or catastrophe. Even if you simply want to borrow money to start a business, you will need a business plan with an executive summary that outlines how much money you will need, how long you will need the money for, and how you will pay back the bank. Here again, you'll need some sort of credit history, or you're going to have a hard time finding somebody who's going to give you a loan at a reasonable interest rate. That's not to say that you couldn't get by, but a credit history is a proven track record to the lender.

What to Do if You Have No Credit History

If you've always rented and have never bought a house (or any other property), then you've never paid a mortgage, and mortgages help you establish credit. If you're making mortgage payments on your personal residence, you have a credit history: you're making payments every month. But if you own your property free and clear, there's nothing for your creditors to really look at, except for the fact that you own a property. If you've never bought a car on a payment plan, then you don't have any credit history there, either. And if you've never paid for anything over time (whether it's a new washing machine or clothing or furniture or even books), then you need to establish a credit history.

Some people, believe it or not, pay for everything with cash—and they think that's great because they're never in debt; they're not really using any credit; they're not incurring interest charges on any credit card balance. Paying cash may help you manage your spending (and saving) better, but it doesn't help you invest in real estate, because if you pay cash for everything, you're not establishing any credit history.

If you have a low credit score, that does not necessarily mean that you can't borrow money and invest in real estate.

Similarly, it's not helpful (from a lender's perspective) if you pay all of your bills in full each and every month, without carrying any debt. That's a good way to *manage* your money, but it doesn't help you when you want to *borrow* money, because, again, your creditors aren't seeing any payment history. It's predominantly conventional lenders (i.e., banks) that depend on your credit history and FICO score, because they are looking at your ability to pay back the loan. For example, if I'm going to lend you $300,000, I need to know how you're going to pay me back, over what period of time you are going to do that, and that you are a good risk. The higher the credit score, the better the candidate as far as any lender is concerned. You want to make yourself as good a risk as possible before you go out and start buying real estate. You don't want to find yourself in the situation that some people do, where they find a property that they want to buy, but they can't get it financed.

If you have never carried any debt, the first thing you need to do is get yourself a credit card. If you already have credit cards, but you pay them off in full every month, then you should start by, say, once a year paying your bills over a couple of months so that your creditors (whether they're Visa, MasterCard, American Express, department stores, or other retail stores) can see some sort of a credit history.

This doesn't mean that you should pay your credit cards *late*: don't do that! Instead, it means paying your bills over time—for example, if you charge $1,000 on a credit card, pay $333 the first month, then another $333 plus the interest the next month, and then $334 plus the rest of the interest the next month. This shows that you can carry debt, that you can pay it off, and that you have the ability to make payments regularly and on time. Even though that's only three months of credit history, it's a start—especially if you have absolutely *no* credit history, and if your credit report shows that in the past, you ran a revolving account where you paid every bill in total, every month. Don't do this on a regular basis; my accountant recommends paying credit cards over time once a year for a couple of months, with lower balances so that you are not incurring large finance charges. Finally, Renee Falgout offers her advice, summed up in Checklist 2-3.

Checklist 2-3   What You Need to Know about Your Credit Cards to Improve Your Credit for Real Estate Investing
—from Renee Falgout

❑ Be very careful about having too many credit cards open; four to five open and active accounts seems to be the magic number. Having too many accounts open with lots of available credit seems to be a negative in the sense that a person in this situation *could* get into financial trouble.

❑ Try not to have the balances over 50 percent of the available credit. Having accounts that are maxed to their limits will significantly reduce your credit scores.

❑ Also, it's better to have a $10 balance than a zero balance, as the creditor won't report a zero-balance account actively.

❑ Scores go up the longer accounts are open. Some lenders require that a buyer have three accounts that have been open for at least 12 months and a major account ($5,000 limit) that has been open for at least 24 months.

❑ Always, always pay bills on time. Being 30 days late on a credit card within the last 12 months can bounce a buyer out of all conforming products and mean higher rates.

How to Improve Your Credit Score

As mentioned, if your FICO score is 700 or better, you are in good shape. If you have a low credit score, that does not necessarily mean that you can't borrow money and invest in real estate. You need to learn how to *improve* your credit score, and the way to do that, as mentioned, is to make monthly payments on time. Furthermore, if you can make *additional* monthly payments on your bills, by all means, make those additional monthly payments. Again, you need to *prove* to your creditors that *you can make payments on time*.

For example, I recently did a lease option on a property for a couple who could not get a loan. I owned the property, and I had advertised it for sale. The couple came to me and said that they would love to buy the home, but right now, they could not get a loan. The woman's credit score was in the 500s because she had had some medical problems that had caused her to be late on her monthly payments in the past. She was trying to clean up her credit. She had recently married, but her husband was not a U.S. citizen, so he could not get a loan.

Because I was in no rush to sell the property, I decided to give them a chance to buy the home. I gave them a lease with an option to buy at a fixed price for a fixed period of time. They put up a deposit for the option consideration. I gave them two years to try to get financing on this property. Their mortgage broker told me that if they started making their payments on time and could develop a strong payment history during that two-year period, they would be in a position to borrow the money from a conventional lender, although they might not be able to borrow the money at the lowest interest. With this arrangement, the people treat the home like their own, and hopefully, when the two-year period is up, they will be in a position to buy the home at a price that is fair. (I'll discuss various forms of unconventional financing that investors take advantage of in Chapter 9.)

I'll also discuss leases with an option as a strategy in Chapter 11. In some states, there are legal limits on lease options because some investors have taken advantage of consumers, so make sure you check the laws in the state where you plan on investing before you pursue this approach. You can find that out by simply calling the Department of Real Estate in the capital of the state where you are planning to invest and ask for a copy of the laws that pertain to real estate. You can also get this information through the National Association of Realtors: contact the local board of Realtors where you live and see if it knows of any new law changes. A Realtor should know whether lease options are doable in the state or not.

Lease options are a very good strategy for investors who either are just getting started or want to tie up a property at a negotiated price for a nego-tiated period of time. The investor has the time to find the right buyer for the property or to sell the option to another party.

What Are Your Goals for the Property You Are About to Invest In?

Another thing you need to do before you invest in any real estate is to con-sider what you want to do with a property. If you're planning to keep the property for the long term, are you interested in managing the property yourself, or are you going to get a property manager? I discuss the details of this decision in Chapter 8, but you need to at least consider this now, be-fore you start buying property. Property managers charge a monthly fee, which obviously adds to the costs of ownership that you will need to cover as well as the money you need up front for that property. So if you want to know how much cash you're going to be putting up and what your cash-on-cash return on the transaction of real estate will be, you need to factor in the expenses that are associated with the property, which includes manage-ment after the acquisition.

If you're interested, but you're not sure about buying a piece of property and holding it for the long term, do a rental survey in your area to determine what the vacancy rates are and what the property management fees are. You can do that by calling property managers in the neighborhood where you're trying to buy and asking them what they charge to manage property and whether they have any statistics on what the vacancy rates are in a par-ticular community.

When you look at a property, you need to do an analysis based on your income, your expenses, the financing you will be able to get, and the price.

Property managers' fees vary from region to region and city to city; in general, they can run anywhere from 5 to 25 percent of the gross rent that is charged on a monthly basis. If you're dealing in resort property, the property manager's fee can be even higher than that. A good rule of thumb is a 10 percent property management fee. If you can negotiate less, then you are doing okay.

Know Where You're Going to Get Money to Invest

Once you have assessed your current financial situation, clearly identified the financial goals you hope to achieve via real estate investing, and learned what you need to know about your credit history, you should consider where you're going to get the money to invest in property. I touched on this briefly at the beginning of the chapter; Checklist 2-4 provides some additional questions to consider.

Checklist 2-4   Know Where You Will Get the Money to Invest in Real Estate

❏ Are you going to use the equity in your home?

❏ Are you going to look at equity in other properties or in other things that you own and can sell to start raising funds?

❏ Are you going to use your credit cards to buy property?

❏ Are you going to use your pension or your IRA? This approach is one in which you can use your self-directed IRAs or 401(k)s to buy real estate or to generate other types of cash flows. (I discuss this in more detail in Chapter 9.)

❏ Are you going to consider approaching private investors, such as relatives or others, to lend you money to get you started?

Know where you're going to get the money *before* you start looking for any property or make any deals. Remember, your reputation is everything. If you cannot follow through on a negotiation, the seller and the Realtor associated with the seller most likely will not forget. The saying "it's a small world" is really true.

Know *why* you want to buy real estate in the first place—

- Are you investing in real estate to establish future financial security?
- Are you trying to capitalize on the numerous tax benefits?
- Are you hoping to use your real estate investment income to replace other income that you currently have (e.g., from part-time or full-time work)?

Next, determine what outcome you are trying to achieve before you buy. When you look at a property, you need to do an analysis based on your income, your expenses, the financing you will be able to get, and the price—because nine times out of ten, you will make money at the time you buy a property, not when you sell it.

For example, Joanne is a real estate investor who lives in Colorado. She's self-employed, and she needed to earn a certain income off of her rental real estate because she wanted to be able to develop her professional speaking career. She could not work at a conventional nine-to-five job, because in order to fulfill her dream, she needed to be promoting herself full-time. Joanne developed a game plan by determining how many properties she would need to buy in order to bring in $5,000 per month fairly quickly. To meet that goal, she needed to decide whether she was going to buy property, fix it up, and resell it, or whether she was going to buy property for the rental market. She ended up buying properties, holding them for a short term and fixing them up, and then selling them for a profit so that she was able to build some capital.

Eventually, she started buying properties and holding them for the *long* term and renting them out. Her tenants helped her make the payments on the properties every month, and because their rent was more than her mortgage payment, she earned income. In only four years, Joanne became successful enough in her investing to have built up enough cash reserves and monthly income to replace the income from her old job, and she was able to devote 100 percent of her time to her professional speaking business.

Joanne got started in real estate investing by refinancing her existing house and taking the cash to invest. In her game plan, she talked about how she was going to acquire $50,000, so she was able to take that $50,000 and keep building off of the seed money: she reinvested the capital from one property in other properties. She did that by buying starter homes, fixing them up, and then selling them for cash. She would roll the original principal amount and a small percentage of her profit into the next deal.

> *If you're asking relatives for money, you want to proceed with caution. Money can be an emotional issue for a lot of people, so think about how you want to approach your relatives for help.*

Beth lives in Los Angeles. She has been a real estate investor for 30 years. She's made her money by using equity from other properties she owns (but not her own family home). Beth has leveraged those other properties. She buys a property, she and her tenants pay down the loan to the point where there is significant equity in the property, and then she refinances the property because it's gone up in value. Beth takes the equity out of that property and purchases another investment property. She's built one on top of the other on top of the other, just with that strategy of taking out equity in a couple of her rentals to keep building more property value and buying more properties for herself. That's a phenomenal strategy.

However, a word of caution: when you take this approach, you are leveraging yourself and putting yourself at risk, because if the market turns and goes sour, you're upside down: you owe more than the property's worth. And if you have to sell the property for any reason, you could have a financial loss.

Pension and IRA Funds

Using your IRA or 401(k) to buy real estate is a phenomenal tool. Many people don't know that you can draw on these funds to make a down payment on a property, yet you can. However, you can't draw on a 401(k) to which a major corporation is making matching contributions; you can draw only on an individual retirement account or a *self-directed 401(k)*, which allows you to buy an asset in the name of the IRA or 401(k). You must have a custodian that will allow you to do this type of investing. (Chapter 9 will cover what the role of the custodian is, how this process works, and why real estate and other alternative cash flow instruments such as mortgage notes are a good way to invest.)

Borrowing Money from Relatives

Relatives can be an invaluable asset to you, but if you're asking relatives for money, you want to proceed with caution. Money can be an emotional issue for a lot of people, so think about how you want to approach your relatives for help. First of all, when you are initially setting your objectives, you should communicate what you're trying to accomplish to the people who are near and dear to you. When they realize what you're really trying to do, they may volunteer to help you out financially. If you can explain to your relative(s) why it would be effective, important, and positive for them to lend you money, you may develop a financial resource. If you plan on borrowing money from a relative, however, you want to make sure that the person you're borrowing from is secured. There are several ways to ensure that your relative is secured. A good attorney can help you with the right legal structure so that the person you are borrowing from is protected.

Borrowing money from relatives is a very personal issue. For myself, I don't like asking members of my family for money. I don't want to be "in bed" with my family, because it can be a very touchy situation.

Here is an example. I have friends who live in Mill Valley, California; they recently got married, and bought their own home. The house cost $1.1 million, which was more than they could afford, so they borrowed $100,000 from the husband's parents and put a first and a second mortgage on the house. They had none of their own cash in the deal. The parents simply lent them the money, with no interest and a request that they "just pay it back when you can."

When the couple moved into the property, they found that it needed work. They hired a contractor, who told them it would cost about $100,000 to do the necessary renovation, so they tapped their parents again, and their parents gave them another $100,000. The contractor who is doing the work has now spent well over $250,000 on this project. The parents have run out of money, and the two young people have no money of their own. They owe more on the property than what it is worth. The couple ended up suing the contractor in court because he went way over the original fix-up costs that he had given them in writing.

Hard-money lenders are a good source of money, but you should use them only for short-term financing. You don't want to borrow from them for a 30-year loan.

The parents had no security for the loan they made to their children. The young couple felt very guilty about this situation, but because they were in a financial crisis, and because they owed a lot more money than the house was really worth, they were stuck. No one won. At this writing, the case is going to court, but it will be years before the property is worth the money they have put into it. And the poor parents—well, fortunately, they can afford to lose the cash if they had to.

This situation is not unusual. It is fairly common for parents to lend their children money without having any legal protection. Moreover, most parents will give their kids a loan (if they're financially able to), and most parents will charge them some interest, but many parents don't require documentation on such loans. To protect themselves, the parents should have been put on the deed (unless they didn't care that they might lose their money). Relatives are a good source of money if you can convince them that the property is a good investment and it's a good deal, and in order to do that, you can offer your relatives or anyone you borrow from security for the loan. Unfortunately, in this particular example, this investment was not a good investment; in fact, it was a horrible investment.

If you're going to borrow money from any private party, you should discuss all possible scenarios. In general, people who lend money to someone else usually have enough money so that if they run into a problem with the borrower, they are prepared to suffer any losses. After all, they did not lend their last dime.

Getting Money from Hard-Money Lenders and Private Investors

There are also hard-money lenders who charge points and a higher interest rate (than conventional sources of funding, like banks—or relatives) for investors who need immediate cash or for individuals who are in dire straits and need money fast. Typically, hard-money lenders are private individuals. They are a good source of money, but you should use them only for short-term financing. You don't want to borrow from them for a 30-year loan.

There are also private investors who will lend money at a lower interest rate, sometimes with no points or fees associated with the loan. Many people would rather lend money than own any real estate themselves. Such people are a great source.

If you're going to look for this type of investor start with networking through the local Real Estate Investors Association, start going to meetings and listening to others networking. Try to absorb as much information as you can before you approach anyone. Then, ask around to find out which of the people in the room are interested in lending money on secured property. Arrange a first meeting with those investors, one on one, and find out the terms, length of time, and cash limit to their private lending requirements. Work with them on an individual, one-on-one basis, because your first deal with an outside investor may require additional collateral or funds than future deals. You have to develop a track record. If investors see that you can perform, they may be less stringent on future deals than they are in the beginning when they don't know you.

If you have all your ducks in a row, share your plan with the investor. Ask, "Would you be willing to work with me? And if so, what would be your criteria for our financial arrangement? What is it that you're looking for in terms of interest and term? How can I make you feel comfortable doing business with me?" It may take you several months to convince an investor to work with you; it's not going to happen overnight. You need to be out talking to the right people, developing a name for yourself and being seen. Show that you are serious about real estate investing so that private investors will take notice. Stay away from advertising for investors. Networking and word of mouth are the best ways to find an investor who would be willing to work with you.

Years ago, when I first moved to Colorado, I met an investor at a real estate conference. He had spent 33 years as a bond broker in New York. He had then retired and moved to California. He was interested in looking at investment opportunities, but he wasn't interested in managing them. I had not bought investment property in Colorado as yet. I was new to the state, and needed to learn my way around my local marketplace before I would consider buying investment property. At the time he came to visit, the Colorado market was undervalued—which he recognized. We went out shopping for properties, and he said, "This is a great market. I would like you to buy me *X* number of properties, and I'll pay you $750 per property." And I said, "Why would I do that? Would *you* be willing to front me or lend me some money so that *I* could go out and buy property?"

Because lenders need to know what you can afford, . . . have your tax returns available; a lender will want to see what kind of income you're currently earning, what your debt ratios are and your ability to pay your loans timely. This is how they assess you as a credit risk.

We ended up owning property together. If you want to utilize private investors who understand what you are trying to accomplish, you can establish comfortable ground by having the proper information that will put them at ease:

- Where the property is located
- The facts about the property,
- How much the property costs
- How much you need to put down
- What you can rent the property for
- What amount is needed for financing
- How long you will need the money

Once the private lender looks over the information you supply, he or she will evaluate whether they decide to either go ahead and lend to you or not. (Working with private money, other than hard-money lenders, can be tricky; more on this subject in Chapter 9.)

Get Your Tax Returns and Other Financial Information Ready to Show Potential Lenders

Because lenders need to know what you can afford, you need to pull together various financial documents:

- Have your tax returns available; a lender will want to see what kind of income you're currently earning.
- If you're renting your home, you may also need to provide potential lenders with a payment history from your landlord.
- If you're employed, you will need either a current W-4 or a letter stating that you're employed and in what capacity and that the probability of your continued employment is good.

In short, you need to look like a good credit risk. If you provide everything that the lender wants in a complete package, you will make yourself look stronger in the eyes of the lender. When working with Realtors, provide a preapproval letter if possible. Realtors will feel that they have a strong prospect and will work with you as they realize you already are approved for a loan. This makes their job much easier.

Make Sure You Have the Time to Devote to Real Estate Investing

Don't rush into real estate investing—just as you shouldn't rush into anything that affects your financial future. Make sure that you clearly establish your game plan and what you're trying to accomplish—both of which help you make the decision that is right for *you*.

If you are considering doing your own property management, when you are determining how much time it will take to invest in real estate, include the time required to find tenants, screen the tenants, and follow up or be available to the tenants. There are strategies to minimize property management to the point that you spend a smaller amount of time in managing property (and I'll cover these topics in Chapter 8).

This isn't a question of how many hours a week you're going to be spending. Instead, the most important factor to your success as a real estate investor will be the discipline to get out and start to look at property, farming your targeted areas, and looking for the right opportunity before making offers. All of this takes time. Some people spend only weekends, going to open houses; that's their strategy, and they make offers that way. Other investors use the newspaper or the Internet, and they find deals that way. You need to decide how much time you realistically have to devote to this business.

You also need to know what approach you're most comfortable with. For example, some investors hate talking to other people; therefore, they would rather do all their research through the Internet. Others enjoy visiting open houses and talking to sellers.

Time is a consideration. Finding good properties at great prices takes time. Be realistic about the amount of time you can spend doing the research, visiting properties, negotiating the transaction, and doing the due diligence to close the transaction. Try not to make up a number out of thin air. Whether it's 2 hours a week or 20, that's up to you, but factor your time constraints into your action plan.

There is no such thing as a minimum amount of time. Only you know what will fit with your work, family, and other obligations. Time is precious. Also, if you plan to put in 20 hours a week, but you can't spend that much time one week because other things have gotten in your way, don't feel guilty. You're going to do what you need to do to get the job done. You decide what that is. If you can spend just five or six hours a week doing what you need to do to continually market yourself and promote your real estate business, you will be fine. Just make sure that the goal you set for yourself is measurable and achievable and realistic.

Your formula for success can always be modified: You can change any action items, timelines, or other strategies any time you want to. Nothing is etched in stone. What you're trying to do is come up with a real estate investing strategy that's going to be successful for you, so that you can do the things in life that you really want to do.

Conclusion

The bottom line is that women make excellent investors: we are very good at setting up checklists and creating a game plan. We are skilled listeners and great negotiators, and we have the ability to accomplish our objectives with a detailed plan of action and a "to do" list. The true formula for success in real estate is your ability to find, negotiate for, and fund property, then either turn around and sell it or keep it for some period of time. By answering the questions I outlined in this chapter and coming up with a strategy that matches your needs, you will march on to success and have fun becoming an investor you can be proud of.

Finally, once you decide what type of property you're most interested in investing in, you need to farm a community or know the area that you're going to be buying property in. This is vitally important. Don't just go out and buy property anywhere; there are many horror stories illustrating the problems with this approach. Too many people trust other people who tell them, "This is a great area [to invest in]." Either they go out and buy something sight unseen or they buy the property because it looks good to them. In either case, they have no idea what they're getting themselves into, and then the market turns on them.

What's even worse is when a neighborhood turns on you, and you find that you have an investment that's worth a lot less than you anticipated, and you can't recoup your expenses. So, you really need to understand the market that you're going to be farming or focusing on before you go out and invest in any opportunities. In the next chapter, I will show you how to do just that . . . know your market, and you will know opportunity when it knocks.

3

What Type of Property Do You Want to Invest In? Determining Your Investing Strategy

You've developed your financial plan, you've identified your financial goals and what you hope to gain by investing in real estate, you know your credit history, you know your financial comfort level, you know where you're going to get the money to invest in real estate, and you have all the necessary financial documents in order. The next step in preparing to succeed in real estate investing is to decide what type of property you want to invest in. This decision determines your investing strategy, and this chapter describes various options for you to consider. This chapter also shows you how to identify real estate opportunities and find properties that fit your strategy. And it describes a fundamental principle of real estate investing: that you make money when you *buy*, not when you sell.

Decide What Type of Property You Want to Invest In

Before you look at any property, ask yourself the questions in Checklist 3-1. Understanding what you want to buy will help you identify opportunities, because you will then look *only* at properties that you would consider investing in, rather than wasting your valuable time looking at properties that don't fit into your plans. For example, Realtor Tami Spaulding works with one investor who loves to buy old farmhouses, hold them for two or three years, strip them, remodel them, and make good money. You need to decide what *you* want to invest in. Or, consider this advice from Tracy Rewey, who specializes in real estate notes and owner-financing deals:

> *Try something new! Don't just think of real estate in the traditional sense. Think mobile homes, land, notes with interest income, owner financing, or tax deeds. There are all sorts of opportunities related to real estate outside the rental market or fix and flips.*

Checklist 3-1   Determining Your Investing Strategy

❑   What type of property are you interested in buying? For example:

    ❑   Do you want to buy single-family homes?

    ❑   Do you want to buy multifamily homes?

    ❑   Do you want to buy mobile homes?

    ❑   Do you want to buy storage units?

    ❑   Would you consider preconstruction or working with builders?

    ❑   Are you interested only in residential properties?

    ❑   Are you interested in commercial properties (especially "soft" commercial properties, which are office buildings rather than, say, factories)?

❑   In what area do you want to invest?

    ❑   Are you interested only in suburban locations, or in downtown urban neighborhoods?

    ❑   Are you looking at areas that are gentrifying?

    ❑   Would you consider marginal neighborhoods?

What Type of Property Do You Want to Invest In?

❑   Are you interested in retirement communities?

❑   What exactly are you looking to achieve in investing?

❑   Are you going to buy only one property a year? Or more?

❑   Are you going to turn around and sell the property? Or do you plan to hold onto it and rent it out?

❑   Do you plan to "flip" it?

❑   Do you want to rehab it and resell it?

If You Want to Invest in Single-Family Homes.   Investing in single-family homes was my personal real estate strategy when I lived in Ft. Collins, Colorado. I focused on four distinct communities; all were residential—not starter homes, but the next step up, and within walking distance of elementary schools with crossing guards on the street corners. Moms could go shopping at the grocery store, which was a short distance from the home. Major corporate centers were not far away, and the homes were close to the interstate for commuters. In other words, the neighborhoods had all the benefits and amenities that people look for in suburbia. They were nice neighborhoods, where people owned, not rented. I focused on buying in neighborhoods where people would want to stay for the long term: tenants who would take good care of my properties, who would treat the property like it was theirs, and who would have no motivation to leave.

Determine your strategy before you buy. Knowing your focus will help you to first identify the areas you want to target; then look for the opportunity.

If You Want to Invest in Urban Real Estate.   Another investor's strategy may be to buy property in a city, rather than in suburbia. There are many investors who invest in urban real estate, either in low-income housing or in up-and-coming neighborhoods. There are many good reasons to invest in urban real estate, especially if you live in the city. One reason is that the rental market is usually pretty strong because people have to work in the city, and there are always people who want to live near where they work. Also, if the city has good mass transit, that makes urban real estate more desirable. On the downside, however, the city may impose taxes that can cut into your cash flow.

If urban real estate is part of your investing strategy, you should look at areas of the city where you're seeing gentrification, opportunity for growth, and momentum in terms of positive changes. Chapter 5 offers more information on gentrifying communities, which are often great opportunities for rehabbing, and Chapter 8 offers guidelines on how to buy Section 8 housing, which is government-subsidized property (and is usually urban but can also be suburban).

Be careful . . . about investing in retirement communities, because they obviously limit the market of occupants to people of retirement age.

If You Want to Invest in Retirement Communities. Another strategy is to look at retirement communities, where people are trying to downsize into condos, patio homes, or small villas because they don't want the big house with its maintenance problems. Focus on significant retirement communities that are already in place so that you can capitalize on somebody's desire to downsize or move into a community.

Be careful, though, about investing in retirement communities, because this strategy obviously limits the potential occupants to people of retirement age, and this may make it more difficult for you to rent—or resell. For example, my friend Howard bought in an over-55-year-old community. He felt that this would be a great marketing strategy for him, because when he developed his investing plan, he decided that he wanted tenants that he defined as "safe" tenants—i.e., tenants without kids, tenants who are older. He felt that older people would cause less wear and tear on a property than, say, a family with three kids running around, who would be more likely to eat up your carpets, ruin your bathrooms, and so on. Instead, Howard wanted to rent to nice, older tenants who would sit in their rocking chairs and look at the sunset every night. So that became his strategy.

What Type of Property Do You Want to Invest In?

He started farming in over-55-year-old neighborhoods. Almost a year ago, he found a house and paid $165,000 for it. He had close to 100 percent financing on this property. He borrowed the money from one of his business partners, who financed the sale for Howard at 6½ percent with an adjustable-rate mortgage. He rented the property out to a tenant for $1,200 a month. With the mortgage payments he's making, Howard is breaking even on the mortgage payments versus the rental income received.

Recently, Howard's tenant decided to buy a property instead of continuing to rent. The tenant bought his own property with a fixed-rate mortgage so that he would not have to pay Howard rent increases each year. The original tenant didn't stay even a year, and now he's leaving. Unfortunately, Howard can't find another 55-year-old tenant who's willing to pay $1,200 a month. So far, when he has shown this property, he hasn't been able to get more than $1,000 a month, so it turns out that Howard will owe more on his monthly mortgage than what the property will rent for.

The bottom line is that Howard narrowed his tenant pool too much by investing in an over-55 community, because many older people still have the money to buy property. He also did not consider the possibility that his tenants might move out, and that in the current real estate market, where interest rates are still low, they might still be able to afford to buy. Instead, Howard thought he'd have a tenant for life who was just going to sit there and maintain his property for him. That was his biggest mistake. Finally, if he wanted to invest in an over-55 community, $165,000 was the wrong price to pay because his numbers didn't work out to allow him to make money.

So what should he do now? He should sell that property, using a lease with an option to buy, and get out. He should have the option expire in a year; hopefully, his lessee would exercise the option. If he could get a $5,000 option consideration, that would make up the difference between his mortgage payments and $1,000 or $1,100 per month for a year. With this approach, he would get $5,000 up front. He would have a $200 per month negative (i.e., if he leases for $1,000 per month and his mortgage payment is $1,200 per month), or $2,400 that he would lose during the year, but he would still be ahead by $2,600 because of the $5,000 up front, and he could get out of this property.

Then, he should never again buy in an over-55 community so as not to narrow his market. In fact, he told me he's probably never going to buy rental property again because he's too busy to attend to it himself, which means that he would have to turn it over to a property manager, but he doesn't have the money to pay for that. This is why you need to determine your strategy before you buy. Knowing your focus will help you to first identify the areas you want to target; *then* you can look for the opportunity.

If You Want to Invest in Less-Expensive Property, Mobile Homes, or Starter Neighborhoods. The strategies just described all focused on established (i.e., stable) communities and up-and-coming neighborhoods, but that doesn't mean that you need to avoid any kind of marginal neighborhoods. In fact, some investors' strategy is to buy *only* in marginal neighborhoods. The point here is that *you* need to identify the type of communities in which *you* want to invest.

If your goal is to invest small dollars and have positive cash flow quickly, mobile homes are a great way to invest in real estate.

For example, I know one investor who buys nothing but mobile homes. Martha buys mobile homes at estate sales, puts them on mobile-home lots or on spaces in mobile-home parks, and then turns them on a five-year rent-to-own program, at an interest rate that's fair. After five years of timely payments, the tenant becomes the owner. This is Martha's model; it's the only type of real estate investing she does. The mobile homes she buys cost under $20,000, and she often gets the owner of the home to finance the sale for her. She's made a nice profit on this type of real estate, using very little of her own money.

This strategy might not appeal to everyone. There are potential disadvantages; the big one is her concern that her tenants may not pay, or may even leave in the middle of the night and abandon the property and what they owe her. But Martha is comfortable with this kind of risk, because mobile homes are cash cows. Consider the math:

What Type of Property Do You Want to Invest In?

- Suppose she puts $2,000 into an estate-sale mobile home and moves it onto a lot.
- She pays $200 per month rent on that lot.
- She then sells the home through her rent-to-own program for $500 per month for five years plus 12½ percent interest.
- She has $2,000 in the deal, and she's already getting $6,000 back ($500/month × 12 months) without the interest in year 1. She's made an infinite yield on her money.

If her initial tenant skips in year 2, she can get another tenant, but she's already more than recouped her investment, because she's made $500 per month rent in year 1, or a total of $6,000 for the year, which earns her a $4,000 profit.

This strategy works very, very well in the southeast part of the United States, or in other areas where mobile homes are very popular. And estate sales are a great way to buy the homes, because the heirs just want to get rid of the property. You buy them, put them on a lot, rent to own, and make a positive cash flow every month off the investment.

Again, there are downsides: people don't pay the rent, so you've got to go chase them; they get up and leave in the middle of the night; and/or they don't take care of the property. There are downsides to any situation. You need to assess the decision in terms of risk, time, and cash flow. If your goal is to invest small dollars and have positive cash flow quickly, mobile homes are a great way to invest in real estate. With this strategy, your marketing plan would be estate sales and mobile-home communities. You can talk to mobile-home owners about putting your homes on their lots. Or, you can buy lots yourself and get monthly income off the sale or rental of the lot as well as the home. For more information on how to invest in mobile homes, pick up the book *Deals on Wheels* by Lonnie Scruggs, a master of this strategy.

If You Want to Invest in Preconstruction. Another strategy for some investors is to buy preconstruction condos or apartment buildings. Here, you are purchasing a property either while it is still under construction or, in many cases, before construction begins. Investing in preconstruction property can be an opportunity to get in on the ground floor by putting up just a little bit of money now as a deposit. Then at completion of the unit, you will put up the rest of the money. This gives you time to get the property financed, and you are betting that the property will appreciate in value.

Let's look at an example of how this might work. You buy a property for $250,000; in one year, when the unit is completed, you obtain permanent financing. The property may have appreciated; in this example, let's say, it is worth $300,000. You can sell the property or assign the contract (if it is assignable) before the unit is completed, or you can obtain permanent financing. This has been a popular strategy in the recent past. In fact, broker and third-party property manager Jaime Raskulinecz says that "in the right market, [preconstruction] can be a great investment. You have to know the market and the area in order to make an informed decision."

What are the downsides to this type of investment? The transaction may not be assignable. If the market flattens or turns, that condo that you bought for $250,000 may be worth only $200,000; in that case, you may owe more than the property is worth. Realtor Tami Spaulding also mentions that if you invest in preconstruction property, keep in mind that you may need to spend a lot of money on appliances, the yard, drapes, and so on. Mortgage company operations manager Renee Falgout cautions that "with new construction, builders usually have buyers pay their portion of the closing costs that include, but are not limited to, the impact fees, stamps on the deed, and the owners' title policy, which can be an additional $7,500 for a $150,000 home." Finally, here's what broker and trainer Magi Bird has to say about preconstruction property:

The first four homes I ever bought were preconstruction. But they were bought with the intention of occupying first and renting out later, a requirement of the loans I placed. After watching the effect of investors reserving preconstruction units, closing them, then marketing them as resale property, I have had an opportunity to see the damage done by such speculation. I think that speculators in a marketplace drive up pricing and affordability to the level that there is a recoil and a corresponding drop in property values. The law of supply and demand is one they have yet to amend or repeal. Therefore, due to supply at the higher price having outstripped the affordability of those with a demand for housing, prices go down, and everyone, including the investor, is the poorer for it.

Any investor must bear in mind that new housing is being purchased at the top of the market, as the investor is paying today's inflated materials and labor costs. Better buys can be made by an equity investor in the resale marketplace. As an investment philosophy, counting on appreciation is the most speculative avenue of approach in use by investors and a poor platform on which to build financial solvency. It is not a practice that I support, except in the case of an owner-occupant.

Checklist 3-2 offers some guidelines to protect yourself when investing in preconstruction.

Checklist 3-2 How to Protect Yourself When Investing in Preconstruction

❑ Know the market.

❑ Know the economic forecast for the immediate future.

❑ Check out the inventory of other projects on the market to make sure that you are not in a situation where there is a lot of inventory.

❑ Check out the builder to make sure he really does what he says he does; check the Better Business Bureau, Department of Real Estate, or wherever the builder was issued a license to make sure his license is current and in good standing.

❑ Find out what is in line for permits.

For example, Cheri is a recent college graduate who was offered a job in Oregon. She was not planning on moving for six months. She bought a home in Oregon that was under construction by a national builder. This was supposed to be completed during the six-month window so that she would have a place to live when she moved. It did not work out that way. Many months later,, she is still renting an apartment and waiting for the house to be completed. Interest rates have gone up, so she will have a harder time getting financing, and she now needs a higher down payment. Finally, there is a chance that when she gets ready to close, the value of the home will have decreased. Needless to say, she is frustrated.

Always remember the real estate golden rule:
do due diligence, and go in with your eyes wide open.

I know of another investor who bought a condo in Tampa at the beginning of a construction period. Tom lives in New York. He negotiated and signed a contract to buy a condo for $200,000 as an investment. He wanted to start building a portfolio of rental property in the Tampa Bay area, because he plans on retiring to Tampa in five years. He put $20,000 down, and he arranged for take-out financing. The builder started construction on his condo.

Six months into construction, a hurricane came through the area. It didn't wreck this particular construction site, but it slowed down the process considerably: the hurricane caused a lot of damage *south* of Tampa, so contractors from Tampa went south to help fix properties. The Tampa condo construction stalled for *another* six months.

After fourteen months, the condo is just about finished. But the real estate market in Tampa has softened. Tom is concerned about the future of this investment. When will the condo be completed? What is its true value? Will he be able to rent it out? If so, will he be negative (in terms of cash flow) every month? Good questions! What are his options at this point? He basically has two options:

1. He can walk away from his $20,000 investment and sell the condo for whatever he can get. If the condo is worth $190,000 today, he would lose $10,000 on the deal, but the advantage of this option is that he doesn't have to tie up his credit and get permanent financing.
2. The other option is to move forward; he can get a loan on this property, plan to sell it sometime in the future, and hope to break even. If Tom holds the property for the long term, chances are that it will go up in price. Tampa Bay is a solid area (at this writing) from an economic standpoint. More than 1,000 people are moving to the state of Florida every day.

What Type of Property Do You Want to Invest In?

Which option is better? I know several people in this situation right now, which demonstrates that you must be very careful if you choose this type of investment because of changing market conditions—and unforeseen circumstances, like hurricanes. In these cases, there wasn't really much due diligence Cheri or Tom could have done to foresee a slowdown in the real estate market or a delay in construction.

This is not to say that investing in preconstruction is not a good strategy. Always remember the real estate golden rule: do due diligence, and go in with your eyes wide open.

Rebecca McLean, executive director of the NREIA, confirms this advice:

Do your due diligence! Make sure you have the knowledge and information that you need. Have a team of professionals (attorneys, Realtors, and tax professionals) and use them! The biggest mistakes I've made were because I just wasn't thorough enough.

Be careful about making decisions under pressure. Never short-circuit your own systems because of a "desperate" situation. You would be amazed how quickly you can move through your own systems if the deal needs to be executed quickly.

There are many investors around the country who are doing very well in preconstruction investments. There are courses on the subject. Patricia, an investor from Orlando, Florida, is on her third preconstruction deal. She puts money up front, makes sure the contract is assignable (meaning that she can transfer the contract to someone else), and assigns the contract while the property is still under construction. This way, she takes no permanent financing. Tricia makes a profit on each deal. That's a great way to invest.

Buying Land, Lots, and More . . . Subdivision. Buying a property before the subdivision has been approved can be a problem: in many states, buyers can make reservations on homes, but they can't complete them until the subdivision itself has received final local and state approval. This is very important because builders and developers will say they're building a subdivision and start advertising it, but if they do not have the permits and approval, this could slow or stall the development.

Until such time as permits are issued, the buyer does have the right to back out of a purchase and receive a full refund. Some investors love the idea of buying new homes that have warranties on them, so that there is no maintenance or repair in the beginning. Also, investors love to buy land, hold that land for appreciation, then turn around and sell the land. However, if the local government decides not to zone a property, and you go ahead and try to market the property anyway, you could be in trouble.

Sheila in Macon, Georgia, bought 10 different lots at about $5,000 per lot in 2002. Three years later, those lots were worth $37,500 each. That's not a bad return if Sheila wants to sell. Buying land to hold can be another great investment strategy, especially in areas where people are relocating.

If you're interested in investing in international markets, know the law, and retain the services of an attorney in the country where you want to acquire real estate.

Sally was interested in buying lots on the water in a neighborhood in Port Charlotte, Florida, because it was absolutely gorgeous. She researched the property and found that environmentalists had been successful in changing the zoning: the state had mandated that no lots could be sold because that particular area was a nesting site for rare birds. The environmentalists got together to get the area rezoned *after* the builder thought he could start building single-family homes in the area; he had already been selling the lots and was trying to develop out this subdivision. The builder did not disclose what the environmentalists were trying to do, which would have been a real problem for Sally if she had not done research on zoning.

Rita has a property in Colorado, and she has decided to try to sell it. She bought raw land that had no water and no water rights. If the property will not perk (i.e., if you can't dig down into the ground and hit water), she won't be able to have water coming into the property. What is the property really worth? Zip. You don't want to buy something until you really do some background research to check out what is reality.

Some investors have had success buying in subdivisions, however. Barbara O'Connell describes two such investments, the first of which went well:

What Type of Property Do You Want to Invest In?

Early in my career, I put a deposit on a single-family home in a brand-new subdivision in Fremont, California, a very nice city I was living in at the time in the east bay of the San Francisco Bay area. At the time, the market was neither a seller's market nor a buyer's market. It was just an average typical market. The builder was a small builder that was doing a small "in fill" subdivision in a very desirable area of town that had the best school profiles. This builder was new to the area and had slightly underpriced his inventory for the first-phase release. The prices were good, and the location was excellent, so I put $500 down as a "reservation' and was told the house would be completed in six months. The house was actually delivered in nine months.

The market started to become a seller's market while the house was under construction, and the builder increased his prices by $50,000 for the same model in the next release. I purchased the house for $188,000. When I closed on the property, the same model was selling for $256,000. Since prices were still increasing, I held on a little longer, and I sold the property for $318,000 about seven months after the house was complete.

That was in 1988. Last time I checked, that same model is now selling for over $900,000. Even with price declines of at least 20 percent in the early 1990s (from 1990 to 1994), this house appreciated more than $700,000 in an 18-year period. Not bad for an initial investment of $500. If I had only held it longer! Yet in 1989, I thought I was pretty smart making $130,000 profit on a $500 investment in less than two years!

Her second investment did not go so well:

Thinking I was a brilliant property investor, I decided to try it again. I took the $130,000 profit from the house in Fremont and decided I would parlay it into multiple properties. The market was still rising fast. The Fremont area had gotten too expensive, so I decided to move to an outlying area that was less expensive. I put de-

posits down on six properties in one day in different subdivisions in Brentwood, Antioch, and Tracy. All three towns were up-and-coming towns with massive amounts of building going on. All six properties were in new subdivisions, and the houses were yet to be built. One by one, as the houses were completed, I bought each property. Each property had gone up a small amount during construction.

In addition to these six properties, I had also bought a number of resale homes dating from the mid-1980s until 1990. So with the 6 new properties, I was the proud owner of 23 single-family homes in and around the bay area. I remember thinking that perhaps my husband and I should retire. After all, we had millions of dollars in equity in our homes!

Lesson 1: What goes up can come down—fast. *The market turned within months of my closing on the last home. Instead of multiple offers at rising prices, there were no offers and declining prices. The average price of homes in the bay area declined by 20 percent in less than three months and declined by 50 percent in southern California. I had bought about half of my properties at the peak of the market cycle. Half of the properties had negative equity in 1990.*

Lesson 2: Equity and appreciation will not pay the bills. *In the late1980s, most investors, including myself, ignored the fact that the properties had negative cash flow. The property generated less income than the mortgage, never mind maintenance and vacancies and nonpaying tenants. We all tolerated this because the appreciation more than made up for the monthly losses, and we got huge tax deductions because of the properties. Or so we thought.*

Once the market was no longer appreciating, investors and speculators and some owner-occupiers stopped buying. As a result, not only did home prices decline, but there was now a flood of rentals where there had been a shortage of rentals. Investors who could not sell their homes turned them into rentals instead. The same thing happened with sellers who had to relocate, and there was a mass exodus from the state at the time. Most could not af-

ford to leave their houses empty, so they either lowered the price drastically or turned their properties into rentals. This pushed rent prices as well as selling prices down. To make matters worse, landlords had less choice in whom they accepted as tenants in order to fill vacancies that started mounting.

Remember, at this time, I had 23 rentals, all with negative cash flow. In good times, the properties averaged $200 per month negative cash flow each. That meant if I had them all rented at top market rent with no vacancies or maintenance, I was paying $4,600 per month in negative cash flow. When vacancies started increasing and rents started declining, the problem got worse—a lot worse. Many of the properties were vacant, and it was hard finding good tenants.

Lesson 3: Don't count your chickens. Six months earlier, I had quit my marketing management job with a Fortune 100 company subsidiary. Why not, I thought: I was making significantly more money in real estate investing than as an employee of a major corporation. At the time I quit my job, I was making a six-figure income; we had moved into a $1.8 million home about the same time as well. No job, huge negative cash flows, big mortgage payment, declining home prices. Could it get any scarier? You guessed it. My husband got laid off from his job after being employed at the same company for over 21 years. The company decided to shut his division down. His salary was substantial and had been supporting the negative cash flows! Six months earlier, we had been talking about retirement, and now we were potentially facing bankruptcy. Half the portfolio had negative equity. The other half had only a little equity. It would be very difficult to sell everything quickly enough to survive.

Nevertheless, Barbara continues to be optimistic about subdivisions:

One of my favorite techniques during a fast-moving market is still to reserve a home that is about to be built in a new subdivision and allow the house to appreciate while it is being built. The longer the *lead time, the better, as far as I am concerned. I recently bought some homes in Florida after a hurricane, and it took the builder about 18 months to deliver the homes. In the meantime, there was a shortage of homes in the area, and prices went up about $80,000 from the time we put our deposit down until they delivered the homes. Some of the homes were delivered during the peak of the market cycle, and we could have sold them the day we closed for a tidy profit.*

In the meantime, the market has turned; there is now too much inventory, and prices are headed downward for a while again. Even so, if we wanted to sell now, we would still make between $50,000 and $80,000 on each house. Considering that our initial deposit on these deals was usually $5,000 and we did not have to get involved in construction financing, the return on our invested funds has been excellent. But I am a long-term hold person, and I prefer to hold most of the homes for the long term. Many baby boomers are retiring to Florida, and I would not be surprised if prices doubled again in the next market cycle. I will say, however, that because of the excess inventory at this time, it may take a few years for the next cycle to begin again.

If You Want to Invest in Commercial Property

Commercial property is an excellent investment if you've got the mentality to deal with it. There are advantages to buying commercial property:

- Commercial property generally has much longer-term leases than residential property.
- The tenant is usually a business, instead of an individual or family.
- That business is going to pay a larger amount of rent.
- The business will help pay for the upkeep.

If the property has executive suites or office condos, keep in mind that the tenants will also be paying for the receptionist and other types of amenities that the building may offer. That's an additional cost that you need to factor when you're buying commercial property so that you can determine your net operating income (i.e., what you're really going to net out of the transaction).

If You Want to Invest in International Markets. Some people believe that the investment climate in the United States is getting worse. They look at investing outside of the United States as an opportunity to grow their net worth. Central America is very popular at the moment: Costa Rica, Panama, Mexico. For example, Heather decided that she wanted to invest in Panama. She checked out the market and decided to focus on one particular area where there seemed to be a lot of American and Canadian expatriates who were interested in investing in and eventually retiring to this area of Panama.

Heather bought land from a developer. She held onto the lots until a couple of homes were built and sold. She then decided to sell her lot back to the same developer for a nice profit. Because property is still less expensive in Central America, and there seems to be growth (especially from retirees who can move there and live well off of their fixed incomes), many investors are interested in acquiring investment-type property. I recently spoke at a Central American conference on real estate: 30 percent of the Realtors in the audience who were not from Central America bought condos in Panama City, Panama. That was about 50 people. *Caution:* If you're interested in investing in international markets, know the law, and retain the services of an attorney in the country where you want to acquire real estate. Every country has different rules. For example, it is necessary to be a corporation to buy property in Panama. In France, you must go through a *notaire*, who does the due diligence all the way from the time when the property was first built to the present. Closings in France can take months.

This example illustrates why it's so important to develop *your own* investing strategy and to identify where and what type of property *you* want to invest in. I would certainly not recommend that anybody look outside his or her neighborhood and buy in another state or region or another part of the world without doing really thorough due diligence. Investing internationally isn't exactly ideal for beginning real estate investors—unless you know the laws of the country you are investing in.

Making Your Decision about Property Types. To sum up this part of the chapter, on deciding what type of property you want to invest in, the basic assumption of this entire book is that women can be successful real estate investors—whether you're a beginner or an advanced investor. You can be successful even if you've never invested in your life—as long as you have a good head on your shoulders and common sense. When considering an acquisition, ask yourself: if you bought it, would you live there? Look at each opportunity from an objective standpoint, not an emotional one. Consider:

- The type of property you want to invest in, based on your specific needs
- The demography and the studies of the area you're investing in to make sure that area has a growth opportunity

Earlier, I gave examples of buying mobile homes or preconstruction because both those situations require smaller sums of cash to get into. With preconstruction, you don't need to finance the purchase until the end, (unless you are paying some of financing/draw costs of the construction) when the building is done. Instead, an investor needs only to put down some money now and some money later. In the example of the mobile home, that investor bought from estate sales on a very inexpensive $2,000 average sale, and she generated immediate cash flow.

What Makes a Good Deal

To determine what makes a good deal (regardless of what your strategy is), you need to consider *all* costs of getting the transaction completed. Checklist 3-3 provides a list of what to ask. All of these fees need to be considered as part of the price of ownership.

You also need to do an estimate based again on what you're going to do with the property. Consider the following:

- If you're going to turn around and resell the property, how active is the market? That is, how many days are existing properties on the market (listed to sell)?
- If you are going to keep the property, what kind of current rental income are you going to be able to get from that property?

In short, when you identify opportunities for investment, consider all of these items as part of acquisition costs, along with your down payment and

Checklist 3-3   Know All Costs of
Doing a Deal Before You Buy

❏   If you're going to get a loan, how much is the application fee? (This can fluctuate.)

❏   How much is the appraisal fee? (On average, this is $250 and up.)

❏   What are your loan costs? (These are negotiable.)

❏   What will any recording fees be? (These are fees to legally record the deed, and they vary depending on the local government, which fixes the cost of recording fees based on the price of the property.)

❏   Are you going to be charged any origination fees? (An origination fee is a fee that a lender charges for originating the loan. It's usually a point or a point and a half, depending on who you go through for your loan).

❏   Will there be any escrow, title company, and credit report fees?

inspection fees. You need to factor in all the costs of being able to tie up the property before you actually go out and buy a property.

Identifying Real Estate Investing Opportunities

Once you've identified the type of property you want to invest in and you've calculated all the costs, you can start to look for opportunities to buy. There are many, many ways to do that. The following are some common ways that people find property.

Investing in Foreclosures

A lot of investors like foreclosures (or preforeclosures, when people are in distress and behind on their payments—savvy investors will try to work out a deal with distressed property owners who have fallen behind in their payments to the bank). At present, some states are changing their laws to protect borrowers who have defaulted on their payments. This is due to investors who paid pennies on the dollar for property and the perception that the borrowers were cheated out of all equity they built up while owning the real estate. We will probably see more legislation as interest rates continue to rise and more property owners fall behind on in their mortgages (Lisa's projection).

Caution: Watch out for

- Paying too much for a foreclosure.
- Not doing the proper due diligence. For example, there might be mechanic's liens against the property. Or the owners might not have paid their taxes, so the IRS put a lien on the property. The poor soul who buys a foreclosure with a problem like this and didn't do the right due diligence can get stuck.

There is a lot of work involved in buying foreclosures. If you're just starting out as a real estate investor, you should definitely go to the courthouse or go online to find out what the foreclosure rate in your area is. In fact, if you're just starting out, I would not recommend foreclosures as your number one strategy.

That said, there are three stages of foreclosure that we will explore later in this book.

1. Preforeclosure, when the borrowers are behind on their payments and the bank is taking steps to foreclose and get them out of the property
2. Purchasing property on the actual day of the foreclosure (from the courthouse steps this is a bid process)
3. After the foreclosure, when the bank that is in control of the property contacts a Realtor and puts the property on the market for sale

If the lender takes a property back at the courthouse steps, it becomes an REO (Real Estate Owned) by the bank. The longer the lender has to hold it, the worse it is. The lender needs to get that property off its books. After all, it can't pay depositors with loans that it's not getting paid on. So the lender needs to unload such properties as soon as possible.

Buying Property through Probate. Estate sales are good places to buy property because heirs are typically motivated sellers. Most investors don't think to use probate sales as a marketing tool. You can buy property through the probate courts. You don't get a lot of competition there because many people basically are not sure how to do it, but you certainly can go to the courthouse and find out how to do it. You need to know at what point in the probate process the heirs can sell a property. The property is advertised in the newspaper. There are regular opportunities for investors to find property that comes through the probate process. Moreover, you can usually buy property at a discount. The heirs get their cash, and you get a property that cash flows!

Finding Properties through Relocation Companies

Another way you can find opportunities is to work through relocation companies, which assist corporate employees who are being relocated to a different area of the country. A company that is relocating employees is a motivated seller because it's going to get stuck with the property if it can't sell that property. You can contact "relo" companies that are working with major corporations and tell them what your parameters are for the type of property you're interested in. Then, if the relo company needs to transfer someone who is unable to sell his property for the price he wants, you have an opportunity to buy in., The relo company may be willing to contact you first, before it has to incur any additional fees, because there are carrying costs for the lender and, in this case, the corporation.

Checking Out Open Houses

Open houses are another source of great opportunities to find property—the best time to visit an open house is at the beginning or the end of an open house, when the Realtor has time to answer your questions. Open houses are a fun thing to do with your spouse or significant other. Also, you can find great decorating and design ideas at open houses. If you are interested in the property, be sure to find out whether the owner is motivated to sell. At times, sellers will test the market to see if they can get an inflated price for their home. *These are not motivated sellers.* Motivation = opportunity.

For example, people who are trying to move up to more expensive housing may need to sell their existing home first. This is a contingency that is put into the contract for the more expensive home in case they cannot afford to carry both mortgages for the long term so they can qualify for the new loan, and can move into the more expensive home. That's an outstanding opportunity for real estate investors. These sellers are motivated *emotionally* to get rid of the house so that they can move into the new house, and they're motivated *financially* because they need to be able to qualify for the new loan. They have to get rid of their other property in order to qualify. This becomes an opportunity for you because such sellers tend to be more motivated and flexible.

A deal becomes more valuable when you have motivating factors and a motivated seller. You win when you know you're at the right place at the right time—and I'll discuss this point further in Chapter 5.

Checklist 3-4   Tips on Finding Investing Opportunities

Follow this step-by-step checklist for doing a real estate transaction. Persistence and follow-up are key. Let this checklist be your road map to success.

- ❏ Get the assistance you need from the financial side. (preapproval letter)
- ❏ Evaluate your local market.
- ❏ Get out and start making offers at open houses where homes are being shown.
- ❏ Get on the phone and call ads in the newspapers.
- ❏ Go on the Web and see what's for sale by owner or Realtor.
- ❏ Start making offers on property.
- ❏ Ask the right questions to find out what each seller's motivation is.
- ❏ Do the due diligence before closing the transaction.
- ❏ Close the transaction. You now own the property!

Wise women prepare by doing the following:

- ❏ Decide on your objectives, and identify what type of property you're interested in and where you're going to buy. These decisions are vital to your success, no matter what strategy you use.

What Type of Property Do You Want to Invest In?

- ❏ Look for areas and avenues where people don't always go. Walk a different path where the competition is not as fierce.

- ❏ Research the demographics of a community that interests you, the school systems, the crime rate, and other factors that might be important to you as a real estate investor. (Chapter 4 provides more information on doing due diligence when you're researching your target markets.)

Wise women tip: when you're looking on the Web to find properties for sale, keep in mind that everybody else is looking at the same sites you are. Do something different to find real estate opportunities that will be good for you and match your investing strategy.

You Make Money When You Buy, Not When You Sell

You definitely make money when you buy, not when you sell, and that's an important thing to keep in mind. You can also make money on creative financing of the property. You may offer the seller their price if you can get your terms.

For example, you might try to get the seller to finance the sale. Remember the example I gave that in Chapter 2 of a woman who was downsizing from the home that she had lived in for 45 years, the house where she had raised her children. Her motivation was emotional, not financial. She wanted to make sure that the property she was selling would be well taken care of years down the line because she had an emotional attachment to it. She didn't want to see weeds in her yard.

In this case the price wasn't the main issue for me; instead, I was more interested in her ability to owner-finance the sale of this property. I asked her if she would consider this. This is an example of being in the right place at the right time and buying a property at the right price. I can pay full price, if she would finance the sale and allow me to make monthly payments to her. Doing it this way would allow my payments to be more affordable than they would have been if I had gone to the bank and gotten a loan. Plus, I did not have to incur origination fees and other costs associated with conventional financing. When the seller is willing to finance the sale, interest rate, and price are always negotiable.

At the same time, the seller was able to get her needs met: she receives monthly income, and she knew that her property would be taken care of. There wasn't a contract between us that specified that the property would be cared for well; you can't do that in a contract or in a purchase offer. She simply trusted me, because when we met, I was prepared. I brought a binder containing pictures of other properties in my portfolio, so that she could see the condition of homes that I have purchased in the past, and feel comfortable with me and our transaction. I told her that she was welcome to drive around to any of the properties and take a look at them at any given time. That made her very comfortable with financing the sale and with me.

Women are great at being organized and prepared. When you buy right—i.e., when you make a good deal—you get to take advantage of the profit, whether you keep the property for income or sell it for immediate profits. You should take all of these factors into consideration because they'll help you make the deal that is most profitable for you. In this case, if I decide to sell that property, I will definitely make money on the back end of it, and in the meantime, I'm making $700 net on the front end every month—which is good enough for me. By knowing what you're trying to accomplish before you buy, you will have a plan for the property and have a good estimate of your realized profit. And that is what constitutes success in real estate: profit, income, and cash flow, so that we can pursue what is really important in our lives.

There is nothing wrong with borrowing money to buy property, but be careful, especially in an area where real estate prices are volatile.

Here's another example. Suzanne was trying to sell her property fast. She was getting married to an out-of-town professional, and she needed to relocate. She was emotionally struggling with the price because this was her first home. I offered to pay full price if Suzanne would finance the sale. I put 10 percent down, and Suzanne financed the property for 15 years at 6.5

percent interest. The rent I received gave me $150 per month more than my payments. Three years later, the tenants wanted to buy the property. I sold it to them, and I was able to make a $50,000 profit.

Suzanne's flexibility resulted from her need to move on with her life, but she did not want to sell the home she cherished at a discount. I found Suzanne through the son of a Realtor friend who was knocking on doors looking for listings for his mom. Suzanne was not interested in working with a Realtor because she wanted to sell the property quickly and did not want to pay a commission.

In today's marketplace, we will see more of these types of transactions where the seller is open to doing some financing of the equity rather than receiving all cash if it will solve the problem. People will do nothing unless they are motivated.

What You Need to Know about Leverage

There is nothing wrong with borrowing money to buy property, but be careful, especially in an area where real estate prices are volatile. If you are not careful, you could end up owing more than the property is worth. In this case, leverage (the payments you have to make to the banker every month) will haunt you. That's how most real estate investors are doing it today, by leveraging themselves to the hilt.

If you are borrowing $100,000 on a $100,000 property, you have no equity in the deal. Next year, if the property's worth $105,000, you have made $5,000, on paper. But if you had to sell this property, would you be able to get that much? For example, I built a house that cost me $235,000. I was told that I could sell it for $285,000. The house finally got finished, and it was appraised for $306,000. Isn't that great? Unfortunately, I couldn't sell that house for more than $270,000. You need to think about securing your financial future first before you jump the gun and start buying just for the sake of buying.

Deferring Tax

It's also important to consider the tax consequences of different types of investments. One way you can make compound wealth by investing in real estate is by doing what's called a *1031 exchange* (described in detail in Chapter 9). Instead of simply selling the property and paying the tax on your profits, you can exchange it for a similar kind of property, which allows you to defer your tax to a time when you may be in a lower tax bracket; then you can pay the tax when you sell your final property. The 1031 exchange can be structured to suit your needs. There are rules on 1031's that are put out by the IRS that we will explore in more detail in chapter 9.

Final Tips on Buying

There are other strategies you can explore that will let you make more money when you buy and sell. Checklist 3-5 lists a few points to keep in mind regarding buying.

Checklist 3-5   Advice on Buying

❑ Don't be emotional—i.e., don't fall in love with an investment.

❑ Be on the straight and narrow; be honest and up-front. If you say you're going to follow up, you should follow up; don't leave a seller hanging. In this business, your reputation is everything.

❑ Look at every investment that comes your way as an opportunity. In other words, you don't have to get the lowest price if you can get the terms you want.

❑ Look at alternative financing strategies. If they are available on that property, save your credit for another deal.

❑ Evaluate properties to see if they make sense given the income goals that you're trying to achieve from your properties. In other words, analyze your investments by the numbers. Don't analyze them with emotion.

If the numbers don't work, don't buy the property. For example, a lot of real estate investors like to use the "1 percent rule" in rentals: if you pay $200,000 for something, you should get $2,000 per month in rent. This rule is no longer applicable as market conditions have changed. If the numbers don't work, don't buy it. Here's what I mean. If I pay $235,000 and my costs are $1,600 per month, but I can get only $1,300 per month in rent, I need to decide if I can afford the $300 per month negative cash flow. If I can't, then I would not buy the property. *Don't do anything that's going to put you in a financial bind.*

There are too many examples of people out there who have done just that: They buy strictly for appreciation, but when they need to sell, they may end up breaking even or, worse, losing money on the deal. Evaluate each potential situation before you buy. If the property cash flows, you know you will get the income so if the property does not appreciate in value you can always rent it until the value comes back to where it makes sense to sell and profit.

Conclusion

Develop a checklist of what you will need to do to become a successful real estate investor. Number one is to farm your area. Identify neighborhoods where you want to buy. I recommend focusing on no more than four neighborhoods and studying them so that you know what to expect, how desirable a community each one is, and how each neighborhood fits into your plan. Today, I buy property in Florida; I focus on only a couple of areas, a couple of cities within Florida. I do not focus on the whole state. Moreover, within those cities, I focus on a couple of different neighborhoods. And when I go down there to buy, I look around based solely on my criteria.

As mentioned, I happen to like areas where the homes aren't starter homes, but they're also not the Taj Mahal. They're areas where the price range is above the starter-home sales range, but the houses are affordable, so that if I wanted to sell, I would know what to expect in profit. The first place I would try to sell a property is to my tenant. The communities I target have good schools and amenities that make the location desirable. This is an important part of my checklist. However, that's *my* strategy; I know many investors who buy only starter homes and have made a fortune.

The secret is to have a game plan that is unique and specific to your needs. Create your to-do list of what you will need to set yourself up to be successful as a real estate investor. Then get moving.

4

Research Your Target Market

Now that you have determined your investing strategy and you know what type of property you want to invest in, you should start researching your target market. First, you should check out the leading indicators of the real estate market in general in the area in which you're interested—what homes are selling for, how much new construction is being built, the rate of foreclosures and mortgage defaults—and also how the U.S. economy is doing overall.

After doing that, you can start looking for deals—in the newspaper, online, in your target communities, through referrals and other contacts, and by attending open houses. In addition to knowing *where* to look for property, you should know a little about *when* to look for deals. Finally, the chapter concludes with five suggestions to keep in mind when looking for deals.

Wise Women Do the Necessary Due Diligence to Get a Positive Outcome

Before you invest in any piece of property, you need to understand the value of that property. You need to know the local market so that you can determine an appropriate price. Therefore, you should get information on four key indicators in your target market (i.e., the area where you're going to be farming—concentrating your time and energy to pick up property; many Realtors refer to this as farming—to find the right deal) because there are certain factors that you need to consider.

Indicator 1: Find Out What Existing Homes Are Selling For

The first indicator is *existing home sales*; look for the "sold comparables" in your area. What is really happening in your local marketplace? This is the leading indicator, the most important factor. For example, the real estate market in the Northeast might be good, but the market in the West may have gone down 10 percent in the last two months. You've got to look in your own backyard, though, because the neighborhoods you're looking at are going to dictate how you're going to buy the property.

Find a real estate agent and ask your agent for a market analysis of what has happened in the area where you're trying to find property. Ask the agent the following questions:

- Have real estate sales increased?
- Is there a backlog of inventory in your area?
- How long is it taking, on average, for a property to sell?
- Are sellers getting close to their asking price?
- What percentage of their asking price are sellers typically getting?

Let's look in more detail at some of the factors that you need to investigate.

Before you invest in any piece of property,
you need to understand the value of that property.

Look at the Sold Property Data.   What has sold in your target area in the last 90 days? You can research this online, or you can get the information from a real estate agent. Either way, you need to assess the correct information concerning the costs so that when you make an offer, you're in a position to know exactly what has sold; this way, you are buying with knowledge.

Look at the Number of Current Listings in Your Area and How Many Days They've Been on the Market.   This is very, very important. The longer something sits on the market, the more motivated the seller will become, and the better the opportunity for you. If you're in a hot area, obviously things are not going to sit on the market very long.

For example, in parts of California in 2005, suppose the asking price for a home was $500,000. Somebody might offer $550,000, and somebody else might offer $600,000. Buyers actually bid up properties over the asking price. Is that a good place to be investing in real estate? I don't think so. If properties are selling in a matter of days rather than months, you will not get as good a deal on the property when you go in to buy.

Look at Expired Listings of Properties.   In other words, look for properties that never went under contract and sold. Here's what I mean by expired listings. A Realtor has a listing agreement with a seller to sell her property for *X* dollars. The seller signs an agreement with that Realtor, under which the Realtor will represent her and try to sell her property for a period of three or six months. At the end of that time, if the property hasn't sold, the listing expires. Then the seller has the right to either renew the listing or let the listing die. Most sellers will let the listing die, because if the Realtor (or whoever the seller listed the property with) didn't sell the property in the period of time it was under contract, obviously the seller probably won't want to continue to work with that Realtor.

The number of expired listings is valuable to you because those properties may be great opportunities for *you* as an investor. Are the properties still available for you to look at? Why didn't they sell? Was a property not structurally sound? Was the floor plan lousy? Did it not meet potential buyers' expectations? Was the property in a bad location, such as on a busy street? Look at these factors to help you acquire real estate below fair market value.

Look at Appreciation Rates.   Is your market a hot market, is it growing at single-digit rates, or is it now flat to negative? Appreciation rates are currently in the single digits to zero because we are in a slow market, which is actually good for trying to pick up a deal. Again, you make money when you buy, not when you sell. These are factors to take into consideration when you're buying.

Look at New or Planned Developments in an Area.   When you buy a newer piece of property, sometimes you can get a better deal. The great thing with a newer house is that you are not going to have the wear-and-tear maintenance issues that you would have with an older property. So, when you're calculating your future cash flows, you may not incur as much expense with a newer building than if you buy a building that's, say, 50 or 60 years old.

If there's a high vacancy on rentals, it is going to be harder for you to rent the property you're investing in for a good price that's going to make you money.

Also, look at what's going up around that development. For example, in 1994, I bought a house in a development in Colorado where there was a lot of land around the development. I bought the house from a builder who was in trouble. He needed to sell the property because he was going through a divorce. My number one question to the builder was, "What's going to be built around this subdivision?" It was a nice-sized subdivision, with approximately 400 houses at the time. The builder told me, "Oh, there's probably going to be a park—but I'm not really sure." As it turned out, an apartment building complex went up across the street; then storage units went up on the other side of the street; and then down the street, other builders put up a condo and town homes.

If you are going to consider buying in new neighborhoods, and if you want to buy right, so that you can make money from your investment, you should learn what else is planned for the area around the development you're investing in. To find that out, go to the city planner's office. *Do not depend on the real estate agent or the builder or anybody else to tell you.* Instead, go to the city planner's office and look at the blueprints or ask someone there to tell you exactly what is being planned for this area. The people there know—and you want to find out all of the following:

- What type of usage is the land zoned for?
- Is it zoned for commercial use?
- Is it zoned for residential use only?
- Is it zoned for multifamily housing?

You need to know these things because they will affect what you buy.

Research new-home building permits because if builders in your area are building, one risk that you may run into eventually is too much inventory.

Find Out the Vacancy Rates on Rentals in Your Target Area. This information is important because if you're buying property for the long term, when you buy it, you want to buy it right—you want to be able to make money from your investment. And if there's a high vacancy rate on rentals in the area, it is going to be harder for you to rent the property you're investing in for a good price that's going to make you money.

If It's Already a Rental Property, Review the Lease. If you're considering buying investment property with tenants already in place, review the terms of the tenants' leases. You want to make sure that each tenant has a lease, determine that it's a lease *you* can live with, and know how much time is left on the lease, unless you want to resell the property. If you are buying to resell, the new buyer will also need this information.

Mortgage loan default rates are an early indicator of a trend toward foreclosures.

Often, investors will buy property that already has tenants living in it. The new buyer soon finds that he or she doesn't like one of the tenants—maybe because the tenant has trash all over the place, or because the tenant is too noisy, or for some other reason. Then the new buyer finds that he or she can't evict the tenant. This is another reason, when buying from another investor, to look at the lease: this is important for you to protect your investment and know the income potential.

Indicator 2: Research New Construction

Research new-home building permits because if builders in your area are building, one risk that you may run into eventually is *too much inventory*. If the market goes flat, builders will slash their prices to get rid of their inventory, and you will end up in competition with them. Thus, you definitely want to look at the number of new homes that are under construction, the type of permits that are being pulled, and what the local economy is like. Right now, 15 to 20 percent of the total U.S. economy is new-home construction, so that's a pretty big deal and a serious consideration for real estate investors.

Indicator 3: Research the Rate of Foreclosures or Mortgage Defaults

Go to your local courthouse to see whether the number of foreclosures is on the rise. Why would that be? One reason right now is that many people have adjustable-rate mortgages (ARMs), negative amortization (*negative am* for short; this is a situation where a buyer pays less than the interest each month, with the result that his or her loan amount actually increases), or both. With these types of mortgages, many buyers will not be able to afford their property if interest rates rise because their mortgage payments will become too high.

Recently, the Federal Reserve raised interest rates a quarter of a point. What will eventually happen as a result is that the interest rates on home loans will go up—which means that borrowers with adjustable-rate mortgages will have to make higher payments. When interest rates were low, buyers bought large homes because they could afford the monthly payments, but they did not take into consideration the fact that their mortgage rates could go up if the economy changed. The higher the interest rates go, the more the ability to borrow will be reduced, which spells opportunity for investors. The owners of some of these larger homes may no longer be able to afford their mortgage payments—which obviously means that they can no longer afford to live in the homes they "bought."

Mortgage loan default rates are an early indicator of a trend toward foreclosures. When people lose their jobs or when the terms of their loans change, you will see the local real estate market become flat or, worse, fall in value. For real estate *investors*, though, this is a buying opportunity because property prices are going to reflect what's happening in the local economy.

Estimate the outcome of the investment itself before you actually buy . . . : you need to be prepared.

Indicator 4: Examine the U.S. Economy

What does the financial picture look like for the U.S. economy? Until recently, interest rates were at a 40-year low, but right now, they're on the rise. Things have tightened up in housing; no matter what magazine or newspaper you read or what online service you subscribe to, everybody is saying that the real estate market is tight, and national economists expect real estate to either flatten or go down for some time. Most people look at this as bad news. However, wise women view this as another potential opportunity. At this writing the real estate market has dropped and the economy has softened. Sharp investors are examining buying opportunities as this is a buyers market at the moment.

Study the indicators to determine what your local marketplace is doing *before* you buy, not after—the worst thing that can happen to you is that you buy something, and then find that you've overpaid; if that happens, in the future, when you need to sell that property, you could be stuck.

In short, you need to estimate the outcome of the investment itself before you actually buy by considering *all* the factors of demography, the local marketplace, and your own investment objectives: you need to be prepared before you *look* at a property.

Using the Internet to Research Your Target Market

There are several good Web sites that you can use when researching your target market. For example, both www.HomeRadar.com and www.domain.com can show you what has sold in the last 90 days in an area that you're looking to farm (i.e., a community that you're considering investments in) so that you'll have some sort of idea of what the market will bear.

Is the price that the seller is asking for his or her property way out of line? If you don't want to pay a Realtor to find that out, you can go online to find out. There are certain governmental REOs ("real estate owned," or properties that banks have already foreclosed on and are reselling) that are advertised online through HUD, the VA, Fannie Mae, and even the FDIC; you can go online to find these resources and see about buying property after it's been foreclosed on. But, again (as mentioned in Chapter 3), you need to realize that you're not the only one doing that type of research, so you'll have competition if you look only at these Web sites.

Where to Look for Property

If you're going to be an investor and work on your own, here are the key ways you can go about finding deals.

Newspapers

Most people look at the classified ads in local newspapers. They look especially at the Sunday newspaper, which is the day that the largest number of classified ads for real estate usually run, followed by Friday. Also, in some areas of the country, when yard sales and garage sales are being held, you tend to see a higher volume of ads of real estate for sale and property for lease. Look also at your weekly neighborhood newspapers, which typically run ads more inexpensively than your city's major newspaper.

Online

Another place to look is online. There are several real estate Web sites, including real estate "for sale by owner" (FSBO) sites and auction sites, that you can investigate to find deals. Is that a good idea? Yes and no. When you're dealing with a FSBO, the owner has already built the commission into the sale price. The seller is trying to make as much money as possible, so you should take that into consideration if and when you make an offer. Doing your due diligence as discussed earlier (i.e., those six ways of knowing value) will help you assess whether or not a property is a good deal or whether you want to pursue it.

There are also discount "for sale by owner" sites, such as buyerowner.com and propertysites.com, where owners are encouraged to list their properties for sale for a nominal fee, and there are other niche sites that specialize in foreclosures. These sites give the *perception* that the properties listed have been discounted. Before you go online to research property, however, you need to know what properties have actually sold for in your targeted area. This will save you time, effort, and money. You will be in a better position to make the right judgment call—to make the right offer at the right price.

Here are some Web sites that you can go on when you're looking to buy a home, whether as an investment or for an owner-occupied home:

- The number one site for Realtors is www.realtor.com, which is produced by the National Association of Realtors.
- Another good site is www.homebuyingabout.com. Most people are probably familiar with the "about" pages. This site can give you a little more educational information on the ins and outs of home buying. This is especially good for someone who wants to buy a property as an owner/occupant; it does not go into depth about buying property as an investor.

You should also look at what is the worst time for sellers because that's the time when they're really motivated to get rid of a property quickly.

Placing Your Own Ad in a Newspaper

Another way to find property is by placing your own ad in a newspaper or on the Internet. For example, craigslist.org has sites throughout the United

States (and internationally); it's a great online advertising mechanism that many people use to advertise for anything from cars to furniture to real estate. Place your own ad for the specific type of property you're interested in investing in.

Communities That Interest You

You can farm a particular neighborhood (as discussed in Chapter 3). Pick one or several different communities in your area. Get to know those communities inside and out. Know what types of homes, condos, or town homes are available—whatever type of property you are interested in. Because you are putting the effort into getting to know these neighborhoods, you will know what goes on sale before anyone else does. By focusing on the specific communities that you wish to invest in, you will have the key advantage of knowing those neighborhoods like the back of your hand.

Personal Contacts and Referrals

Networking with personal contacts and referral sources is great if you're trying to buy a piece of property as an investment. These contacts can include Realtors, attorneys, financial professionals, churches, friends, people you work with, and so on.

Open Houses

Personally, I love open houses, whether the property is a FSBO or listed through a Realtor. Going to open houses on Sunday (they're almost always on Sundays) does two things for you:

1. You're able to see the condition of the inside of the property without being harassed by the Realtor, the seller, or anyone else—that is, no one will pressure you about this particular property or any other property, and you can look around anonymously; you're just walking in without an appointment, and you can look around freely,
2. You will get a good feel for the street, the development, and what's around it; also, you may meet a Realtor that you would like to work with.

When to Look for Investment Properties

If you are trying to sell property, the best time of year to market your property is usually February through August (late spring and early summer), as people are trying to relocate their families before school starts. However, you should also look at what is the *worst* time for sellers because that's the time when they're really motivated to get rid of a property quickly.

For buyers who are looking for great opportunities, there really is no "worst time." During the winter holidays, naturally, business does tend to slow down; you don't find as many properties for sale. On the other hand, those sellers who are willing to show their property in bad weather or during the holidays will be *really* motivated to sell.

In Checklist 4-1, Barbara O'Connell offers some advice on how to know when a real estate market cycle has reached its peak and is about to go the other way—which means that there are opportunities to invest.

Checklist 4-1   Warning Signs That the Real Estate Market Has Peaked–which Means Buying Opportunities for Investors
—from Barbara O'Connell

❑   The inventory of houses on the MLS and for builders increases, compared to the same time of year in the previous year.

❑   Houses start taking longer to sell.

❑   Multiple offers stop.

❑   Builders and sellers start offering incentives to purchase their homes, such as offering help with closing costs or extra upgrades at no cost.

❑   Closing prices on similar houses in similar neighborhoods do not go up for a period of time.

❑   Prices actually start deteriorating.

❑   Only houses in good neighborhoods that are in top condition continue selling.

Broker Jaime Raskulinecz has done transactions during good markets and bad. Here's her advice on when to buy and where to look for help:

With some markets softening, this is actually a good time for investors to start thinking about buying. I always recommend that new investors join a local real estate investment group in order to be around people who are actually working as investors, if only part time. These groups are a great resource, as some of the members have a wealth of knowledge and are eager to share with newcomers. Get as much knowledge as you can to be able to analyze an investment and then go out and make your first purchase.

Century 21 Realtor Anna Mills confirms that there's no bad time to buy:

When the economy is good, real estate is good. When the economy is bad, real estate is even better! There is no "bad" market; there is only a buyer's market (which the sellers think is bad) or a seller's market (which the buyers think is bad). For investors, it's a business, not a one-time sale, so business should be done according to the markets, not fighting the market.

New investors always think they're too late: the deals are all bought up; there are too many investors; the economy isn't perfect. Once they become investors, their only thought is, "Why didn't I start sooner?"

Realtor and trainer Magi Bird also emphasizes the importance of just getting started:

Buy a house as soon as possible, live in it, fix it up, write a note against the equity to make a down payment on a new home, and rent the old home out behind you. Repeat as often as you can.

Investor Jennifer Dizmang also suggests just getting started:

Research Your Target Market

I think the first step is to start small and create a habit. Take some money, $1,000 for instance (not enough to break the bank, but enough that it is important), research an investment that is of interest to you (possibly a stock or a real estate option), create a performance goal and an exit strategy, and then invest. It's amazing how quickly [you] learn when [your] own money is committed.

Another step in overcoming this obstacle is to understand that when you are an investor, there are times when you are going to lose money. It is not the end of the world, but I think women especially spend a lot of time beating themselves up about making the "wrong" decision or second-guessing what they could have done differently. Look at it for what it really is: a meaningful learning experience that will take you to the next level of development. It is merely the cost of learning in the game called "life."

Finally, Barbara O'Connell also recommends just getting started:

Start simple. Buy a single property, and get some experience managing or selling that property before you go into multiple properties. You should find out what mistakes you made in the previous transaction before repeating the same mistake on the next one. If you find something that works for you, repeat what you did that was right, and correct the mistakes on the next transaction.

If the market is white hot and prices are rising fast, just make any "OK" deal in the best location you can afford. Today's "OK" price is tomorrow's bargain in a fast-moving market. Don't worry about getting the best deal in a fast-moving market. Just put a deal together that you can live with and hold on for a fast ride. Most of the appreciation is made in only a few years in any market cycle. You want to own any house in a decent neighborhood during that time. It is almost impossible to lose in a fast-rising market. However, you must understand the actual market value of what you are buying, and don't pay twice what it is worth. If you plan to sell immediately after closing, make sure you are not near the top of the cycle.

Wise Women Invest in Real Estate

When the market shifts to a buyer's market, take your time and look for a bargain. It may be a very long time before the market moves up again in any significant way. Do not buy a negative-cash-flow property in a buyer's market unless you are prepared to hold the property for a very long time before you make a profit or unless you get the property significantly under market. Just remember, in a slow market, prices can just as easily go down as up from the price where you buy it. I tend to stay away from negative-cash-flow deals unless there is significant upside potential in the very near term.

Be aware that prices can and many times will come down at some point, and sometimes for a long period of time. Change your strategy for a slow market. You can lose money if you buy at the top of a market cycle and have to sell in the short term. I personally have a strategy for every market condition. I rarely buy property for a short-term gain. Generally, I personally like to buy and hold properties for the long term; if I make a profit in the short term, I consider it a bonus.

The nice thing about real estate is that if you hold it long enough, you can usually make a profit even if you made a mistake initially buying it. Real estate has an intrinsic value based on its utilitarian value in most areas. That means that, unlike stocks, people can actually use the real estate they buy to live in or for recreation or business purposes.

It is my experience that the value of the land almost always goes up substantially over time—provided, however, that the land is located in an area that can be used for its intended purpose, of course. Even residential land in the middle of the desert has turned into valuable land over time. Think about Las Vegas or Palm Springs. I bet that in the early 1900s, almost everyone probably thought the desert land where Las Vegas now stands was almost worthless."

The point is that you can make a mistake buying real estate and still come out ahead by just holding on to it long enough for the value to increase. There's an old saying: "They ain't making any more land."

So real estate will always have some value, unlike stocks, which may or may not have any real intrinsic value depending on the company whose stock you buy. I think most people who invested in Enron thought they were making a prudent investment.

When Looking for Good Deals, Pay Attention

Successful real estate investors *pay attention*—to the marketplace where they live, to their local economy, to the neighborhoods they invest in. Admittedly, this takes work, but if paying attention was good enough for the top 20 investors I know, don't you think it will work for you? So here are five strategies to prepare you to pay attention and take advantage of being "at the right place at the right time." The best part is, you will look, sound, and be the expert in your area if you follow these five suggestions.

Don't waste your time in an area that either is out of your price range or doesn't fit your objectives as an investor.

Read the Local Paper

Read it every day. Start with the local headlines. Become intimate with what's happening in your community. Read the classifieds under real estate for sale, real estate for rent, and money to lend, and look at bank advertising. By looking through these ads, you may find sources of money and disgruntled landlords who would like get out of the landlord business *now*. For example, I know one investor who has an ad in the obituary section of the paper looking for estate sales.

Specialize in at Least Three Neighborhoods

Start farming. Drive or walk your targeted neighborhoods at least twice a week. Why twice? Because new listings and signs that appear in a neighborhood are most likely to be posted on Sunday, followed by Wednesdays—or on garage sale days.

You will learn a lot about the property, the neighborhood, and the motivation of a seller by visiting with the person who is sitting at an open house.

You want to know these neighborhoods as well as you know your own. You want to know who lives there on the weekends. Is it a nice quiet community, a family community, or a young singles community that you're looking for? Know what you are really looking for before you buy. Don't take someone else's opinion; get out in the neighborhoods and see for yourself.

Know What the Properties in Your Farm Areas Are Worth

You need to know property values in your areas long before you start looking for property. A great Web site that I recently discovered is www.homeradar.com. You can check sold home prices right on the Net with this site. It is current information, and it is simple to use.

Or you can befriend your local Realtors and ask them for comps. Either way, don't go out there blind. Know what something costs before you shop. Don't waste your time in an area that either is out of your price range or doesn't fit your objectives as an investor.

Call Three Property Managers

If your objective is to buy and hold property for the long term, call three property managers in your area to get an idea of what a property will rent for. You need three opinions on the same address. Why? Because you are trying to determine the fair market rent. When I become interested in a neighborhood that I'm not familiar with, this research is imperative.

For example, I recently received quotes ranging from $250 to $400 per bedroom as a "reasonable" estimate of what I can get for rent at a particular property address. That's a pretty big price swing on a four-bedroom home: from $1,000 to $1,600 per month. In such cases, I always use a number toward the middle to lower end of the range. I use rental information from property managers to help me evaluate whether or not a property will provide positive cash flow. This information can make all the difference to my negotiation strategy.

Go to Every Open House Every Week

You will learn a lot about the property, the neighborhood, and the motivation of a seller by visiting with the person who is sitting at an open house.

As mentioned, I've purchased rental properties from sellers who needed to sell their existing property so that they could qualify for a new, more expensive home. This provides the opportunity for contingency clauses that offer lots of flexibility with regard to price and terms.

For example, in early 2006, I looked at a property that was listed for $325,000. I thought it was at least $25,000 overpriced. The sellers were building a more expensive home and wanted to stay in their existing property until the new home was completed. I offered them $285,000 with a right of first refusal, meaning that if anyone offered more than my price, the seller would have to come to me first before accepting that other bid, and I would have the right to buy it or not at that price. I had a one-year limit on the contract and will be happy to close at $285,000.

The new home was completed at the end of March. The sellers have just moved, leaving this house vacant. I still have six months left on my contract. Because it was springtime, the seller decided to list the property with a friend who was a Realtor. It's now listed at $345,900. I'm still in there at $285,000. Neither the seller nor I have anything to lose.

In summary, when you pay attention, people get to know who you are and what you do. Neighbors, professionals, and others will call you from time to time to see if you can help them solve a problem, let you know about a property that's getting ready to go on the market, or invite you to a variety of functions where you will get to meet others who can be in your sphere of influence. Paying attention could be the key to your success as a real estate investor.

5

Rehabbing and Other Short-Term Investing Strategies

Once you've done your due diligence and research, another aspect of determining your real estate investing strategy is deciding whether you want to invest for short-term profits or long-term appreciation. The real answer to this question is, *it depends*. Before you invest in each particular property, you need to determine what outcome you want to achieve with that property.

To help you make that decision, this chapter begins by describing different types of long-term and short-term investment strategies. If you're more interested in long-term investing strategies, Chapter 8 covers what you need to know about property management, something that you'll need to deal with if you're buying and holding property and leasing it to tenants. If you're more interested in short-term investing strategies, this chapter covers the two main ones. First, it covers *flipping* properties—buying and re-selling almost right away. Then, it focuses on *rehabbing* properties—either giving a property a fresh coat of paint (literally and figuratively) or renovating it substantially to improve it so that you can sell it at a much higher price.

Decide Whether You Want Property for the Long or the Short Term

What is your objective for your real estate investments? What's your strategy? Are you buying property for the long term or for the short term? And what's *your* definition of long term and short term? My definition of long term would be five years or longer, which is long enough to be comfortable with the property, long enough to have rented it out for some period and have a history. A short-term investment is one that's not forever and that you're not married to—i.e., your game plan is to sell it and take the gain.

Generally speaking, on average, properties turn every five years. But some investors don't want to hold property for even that long. Some investors want to rehab—to fix up properties and get rid of them after 60 or 90 days. (I cover rehabbing in detail later in this chapter.) Other investors like to hold property for a long enough period of time to recoup their cost and capitalize on the appreciation potential. So, it depends on the investor's objective. My personal objective is to always hold property for the long term. Rarely do I hold it for the short term because I want to continue to receive income well into my retirement. I look at real estate as my social security. My tenants help to pay off my mortgage over time. Depending on the deal, however, I have held property for shorter periods.

---

*If you're a brand-new investor or just getting started,
I would not recommend flipping properties.*

Also, the longer you hold the property, the better the chances, if you're going through a cyclical market where you've got some volatility (as we are right now, at the time this book is being written), that the market will eventually rebound. Therefore, holding property for the long term can be beneficial. I've held property long enough that, if there's a down market and I don't have any motivation to sell, I can hold on to it until the market comes back up, and then make a conscious decision to sell at a price that I decide.

Decide for yourself what your objective will be in terms of holding on to property: long term or short term? Different investors have different strategies. Let's look at a few of the choices you might make to determine what approach will work best for *you*.

Flipping: A *Really* Short-Term Strategy

Some investors will buy property and then flip it—that is, sell it immediately for a substantial profit. Right now, anyone who wants to do this needs to be *extremely* careful: in 2006, several states passed legislation that will eventually prohibit flipping, so you really need to understand what you're doing. Check the real estate laws in the state in which you're interested in buying property.

If you're a brand-new investor or just getting started, I would not recommend flipping properties. Put yourself in the lender's shoes. If you buy a property for $100,000, hold it for 30 days, supposedly fix it up, and flip it for $200,000, chances are that you're going to get an MAI (made as instructed) appraisal that says that the appraised value of the property is $200,000. But that's not necessarily going to be a *legitimate* appraisal. You can inflate a property to some degree, but to inflate it outrageously is wrong.

There are investors who've flipped property and have taken advantage of poor individuals; they buy a property that was way overvalued and then get into financial trouble because they can't make their payments. In one case, an investor went to jail for 30 days for taking advantage of his buyers. He sold property in Indiana for over 100 percent more than he paid for it (he might have paid $46,000 for a property and sold it for $98,000). The people who bought the property couldn't afford it. Three months into the deal, the buyers couldn't make the payments; the lender took back the property in foreclosure which put the lender in a bad position since they had made the loan to the buyer based on an inflated appraisal, and found that it was completely upside down on the deal. The lender is the one who's in trouble if it cannot resell the property for the amount it has loaned on it. The lender investigated the transaction, found the party who sold the property to the buyer, and took legal action.

However, note that this type of flipping is different from *legitimately* fixing up or *rehabbing* a property, which is covered in the next section of this chapter. I'm talking about people who do nothing but buy property, then turn around and resell it. You should be very cautious about doing this. I'm not saying that you can't do it; people flip properties every day. But I strongly recommend that if you're just getting started in real estate investing, you should be very careful. In fact, I personally would not start my real estate investing career by flipping property.

Renee Falgout (operations manager for a mortgage company) tells this story:

> *One of the most creative investors I've ever worked with is an investor who always buys distressed property at much less than full value, gets the sellers to pay the closing costs and sometimes even hold a short-term second mortgage, and is also able to finance the cost of repairs to the property. Once the property is repaired, it's sold for the improved appraised value, and the investor not only is out of pocket little to no money, but enjoys significant profit.*
>
> *The only thing to watch in these instances where an investor is going to buy and sell a property in less than 12 months is that the investor must sell to a buyer with good credit. Less-than-perfect credit will cause a lender to scrutinize the value of the property in case they feel there is a risk of the buyer defaulting on the loan. Most lenders will not loan on a property if it's had more than one owner in the last 12 months. The lenders that do will either want more than one appraisal from independent appraisers or require that the buyer fit into very high standards. I've seen this cause deals to fall apart on several occasions, to everyone's frustration.*

Rehabbing: Another Short-Term Strategy

Rehabbing can turn your investments into a serious business. For example, Mary is a real estate investor who lives in Oregon. She buys very high-end homes, in the heart of wine country, in very expensive neighborhoods. She buys these properties well below fair market value. She brings a crew in, and they rehab the properties; they put in granite countertops, beautiful flooring, and gorgeous bathrooms and make the property beautiful and marketable. Then she turns around and sells the property for $1.1 million. She does just a couple of these a year. After the costs of buying a property and the materials to rehab it, and after she pays her contractors and their crews, about 30 to 40 percent of the difference in price goes into her pocket. Mary does a fantastic job as a rehabber and is well respected. This is her business; she does this full-time. If she does three deals a year, she's making a lot of money. She's taken the concept of rehabbing (or fixer-uppers) and turned it into a business, and she has been doing that successfully in Oregon since 1997.

Before that, Mary was a landlord. She came into this business as a mortgage broker, became an investor, then became a business owner who specializes in rehabbing luxury homes. She has developed a very astute eye, she buys the properties right, and she does the right type of renovations (which I'll discuss in the next section). She then flips the properties after about six to eight months, because it takes her that amount of time to fix them up and resell them.

The number one way people find properties to rehab is by just driving around and looking for properties that look like they're fixer-uppers.

How to Fix Up a Property and Resell It for a Profit

When you buy a property, you need to buy it right. If you're going to be fixing property up for resale, Checklist 5-1 lists the types of renovations you can make that will give you the largest return on your investment.

In general, California is probably the most expensive state in the country for real estate; in parts of California, the cost to build is $300 to $400 per square foot. In contrast, if you were going to do the same type of rehab in the Midwest, you'd probably be looking at less than $100 per square foot. If you're investing in Ohio, you can buy property for $25,000! Prices for renovations and square footage cost to build depend on what part of the country you are in.

Checklist 5-1 gives few examples of the percentage you can expect to recoup should you decide to go out and invest in a property and fix it up, and that fix-up cost needs to be recaptured at sale. Even in California, where it can cost $25,000 to build a deck, you can get about 85 percent of that in-

Checklist 5-1   Simple Renovations
That Provide the Best ROI

❏ *Bathrooms*. If you fix up a bathroom, you should recapture 85
percent of the cost of that fix-up when you sell the property. In
dollar amounts, if you spend $10,000 on renovating or updating a
bathroom, you should be able to add $8,500—at a minimum—to
the price of the property. And you may be able to get even more.

❏ *Kitchens*. If you fix up a kitchen, you should be able to recapture
approximately 90 percent of your costs.

❏ *Master bedrooms*. If you do a master bedroom, you're looking at
about 75 percent recapture.

❏ *Deck addition*. This is one of the least expensive fix-ups that makes
a difference: your recapture rate on a deck is almost 100 percent.
Of course, the cost of building a deck varies depending on the type
of property and where you're investing. For example, if you put a
deck on a house in California, it's probably going to cost you
$25,000, whereas if you put that same deck on a house in Michigan,
it might cost you only $3,000.

vestment back, because the house to which you're adding that $25,000 deck
probably is priced at more than $1 million. Obviously, spending $25,000 on
that particular property would be a drop in the bucket. Again, it's all relative
to where you live.

Factor all costs in advance. Beth is an investor who looks for properties
that need only cosmetic fix-ups. She wants to fix the landscaping, plant
some flowers, put on a fresh coat of paint, and make the property look like
storybook land, so that she can turn around and resell it. She was very, very
successful doing that in Alabama.

Then she moved to Colorado. Unfortunately, the difference in landscaping costs between Alabama and Colorado put her out of the market. She
didn't make as much profit. As a matter of fact, when she got done with her
landscaping costs—simply planting the right flowers and making the outside space presentable—she just about broke even. She wasn't making as

much money in Colorado as she was in Alabama, where she could get landscaping for almost nothing.

She did her research on the real estate, and she bought the real estate right. What she didn't factor in was the difference in the cost of fix-ups in Colorado and Alabama. Fortunately, she did all right; she just didn't make as much money as she had in Alabama. You need to know how your costs will vary, depending on what part of the country you're investing in, when you're buying property and fixing it up. You need to take all expenses into consideration.

Other Rehabbing Costs You Need to Consider

When you invest in something that needs to be fixed up, like a rehab-type property, there are some financial expenses that need to be covered. The most significant of these costs include the following:

- The down payment
- The origination fee for the mortgage (discussed in Chapter 3)
- Any closing costs (which include the fees to a title company or an attorney's office for closing the transaction, getting title insurance, the appraisal, the survey, and the home inspection)

When you buy a property, you should always put in the contract that the deal is subject to a home inspection or an inspection of the premises, because you can't always spot potential problems—especially if they're behind the walls or in the foundation.

For example, I just entered into a contract on a soft commercial piece of real estate, an office building. When I got the inspection report, I found out that there was moisture in the foundation. And this building is only five years old! Is that mold? Or is it just moisture? Is there some sort of small leak that needs to be fixed? Is it something that can be remedied by a simple caulking process? My inspector is responsible for telling me exactly what the problem is and how I can get it fixed. That's a bargaining chip for me; I can go back to the seller and say, "Hey, you've got to fix this property before I buy it."

Every contract should have language that says "subject to" a home inspection. There's a fee associated with an inspection; depending on the part of the country in which you live, it can run you $250 or more. It's worth it—but you also need to factor in the cost of fixing up the property.

If I like [a] property, I request an inspection of the
property first, before I even make an offer,
to see exactly what I'm getting into.

In Pasco County, Florida, there are big billboard signs on highway US 19 that say, "We buy sinkhole property." A sinkhole is a foundation where the property collapses inside of the foundation. If the damage is not severe it isn't necessarily demolished (as it is in an earthquake or when a property gets torn down), but it can be affected by the ground sinking under it. It is very difficult to get a loan to buy that type of property. Therefore, some investors pay cash for these properties, rent them out, and then, over some period of time, try to get the sinkhole cured and then sell the property.

If you decide to do this (that is, to invest in sinkhole property), you need to know what you'll have to do to get the foundation (which is typically a concrete slab; the majority of homes in Florida are constructed on a slab) to pass inspection and get a certification that the problem has been fixed. Those costs need to be factored into your buying decision. Still, because sinkhole property costs a fraction of what a regular piece of property costs, there are investors with money who are going to these regions of Florida and buying these sinkhole properties. This presents another unique buying opportunity if you like risk.

How to Find Fixer-Uppers to Rehab

How do you find a property that really needs some fixing without having to do a lot of homework? Well, the number one way that people find properties to rehab is by just driving around and looking for properties that look like they're fixer-uppers. There are two types of neighborhoods you want to look in for these properties.

Look for Vacant or Rundown Properties in Otherwise Good Neighborhoods. My preferred approach is to look for homes in good neighborhoods that appear to be vacant or have not been attended to. If you're looking to fix up a property and sell it in six months, this is a good strategy for you. Still, you need to know your market.

In older neighborhoods, look for weeds, broken windows, property that looks like it needs outside work, or property that looks vacant. Get out of your car and look in the windows. You can go around and talk to residents of the neighborhoods you're interested in (i.e., the communities you're farming)—in other words, talk to people who live in those neighborhoods and see if they know of any properties nearby that fit what you're looking for.

Out-of-town or out-of-state owners are phenomenal opportunities, and one way to know if the owners are out of town or out of state is to simply take a look at a property.

Once you find a property that looks like it needs some work—e.g., the lawn looks untended or the property looks vacant—you need to find out who the owners are, and the best way to do that is to research local tax records, which is very easy to do.

If you see an area that is up and coming, and you buy in at the right time, you're going to make money on it.

I've bought several properties that way. I love out-of-state owners because their motivation has changed. When they bought the property, they were probably either living in it or living near it, or maybe they bought it as an investment. Then they hired a lousy property manager, or they tried unsuccessfully to manage the property themselves, and then the property is just left sitting there, with no money coming in. (Chapter 8 includes some horror stories about property management.) Again, it's easy to find these properties: just look around in the communities you're farming. Walk those neighborhoods or drive through them regularly, looking for opportunities. You can see just by looking at these properties that they're not the same as other properties, and then you go to the courthouse and you find out who owns them.

I recently drove through a very expensive neighborhood in California where all the homes were well manicured except for one, where the grass was very tall and the place looked worn. I could tell just by looking at it that it was vacant. This property was in stark contrast to the rest of the neighborhood, which looked fantastic.

So I went to the courthouse to find out who owned the property, and I sent the owners a letter to find out what they were intending to do with it. My letter basically said, "Dear Mr. So and So: Courthouse records tell me that you own this property on 123 East Main Street. I see from the property that it looks like it is vacant. Are you interested in selling the home in an 'as-is' condition? If you are, here's my telephone number; I'd love to talk to you about it." In such cases, if the owners call me, then I make arrangements to get into the property. I've already checked out the outside of the property; now I want to check out the inside. If I like the property, I request an inspection of the property *first*, before I even make an offer, to see exactly what I'm getting into. Then I get estimates for the repairs or the rehab or whatever the project needs.

I run my numbers to make sure that my return on investment makes sense, and then I make an offer. This scenario is a simple, repeatable process that works well. And this type of simple rehabbing is a good way for first-time investors to get started. Later in this chapter, I'll discuss crunching your numbers to estimate the cost of rehabbing a property—and how to find qualified, trustworthy, skilled, competent contractors and construction people. Your costs and your construction team are critical to ensure that you can do good-quality renovation in a short amount of time and for a reasonable amount of money, so that rehabbing as an investment strategy can work for you.

Look for Good Buildings in Up-and-Coming Neighborhoods.

Another way to find fixer-uppers is to look at gentrifying neighborhoods. If you see an area that is up and coming, and you buy in at the right time, you're going to make money. If you wait until that neighborhood has already been completely redone, it's too late. However, many gentrifying neighborhoods have great *future* opportunities—in other words, they typically fit better into a *long-term* strategy (e.g., 10 years or more), where you buy and hold because you're betting that the entire neighborhood will go up in value. Remember, the number one way investors make money is by appreciation.

If I were buying a property in a neighborhood that I thought was undervalued now but would gentrify down the road, I would plan on holding that property well into my retirement. I would look at it as a retirement vehicle, with the expectation that I'll be renting out that property. Finally, an additional factor that you need to watch out for in some regions—especially New York City and Santa Monica, California—is rent control, because that will affect your cash flow. If a building is rent-controlled, you may not be as excited about buying it.

When you're buying and holding property for the long term, keep in mind that property prices don't always go up.

You can tell when a neighborhood is becoming gentrified: people are making an effort to make the neighborhood look better. That's a great investment opportunity. This is especially true when an owner has held a property for many years: you can look at estate situations. In this case, you are working with estate attorneys who are representing people who are trying to move out of their long-time homes because they want to go into a nursing home or an assisted-living community, or because they want to downsize into a condo, or because the original owner has died and the heirs want to sell the property. (You can also look for obituaries, in the latter case.) Those are all great opportunities for finding real estate for this type of strategy when you're buying and holding.

You might also consider buying in severely undervalued neighborhoods, where individual, specific properties or buildings are lovely—for example, you might find and consider buying a fabulous home in what is still on the fringes. If you think that the property itself is valuable, and if you're willing to invest in a neighborhood that eventually—say, over 15, 20, or even 30 years—will change because the properties themselves are high-quality, even though the neighborhood at the time you buy is not, is a possible strategy. In this situation, what you're doing is banking (as most real estate investors do) on appreciation: that in the future, others will see the neighborhood and the properties the way you see them, and that the property will be worth infinitely more than it is today.

In the current real estate marketplace, where the numbers are going down, many investors are nervous about the market because they think they'll lose their money. They may be losing money on paper, but if an investor buys a house that is itself beautiful in a neighborhood that currently isn't the greatest in the world, improves it further, with original detailing, high-quality material such as luxury wood, and the right decorations (i.e., increases the value of that property later on down the road), and holds the property long enough, there is an excellent chance that he or she will make money.

Moreover, the first investor to spot a property like this can actually *start* the gentrifying process. For example, suppose you buy No. 209 on a particular street because it looks fabulous. The rest of the block may look horrible, but you might decide to buy the best building on that particular block. Then another investor will come along, see what you paid for No. 209, and see that it's gone up a little bit in value; that investor might be willing to pay a little bit more for No. 213. When that happens, if you own No. 209, you benefit because you'll see a tiny bit of appreciation in the value of your property as prices increase.

Do not buy a fixer-upper unless you've got the money to fix it up. Be very cautious about your cash flow.

However, when you're buying and holding property for the long term, keep in mind that *property prices don't always go up*. You have to restrain yourself from thinking that you're going to make 100 percent on your money next year. You're not. If you get even 3 percent or 5 percent appreciation, you'll be doing pretty well right now. A few years ago, there were double-digit appreciation numbers, but now that's not that case. You need to have a slow-and-steady mentality when you're buying for the long term, especially when you're buying in a not-so-great neighborhood that you hope will eventually gentrify. Keep in mind that you're buying only that individual property, and you're *hoping*—and risking—that your property will appreciate over the long term. And it might not: the neighborhood you invest in today might not become the upscale neighborhood that you hope and think it will.

Avoid Property in a Bad Location.   This doesn't just pertain to areas that are declining in value. For example, I would avoid buying a property on a busy street, because that's a deterrent when you're trying to sell. Statistically, resale values for properties on a busy street have been lower than those for properties on a quiet cul-de-sac.

Look for Properties That Need Only Cosmetic Improvements

The type of fixer-upper that I recommend for real estate investors who are just getting started in rehabbing is properties that need only small cosmetic changes that can be done relatively easily. I'm certainly *not* recommending that beginners get involved in doing total rehab as a business, where you're gutting a property and making structural changes. Instead, the cosmetic changes I'm advocating are painting, redoing a bathroom, maybe going to Home Depot and buying basic cabinets for the kitchen—in other words, things that can be done easily without having to spend a lot of money and a lot of time, but that will really give a property a fresh, clean look.

Calculate the Cost to Rehab and Renovate Very Carefully

This is a critical factor in how successful you'll be in rehabbing property. First of all, *do not buy a fixer-upper unless you've got the money to fix it up*. Be very cautious about your cash flow. Even if you think you have a lot of money, watch out for negative cash flow, because if you have to spend a lot of money on fix-up costs, this will cut into your cash flow, and you can end up owing more than you think you do. You're not going to get your money back until you've held the property for a period of time, and if that was not your objective, you're going to get burned. When you're calculating how much it's going to cost you to rehab or renovate, make sure that you can stay within your budget.

That budget will differ for each investor, and it varies in different markets across the country; there's no single estimate to cite, such as "make sure you have *X* amount of dollars before you invest in real estate." Instead, you need to decide for yourself what this number is—i.e., what you can afford and still feel confident that you'll have enough money to fix up the property in which you invested.

For example, Marsha bought a property in Austin, Texas. She budgeted $11,000 for fix-up costs. But when she reached her $11,000 limit, she was nowhere near done with renovations. Marsha had bought this property with the intention of turning it quickly. Her logic was that Texas is a hot market, and she was trying to raise capital. Unfortunately, because she knew no one locally, it took her much longer to complete the work. She ended up being out some money and sold the property anyway. Not a good investment. Two lessons: when you are starting out, it makes sense to invest where you know and where you have connections.

Keep in mind that there are nightmare stories of renovation costs spinning wildly out of control. . . . If you don't have the money, don't do the deal.

If you're going to get serious about doing fixer-uppers, you need to really study what the market will bear, and one way to do that, again, is by getting involved with real estate investor associations and doing some online research. There are different online newsletters you can subscribe to that have articles, chat rooms, and other educational seminars you could participate in. There are Web sites where you can review articles that people have written on the subject. These sites allow you to ask questions on discussion forums as well as people who will answer questions pertaining to the specific area that you're interested in investing in.

Keep in mind that there are nightmare stories of renovation costs spinning wildly out of control. For example, suppose you find a good property in a great neighborhood for, say, $250,000. You have the $50,000 for the down payment; you do your research on what it would cost to renovate, and you find that it will cost another $50,000, which you also have and are willing to invest. And you find out that, with the extent and type of renovation that you're doing, you should be able to resell that property for $400,000. Once you're into the renovation project, however, after your $50,000 renovation budget has already been spent, your contractor tells you that the renovation is going to cost twice as much and take twice as long, and he needs another $50,000—which you don't have.

These scenarios do happen, and this is why I advise that *if you don't have the money, don't do the deal.* You need to know, in advance, before you buy and start renovating, what's it's going to cost to fix up that property. In this hypothetical case, you had the money that you were originally quoted. So to prevent such nightmares from happening, you should have between 10 and 20 percent more than you think you'll need, as a cushion. If you're quoted $5,000, you'd better have $7,500 to be on the safe side, because in the end, especially with labor, it may not cost what your contractor originally said it would. Just like in any other business, your contractor may find some reason why you have to pay more or go over your original budget, and you need to have a cushion for yourself. And to prevent such extreme situations, a later section of this chapter offers some guidelines on how to find reputable contractors and renovators in the first place.

What a lot of professional rehabbers will do is borrow money from hard-money lenders—i.e., individuals or companies that charge a higher rate of interest (say, 12 or 12½ percent) for only six months. Hard-money lenders will also charge fees associated with the loan. Rehabbers or people who want to turn property will borrow the cost of fixing up the property. At six months, some hard-money lenders will allow the loan to be renewed, charging more points and extending the loan for another short period. This means that if the investor is not through with the renovation or needs more money, he or she has the option to borrow more money subject to the hard-money lender's approval. Hard-money lenders know what the fixed-up property will go for. They lend based on a percentage of the fixed-up price, generally up to 65 percent, so that there is equity should the hard-money lender have to foreclose because of nonpayment.

Decide what your profitability needs to be and go with that number. If you cannot get that number when all is said and done, don't do the deal. Checklist 5-2 summarizes the key points to keep in mind when looking for potential rehab properties.

If You Decide to Do the Renovation Yourself

One big thing you need to watch out for with renovation is the time required. In general, you're better off hiring skilled people to do the work for you than trying to do it yourself. Nine times out of ten, individual investors will not get the property done in a timely basis—and time is money.

A lot of people think, "Oh, I can fix this. I can fix the wallpaper that's coming off the walls. I'll just peel it off and put new wallpaper on," or they think

Checklist 5-2   Wise Women's Road Map
for Finding Good Properties to Rehab

❏ Drive around the communities where you want to buy, looking for a property that needs a little bit of fixing up.

❏ Once you've identified such a property, find out who the owner is by searching the local tax records.

❏ Follow up with the owners. I like to do that in the form of a letter telling them that I'm interested in possibly buying the home in an "as is" condition. Of course, that would be subject to an inspection.

❏ If the owner says that he or she might be interested in selling, go and see the property, and then request an inspection of the property *before you put your offer in*. You want to get the estimates for repairs and know the different types of changes you want to make on that property before you make an offer.

❏ Remember, when you're buying a property, you make money when you buy, not when you sell.

❏ Know what the end result for the property will be so that you can estimate a profitable return.

they can paint it or even do some minor construction or repair work themselves. Then they get busy with their families or their jobs and they never finish the renovation, which obviously ends up hurting them in the future.

Other investors decide to be the general contractor on the renovation and hire subcontractors to do all the painting, wallpapering, and reconstruction. If you have the time to devote to that, fine. But if you don't have a whole lot of time, you shouldn't be doing this as you may not be in a position to devote the time necessary to completing the job in a professional manner. Remember time is money!

Avoiding Problems with Contractors

Another major concern that many real estate buyers and investors have is hiring a contractor who turns out to be a nightmare. Here's an example.

Rehabbing and Other Short-Term Investing Strategies

Margie is an astute real estate investor living in Idaho. She decided to buy a property on a marina for $625,000. This property was okay if you wanted to live in it "as is," but she didn't like it that way; instead, she wanted to make a lot of changes.

To finance the renovation, she used another property she owned. She sold that property to a contractor on a lease with an option to buy, and she entered into an agreement with this contractor that he would fix up the $625,000 marina property in lieu of giving him a reduction in rent so that he could buy the property through the lease option agreement.

Call the state agency that's responsible for licensing contractors and home improvement handymen. Make sure that your contractor is licensed— and that the license is current.

After eight months, the property is still a complete shambles. She has screamed at her contractor; she has gone to the Contractors Board; she has threatened to terminate the existing lease option that the contractor has (which she really cannot do because he's making his payments). She has no grounds to terminate him, and she's stuck with a mess. Now she's going to have to go out and hire another company to fix it.

When you hire a contractor, make sure the contractor is properly licensed, check the contractor's licenses, and get at least three references. Ideally, you should look at the quality of the contractor's work on other properties at different stages. You want to make sure the contractor knows what he's doing.

Here's another nightmare example. Teresa in Mill Valley, California, bought a house that she wanted to live in, and she hired a contractor. He gave her a price, and he told her that he would put everything in writing. He started work without a signed contract, just an oral agreement. Yet he went 100 percent over what they agreed the price would be, and there was nothing she could do. She allowed the work to continue despite the fact she was over her budget. Clearly, when you're hiring contractors, you have to be very, very careful. Get regular progress reports, and go see the property. Make sure the contractor understands that you are overseeing the work.

Tips on Hiring Contractors

If rehabbing property sounds like a good plan to you, ask yourself what is the best way to go about finding a good contractor. What skills should you look for? Here are some guidelines.

Ask a Contractor for References.   This is the first and most important thing you should do. You don't want to just meet somebody and say, "You're hired." Get references from a contractor—and *call* those references—before you even consider hiring that contractor.

If at All Possible, Look at the Work the Contractor Has Done in the Past.   You want to see exactly what he has done. For example, if he put an addition on a building, go look at the building. You want to look at where he put the electrical work. You want to look at the finishing work to see how he finished it, if it looks good, and if you're happy with the work that he did. Before you hire anybody, go look at that person's work.

Check the Contractor's Licenses.   Next, you want to call the state agency that's responsible for licensing contractors and home improvement handymen. Make sure that your contractor is licensed—and that the license is current. Make sure the contractor is also bonded, so that if somebody falls and gets hurt on the job, the contractor is going to be the one, under his license and insurance, who will be liable, not you.

Find Out if Any Complaints Have Recently Been Filed against the Contractor or His Company.   If so, find out what the remedy for those complaints was. Did the contractor solve the problem? Was the complaint justified? Before you hire somebody to work on a house that you're buying and financing or paying cash for, be sure that you get a deadline in writing.

Get at Least Three Detailed Bids.   Do not accept the first offer that somebody gives you. Get the bids in writing, so that you can assess the quality and the workmanship and determine if the bid is really within the guidelines of what you're expecting to pay. If one bid is substantially lower than the other bids, be careful. For example, Waste Management and other private companies bid on city government trash contracts. Waste Management might come in much lower than everybody else because it's a volume-based business. But if Joe Smith & Associates comes in significantly lower, that should be a red flag to the city. Make sure you look at the bids; they should be fairly close—within 10 percent of each other. If you see a significant difference, I would stay away from that contractor. In other words, run your rehabbing like a business.

Get a Written Contract.   You want everything in writing, and I know several horror stories of cases where people didn't do that, but accepted verbal promises, and then what they expected to happen didn't happen.

For example, Jackie bought a property that she needed to resell within 60 days. She already had a buyer for the property, and she needed to get certain work completed. One of the fixes she needed to have done was a kitchen renovation. All she wanted was to buy cabinets from a Home Depot–type store and put in a new floor. In other words, this should have been a very quick and easy renovation.

The contractor she hired verbally said, "That's not going to be a problem; I'll be able to do that for you. I can install cabinets; this is an easy job." He started on a Monday, and he never came back. She had nothing in writing from this contractor. Jackie had given him one-third of the amount agreed to as a deposit. She lost her deposit money, and she had to find somebody else to finish the job. Nobody wants to take over somebody else's mistakes, so she had a hard time finding another contractor to complete the unfinished work. Because of these problems and delays, she lost a potential buyer. If she had at least had a contract in writing, she still might have lost her buyer when this contractor skipped, but she would have been able to go after him legally and get her deposit back. If nothing else, she could have gotten a judgment against him through Small Claims Court. But she had nothing in writing.

In some states, oral agreements are legal. A fax agreement is legal. However, an e-mail agreement is not necessarily legal. You want something in writing that you can hold in your hand, that this contractor has committed to. It should specify the cost, the time it's going to take to do the job, the work you specifically requested, how the job will be done, and when the job will be completed. In a hot market, good contractors are hard to find.

If There Is a Project Change, Make Sure the Change Is Put in Writing. When you first contracted for the finishing work, you need to need to make sure the contract you sign allows you the opportunity to make changes without incurring huge costs.

If you don't get the changes in writing, your contractor can come back to you later and say, "I did this, this, and this, and this is what it cost me to do it, and you're going to have to pay the difference." And then you have a debate or worse you don't have the money to pay what the contractor says you, owe, he or she can put a lien against your property or sue. Set up your contract right from the start, if uncertain, have an attorney review the contract, and have provisions included for change orders so you are protected.

If Your Contractor Requires a Deposit, That's Fine, but Do Not Pay the Entire Bill until Completion. If you have to pay a third of the cost at the beginning of the project, a third in the middle, and a third at the end, that's fine. However it's negotiated, you want to make sure that you hold something back until the job is done and you have a certificate of occupancy from the city if you need one. You must be satisfied with the work that this person's done.

During the course of their investment career, 75 percent of investors will need to have work done on a property in order to make it resell, make it look sexier, make it more marketable. These guidelines can help you protect yourself—and your investments.

Determine Your Objective for Each *Rehab Property You Buy*

If your objective is to rehab properties, develop a detailed plan, a road map to help keep you on track and keep you on a timeline. Time is money. When you assess what kind of property you're going to look at, determine your exit strategy for each particular property. Keep in mind that your objective does not need to be the same for each property.

- You might want to hold one property for the long term.
- The next one, you might want to rehab.
- The next one, you might decide to flip.
- You might fall in love with the next one and decide to make it that your personal residence.
- The next one you might want to buy may be a commercial building.

You also might look at different types of property—for example:

- You might be looking at land or improved lots that could turn into a development.
- You could be looking at commercial real estate.
- You could be looking at industrial real estate.

All of these are objectives that you need to decide on. First, decide what type of investments you want to do, and then look at each property objectively to decide your strategy for each individual deal. When you use a common sense approach to investing, you will profit.

Conclusion

Investing in a rental property or holding a property for the long term is a great way to build a portfolio. If you do it right, your tenants are paying for your mortgage, and you get the payoff when you sell the property, whether that happens in 5, 10, or 20 years. Investing in real estate can be lucrative and should have slow and steady growth. If you decide to buy for the long term, recognize that there is a downside to being a landlord and there could be a downside to holding a property for the long term (Chapter 8 discusses these in detail). But in the end, if your investment strategy is one that involves holding the property to capitalize on appreciation, to use it as an inflation hedge, or to gain tax benefits of depreciation on your properties, then the long-term strategy can be a beneficial one.

On the other hand, if you decide that the long-term strategy is *not* for you, then you should consider buying, rehabbing, and reselling quickly. It is all up to you. Checklist 5-3 provides some final guidelines.

Checklist 5-3   Wise Women Determine
Their Outcome Before They Buy

❏ Determine both the desired outcome of your strategy and your objectives before you buy.

❏ If you're going to get into the fixer business, try to start out by buying it right in the first place and doing limited cosmetic fix-ups to save cost. Make sure that you get bids from contractors and that the contractors are licensed and bonded.

❏ If you're going to buy to hold, you want to look at the long term, what type of property it is, and the appreciation potential, because the number one thing that investors who buy for the long term are looking for is appreciation.

❏ And then, finally, you make money when you buy. If you overpay for a property, or you buy when the market is at an all-time high, it's going to be much harder for you to make money than if you bought it right in the first place.

6

Working with Real Estate Agents: A Professional Source to Help You Find Property

Realtors are in the best position to help you identify the right investments. They have the opportunity to see potential deals before properties go into the multiple listing service (MLS). In other words, Realtors are often in the right place at the right time and can assist you in investing in property. This chapter covers how to work effectively with Realtors to find investment property.

If you decide that you *don't* want to research potential investment properties on your own, you should consider working with a Realtor (aka a real estate broker or real estate agent). That said, working with real estate agents can be a very time-consuming and tedious process—but it can also be a very positive process. You need to interview the Realtors you plan on working with to make sure they understand your objectives. In general, no real estate agent will work with a seller of a property unless the agent has a listing agreement. On the other hand, if you are the investor/buyer, you will not have to sign an agreement in order to work with a Realtor (unless you are working with a buyer's broker).

The National Association of Realtors (NAR) is the largest lobby in the United States, with over a million members. If you like dealing with women Realtors because you feel there will be more camaraderie between you and you will have a better working relationship, check out the Women's Council of Realtors (WCR), which is a subset of the NAR. WCR is an association of active women Realtors, they offer continuing education programs for Realtors who really want to hone their own skill sets as well as other programs that are geared to the woman professional.

Realtors use the multiple listing service. It's put together by the local Board of Realtors, and the different real estate companies that participate on that local board use it to list and share property information. The MLS will give the following information about the properties for sale:

- The address
- The square footage
- When the buildings on the property were built
- The taxes on the property
- The owner's name
- Other details necessary for you to make an initial objective evaluation of that property

Why You Should Consider Working with a Realtor

Most of the women in the real estate industry that I talked to encouraged working with Realtors. (Of course, many of them are Realtors themselves.) Here's what some of them had to say on this subject:

Many of us who get into the business early may have money to be able to invest, but [we] don't yet have the expertise. You can really get in over your head if you don't know what to look for, don't know how to evaluate the comps, or don't know the neighborhood. This can be downright dangerous.

Also, many of us are doing this as a secondary business. Unless we are truly dedicated to focusing on our investing business, we need the help of someone who will push us along and keep us moving forward.

—Rebecca McLean, executive director
of the National Real Estate Investors Association

An experienced Realtor has access to the MLS and can find properties very quickly that are listed if they have your criteria. An experienced Realtor can also help the novice investor enter the market by helping to provide some of the knowledge necessary to succeed.

—Jaime Raskulinecz, broker since 1994.

It's all about the numbers. Even if you have to train a Realtor on your investment needs, they have the numbers. Thousands of agents have thousands of buyers and sellers and the technology. Computerization has made Realtors a better tool because they can auto-send the "investment pack" you want, right to your personal e-mail, with full pictures, stats, and comps. To get results, offers have to be made in mass; then you can negotiate with the houses that counter back. Using a Realtor as a team member can catapult you into the numbers.

—Anna Mills, Century 21 Realtor for 30 years

When you are with a good Realtor, they will know the market and can find what you are looking for in a short time frame. The Realtor can advise on lenders, inspectors, title companies, and the market.

—Tami Spaulding, Realtor for 26 years

First of all, a Realtor has easy access to the MLS, which can be a strong resource. Secondly, when buying property, the fee is gener-

ally paid by someone else—the seller! Why not take advantage of knowledgeable assistance when someone else is footing the bill? Third, a well-connected Realtor will often know or hear of deals before they hit the MLS or become common knowledge, providing beneficial insider knowledge.

—Tracy Rewey, real estate note
and owner-financing expert

Realtors, by virtue of their 24/7 exposure, analyze thousands of properties over the course of a year, and some are excellent deals because of a certain quantity of benefits, but none of them are everyone's definition of a good deal. Realtors have the advantage of inside knowledge, through their associations and relationships with other professionals in the industry and affiliated industries. In addition, they have the MLS system, word of mouth, rumor, and—in the case of my agents—formal investment analysis training and experience. This is over and above all of the venues available to the proactive investor.

The best position for any investor is to be on the preferred client list of a real estate investment counselor. This counselor will have reviewed thoroughly [your, the investor's] financial position, liabilities, assets, comfort zones, and investment philosophy. This means that [your] Realtor will call [you] each time the Realtor discovers one of his [or her] "deals." I have never minded paying someone to do my taxes if their bill is one-third of the amount they saved me, and a competent Realtor costs far less than that.

—Magi Bird, broker and
real estate trainer/educator

What You Need to Know about Realtors' Commissions

Real estate agents get paid by commission, and these commissions are negotiable. Usually, each state has a general average of what a property owner—i.e., the seller—would pay in commission, which is approximately 6 percent. Still, you should know that Realtors can negotiate commissions. Broker Jaime Raskulinecz confirms this: "Commissions can always be negotiated and are largely dependent on the current market conditions, so it would be hard to pinpoint a [typical] percentage." Century 21 Realtor Anna Mills has this comment on commissions:

Make a Realtor an "investor team member," and your commissions may be very negotiable. There are specialty deals, where multiple properties are bundled together, or repeats, where another property bought every couple months, etc.

However, Anna can't give any information on "typical" commissions because in the area in which she works, commissions cannot be discussed among Realtors, for price-fixing reasons.

Realtor and educator Magi Bird had this comment on commissions:

An agent's compensation is a matter of negotiation between the principal and the agent, and will vary with the type of transaction being undertaken. Most of my agents work as buyer/brokers, and their fees will range from 3 to 10 percent, dependent upon the type of property, the work involved, other brokerage fees to be paid, and the profit expectations of the client. Some of our clients prefer to make their agents a participant in the project, even though that is not a concept I promote.

A lot of Realtors don't like to work with investors because their perception is that investors are cheap. Many investors just want to buy a property at the lowest possible cost; they don't want to have to negotiate any commission. Sometimes, the investor's mentality is, "I could do this myself; why do I need you?"

If you're working with a Realtor to help you find investment property, of course, you may also find opportunities on your own. If you don't have a buyer's broker agreement, you can invest in that property on your own. If you are working with a buyer's agent, Tami Spaulding says, the typical commission is 3 percent. (But if you're working with a transaction broker, the commission should be 0.)

Ask [a] *Realtor* [you're considering working with] *for the names of at least three investors that the Realtor has personally helped become profitable in their real estate investing, and then check them out.*

How to Evaluate Real Estate Agents to Find One Who Is Right for You

If you do decide to work with a real estate agent as one of your marketing strategies to find the right deal, you need to have a "job description" in your mind that will help you assess that Realtor. The rest of this chapter offers some guidelines to help you assess whether a Realtor will be helpful to you.

Find a Realtor Who Has Experience Working with Investors

This is the number one consideration when you are looking for a Realtor who can help you. Measure the Realtor's experience by the number of *transactions* the Realtor has been involved in, not the number of years he or she has been in business.

Also, keep in mind that many Realtors work part-time and have another job, and these Realtors may not know the market as well as a full-time Realtor will. In general, when you're trying to assess who's the right real estate agent for you to work with, it's important that your Realtor understands your needs and what you're looking for. On the other hand, there are Realtors who are trying to find their own investment deals, which means that they may be competing with you for the same potential investments. Therefore, they may not want to spend as much time with you because they're looking out for themselves, and they may cherry-pick the best deals. This is a gray area; you want your agent to have investing experience, but you don't want him or her to be competing with you.

You want to look at the number of transactions the Realtor has done. There's no real minimum for that; it's up to you to determine what you're comfortable with. Broker Anna Mills suggests that investors should "find a Realtor who is an investor. Join your local, state, or National Real Estate Investors Association to network and learn."

Do background reference checks. Ask the Realtor for the names of at least three investors that the Realtor has personally helped become profitable in their real estate investing, and then check them out—*call* those investors. By checking the references of the Realtors you're considering working with, you're going to get a lot more information.

Finally, Tracy Rewey (real estate note and owner-financing expert) has this advice:

> *If you are new to investing, then select an experienced real estate agent (five years' minimum experience). If you are an experienced investor, you might opt for "hungry," which often results in a highly motivated agent. Most agents are motivated, though—after all, they only get paid on results.*

If you as an investor are going to work with Realtors, do your due diligence and research to make sure that the Realtor you choose is reputable.

Look for Realtors Who Really Know Their Market

Get as much information as you can about any Realtor you're considering working with. One good way to do that is to see who is advertising where and how well the Realtor is respected. Is this person the number one producer for his or her company? Does he or she get around the community?

Broker Jaime Raskulinecz has this suggestion: be as specific as possible in relaying your needs and criteria for an investment property, so that the Realtor knows what properties to bring to you.

Check That There Are No Complaints Filed against the Realtor You're Considering

You should also call the Department of Real Estate and make sure that no complaints have been filed against the Realtor you're considering. I bought a property in Ocala, Florida, in the summer of 2005, using a Realtor who is a good Keller-Williams real estate agent. She was relatively new to the business, but she was very thorough in helping me. However, the Realtor who was representing the *seller* was with another real estate company (which shall remain nameless). This particular Realtor misrepresented his client, the seller of the property, who was a widow. This poor woman did not have any idea of what to expect from the process. She was downsizing because she had lost her husband and she couldn't afford to keep the house. And the real estate agency she hired was trying to take advantage of her.

First of all, her Realtor charged her a 7 percent instead of a 6 percent commission; the company had her sign new documents. Next, the company listed her property for much more than it was worth. Finally, the broker/owner was unethical. Here's what happened: after I put in an offer to purchase the property and the seller and I had agreed on the price, the seller's Realtor found someone else who wanted to buy the same property and was willing to pay more for the property than the seller and I had already agreed to in writing. She already had a sale—and we had a contract (signed by her and by me).

I ended up having to hire an attorney to go after the real estate company that represented the seller because the company was trying to cancel my transaction—and the contract I had signed with the seller. An agent can't do that when the seller already has a signed contract. Her Realtor must have thought that I was an idiot. In the end, our contract prevailed. The seller was satisfied with the price she received, but not with the company that tried to rip her off. I ended up reporting the seller's broker to the Florida Department of Real Estate.

I do believe this to be a rare case. My overall experience working with the Realtor community has been positive. The message here is to research the company and agent thoroughly. By checking references in advance of working with a particular company, you should have a good experience. Rates have been low for so many years in the recent past, prices of properties have gone up, that people have become Realtors to "get on the bandwagon" to make a living in real estate. I think as the volatility in the market continues, or if the market continues to go down, it will weed out the Realtors who only got into the business to capitalize on a quick profit.

Working with Real Estate Agents

The point is, if you as an investor are going to work with Realtors, you need to do your due diligence and research to make sure that the Realtor you choose is reputable. Your Realtor should also know enough about the agency rules, commissions, and so on to know if the seller's agent is not fairly representing him or her.

Here's another example—this one pertains to the sale of mortgage notes rather than property, but it also illustrates the importance of doing due diligence. Some people will sell their property and owner-finance the sale for the buyer, with the buyer making the payments to the seller instead of to a lender. Mrs. Jones had a property for sale in North Carolina. She sold her property to Charlene, a real estate agent who lives in Georgia. Charlene resold the property, on a wrap-around mortgage, to Suzanne, who lived in North Carolina.

Suzanne moved into the property and made payments to Charlene. Suzanne thought she was going to get the deed to the property because she had been making payments on the property. But Charlene was still making payments to Mrs. Jones. After three years, Suzanne wanted to sell the property she had been living in and making payments on and move to another state. When she tried to sell, however, Suzanne found out that there was a first mortgage in place by Mrs. Jones. Suzanne had no idea who Mrs. Jones was because she was not a part of her transaction with Charlene. Needless to say, there was confusion as to who was the legal owner. It was a mess to straighten out.

I don't want to paint such a horror picture that it discourages you from getting started in real estate investing. But these examples illustrate why, if you're going to work with a Realtor to find good investments, *you need to be really careful* in choosing whom you're going to work with—checking licenses, references, and whether there have been any complaints filed against that person. In short, do your due diligence on the Realtor before you hire that Realtor to work with you. You don't really know whom you're dealing with—until you ask around. So protect yourself before you decide to work with someone.

Make sure that your Realtor has strong negotiating skills and that she's capable of getting properties for buyers, not just working as a listing agent.

Make Sure the Realtor Understands What Your Goals Are—and Works to Meet Those Goals

The Realtor you decide to work with should also understand what you're trying to achieve so that she's looking for the right kind of property. For example, if your budget is $200,000, you don't want your Realtor to bring you properties that are out of line with your financial requirements. You will run into agents who will say things like, "I found this great property for $250,000; it's a real beauty, and the potential for resale is great; it's going to make you so much more money." If you can't afford $250,000, that Realtor is not serving you and your interests. Your Realtor needs to work within the guidelines that *you* have as an investor. To optimize your relationship with a real estate agent, Realtor Tami Spaulding advises, "Get preapproved for your financing, know what numbers make sense to you, and hire a Realtor who will listen and work."

Also, it's not just your *price* that your Realtor needs to know; she should also know the investment area that you're trying to establish yourself in. She knows the property type you are looking for: single-family, town home, condo, and so on. Your ideal floor plan should also be a factor. If you want to buy only three-bedroom, two-bath homes with a master bath, that is all she should show you. And she should have information on the local schools, amenities, and any and all other factors that you might take into consideration when you're trying to assess whether a particular property is a good deal.

Tami also points out that Realtors should find out what an investor is looking for and do the same search that she would do for an owner-occupied property: "The big difference is, with an investor, it's all about the bottom line, not how they feel when they walk into the kitchen."

Broker Magi Bird has some additional advice on making sure your Realtor understands your investing goals:

> *Be open and honest, and insist that your Realtor get to know you, your financial position, your dreams, your goals, and your comfort zones intimately, so that he will understand what you are trying to accomplish, why, how soon, and what you can handle. Be honest. She can't read your mind.*

Secondly, always do what you say you will do. Never mislead.

Thirdly, be absolutely loyal. This should generate loyalty from your agent in turn. Any client who ever lied to me, I dropped like a hot potato. I sat down with each one of my clients, outlined a plan of action that would lead us to his desired outcome, and expected my client to fulfill his end of the bargain. Any time a client committed an action that sabotaged our plan, such as the purchase of a property from another agent—or even without an agent—or made a retail purchase that harmed his ability to qualify, or failed to make payments that he had contractually committed to, I dropped him.

Your Realtor cannot want your financial success for you more than you want it for yourself.

Don't give your Realtor total authority over your investing strategy, however. Investor Jennifer Dizmang tells this story of how she learned this lesson the hard way:

I was traveling a lot for business, and my real estate broker, with whom I had done 10 transactions the previous year, called me on the road with a "great deal." It was an owner-carry on a five-plex that I could purchase for $130,000 at 6 percent interest, but I needed to act quickly because he had two other buyers on the hook behind me. I bought the property sight unseen, "through his good judgment," and faxed the documents to complete the deal.

Upon returning home and looking at the property, I came to the horrific realization that I had, in essence, purchased a crack house that was falling down and nothing was up to code. Within one month, I received a notice from the state that if the electrical work was not brought up to code, it would condemn the property. I fire-sold the property to a rehabber that was capable of the fix-up and promptly fired my Realtor.

What did I learn: don't let other people make your investment decisions for you, and no matter how much business you are sending someone, remember that they will almost always look out for their best interest before they look out for yours.

Work with a Full-Time Realtor

Another factor that's important to me when I'm using a Realtor to help me find property is that that Realtor works in the business on a full-time basis. I would not want a part-time Realtor. Full-time Realtors spend more time understanding their market. That's not to say that part-time Realtors don't know their markets. However, part-time Realtors have other sources of income, so they're not totally devoted to real estate; they're doing other things. I myself would rather work with somebody who's in the industry full-time, who has the pulse and the beat of the marketplace, and who will be able to contact me immediately when something goes on the market, so that I have an opportunity to view the property before anybody else.

Make Sure Your Realtor Has Good Negotiation Skills, Not Just Selling Skills

Some Realtors are outstanding listers: they're terrific at finding prospective sellers and at convincing those property owners to let them list the property for three or six months or whatever their time frame is. Obviously, the longer that Realtors can tie up a property, the better it is for them. *But that's all they do.* Instead, I want to work with a Realtor who not only is capable of finding properties for me to invest in, but *also has strong negotiating skills*. I don't want the Realtor to also be representing the seller's end of the bargain. I don't want somebody who's just going to go out and be a lister; I want the Realtor to represent *me*. The Realtor can't do both. Therefore, I want to work with a Realtor who has a history and experience working with investors or with people who are interested in *buying* property.

Your Realtor should also have an established network of home contractors and inspectors, preferred title companies, lenders . . . , and so on, so that . . . you [can] get [your deal] closed quickly.

To find this out, just ask her. Ask a Realtor where most of her business is coming from: *listing* properties or working with people who are trying to *buy* property? What percentage of her business is from listings? Also, there are Realtors called *buyer's brokers*; when working with one of these, you do sign an agreement with the Realtor, but her job is to represent you, the buyer. I'm not necessarily saying that that's what you should do. What I'm saying is, you want to make sure that your Realtor has strong negotiating skills and that she's capable of getting properties for buyers, not just working as a listing agent.

Work with a Realtor Who Has a Great Network

Your Realtor should also have an established network of home contractors and inspectors, preferred title companies, lenders (including names of loan officers), and so on, so that if you put a property under contract, your Realtor and her network can help you facilitate the transaction and get it closed quickly. You don't want your deal to be held up because your Realtor doesn't know the right people to help you close that deal.

For example, Tami Spaulding is an outstanding Realtor who has a tremendous amount of experience as an investor herself, plus she has worked with investors in her marketplace, and she has been very successful doing a lot of interesting deals. She has a list of people that she works with, so that if I were to put a property under contract, the first thing Tami would do would be to get a home inspector out to the property. She also has a list of appraisal companies that work with her, so she could get the appraisal done quickly. She has put together excellent strategic alliances that help the buyer and the process go as smoothly as possible.

Make Sure Your Realtor Will Follow Up on Deals and Keep You Informed

If I'm working with a Realtor, I want to be able to know exactly what's happening with an offer that I've put in. When am I going to get a response? How's the process going? What's the flow? *A good Realtor does good follow-up.* (If you're a Realtor, keep that in mind.)

If you're an investor who is working with a Realtor, here is the sequence of events you should expect to see:

- The Realtor gets a listing from a seller who wants to sell his or her property.

- If the property fits your parameters, the Realtor should contact you and set up an appointment to get you into the property as quickly as possible.
- If you like the property, you negotiate and visit the property with the seller present. (Chapter 7 covers negotiations in more detail.)
- You write up the offer with the assistance of your Realtor. Make the presentation to the seller.

This last point is vitally important: you should make your own presentation to the seller regarding the offering price you've come up with, once you feel comfortable doing so. Nobody is going to represent your money better than you can. Remember, the seller's asking price is her first offer, so it's your responsibility to tell the seller why you've come up with the price you're offering. Personally, I will not work with a Realtor who does not allow me to make my own presentations. Many Realtors do not want to work with investors who wish to make their own presentations. If the Realtor can't understand why I want to make my own presentation to the seller, then I won't work with that Realtor.

The Realtor can be there when I make my presentation—in fact, I recommend that she be there. I also recommend that if the seller is working with a Realtor, the seller's Realtor should be there as well. When I make my presentation, I want to tell the seller how I arrived at my offer price and why, what I can do for the seller, and how quickly I can close the deal. Realtors don't like investors to make their own presentations because they don't like the investor to be in control of the situation. Many Realtors think that investors don't know what they're doing. But because I've been around a long time, I like to do my own presentations.

If you're a *new* investor and you are working with a Realtor, you should have enough confidence in your Realtor to make the offer together. Until you are confident that you completely understand your market, that you can assess the value of the property, and that you can make your own presentation, you and your real estate agent should make the offer together. On the other hand, if you want the Realtor to make your presentation for you, you should be confident that your Realtor is going to do a good job for you. If you aren't, don't let your Realtor do it.

Once I've made an offer and the seller and I have agreed on the terms, I will write up the offer, and the offer gets signed. Do your due diligence, which includes a home inspection, a title insurance policy, and the appraisal. If I get a loan on the property, then it goes into escrow and it gets closed with the title company; at that point, my Realtor gets her commission. If I'm planning to rent the property, I will find a tenant or a tenant-buyer. The tenant-buyer moves in, and then, at some point, I'll sell that property to the tenant-buyer. In my ideal scenario, that's the sequence of events that I'm looking for when I work with real estate agents.

Using Realtors as "Bird Dogs" to Help You Find Potential Investments

Another strategy for working with Realtors that you as an investor can use is to have a Realtor be a "bird dog,"—i.e., the Realtor goes out and finds property for you, and then you pay the Realtor a referral fee. Keep in mind, though, that Realtors must disclose all fees that they receive on the transaction; this is specified in their license.

Conclusion

If you're interested in investing in real estate, you should look at every single tool and opportunity that's available to you, including working with real estate agents to help you find good investment property that matches your strategy and meets your financial goals. I'm not necessarily *recommending* that you work with a Realtor; in the end, it's up to you to make your own decision based on your comfort level.

If you do decide to work with a Realtor, you should work with only one in your area. Do not work with multiple Realtors: it's a small industry, most Realtors know one another and talk to each other, and if you work with more than one, you will mar your own reputation. When I was investing in Ft. Collins, Colorado, I worked with one Realtor, Tami Spaulding, because she knew what she was doing, she was an experienced investor in her own right, she wasn't into stealing deals, she knew exactly what I wanted, and there was no reason for me to work with anyone else.

If you're investing in different types of property, however, you may want to work with a different Realtor for each particular property type. For example, if you're interested in buying land, you would want to work with a Realtor who specializes in land. If you're interested in buying soft commercial property (for example, storage units), you would want to work with a broker who is a Certified Commercial Investment Member (CCIM) or a real estate broker who specializes in commercial real estate, because you want to work with the most experienced, most knowledgeable person. If you are working with more than one Realtor because they have different specialties, you should disclose that to the Realtors you're working with. Be open and honest about what you're trying to do. If you don't, and the Realtors find out that you're working with others, that will come back to haunt you, and your reputation as an investor is everything.

Finally, I get the question, "Do you think I should get my real estate license so that I can use it in my investing business?" I know many investors who do this. I never had a real estate license. I enjoy meeting and working with sharp Realtors who know their business. It's a personal choice.

7

Winning Negotiation Strategies for Women

As mentioned in Chapter 1 and throughout this book, I think women make phenomenal negotiators because we know how to use empathy, we are good listeners, we will sit and encourage people to continue to tell their story, and we ask open-ended questions that get individuals to start talking. This chapter covers the best type of questions to ask to help build rapport.

Finding True Motivation: What Does the Seller *Need*?

First of all, in any type of negotiation, no seller will be motivated to sell his or her home at less than fair market value or full price unless that seller has a need. For example, if someone needs to get out of a property because he or she is getting divorced, that person has a need: to sell the property in order to finalize the divorce. That's the need, the motivation to sell.

Or maybe the seller is being transferred to another city in either another part of the world or another part of the country. As discussed in Chapter 3 on working with relocation companies, people sometimes voluntarily request relocations; for example, employees of Hewlett-Packard often request temporary relocations to take advantage of an opportunity to work in India for two years. Those employees need to tie up whatever loose ends they have in the area where they are currently living, so they will either rent their properties out for two years or sell them. Either way, they have an inherent need because they can't leave the property vacant. Some people can't afford to leave their properties at all; they need to sell to get cash to live overseas.

Believe it or not, I even met one seller who refinanced and sold property to finance five plastic surgeries. Whatever the seller's reason is, finding his or her motivation will help you to accomplish a "win": you get what you want, and the seller gets what he or she wants or needs.

In any type of negotiation, no seller will be motivated to sell his or her home at less than fair market value or full price unless that seller has a need.

Therefore, you always want to look at individuals who have a need to sell. Checklist 7-1 lists some of the more typical reasons that motivate individuals to sell—and to sell their property at a discount. Keep these in mind when you're talking to a seller. Many of these reasons involve deadlines—and the closer the deadline comes, the more motivated the seller.

Checklist 7-1 Typical Reasons/Motivations for Selling a Property

❏ A new job.

❏ A divorce.

❏ A serious illness.

❏ A bankruptcy.

❏ The owner may be behind on the payments.

❏ The owner may need to go into a nursing home or assisted-living facility.

- ❏ The owner may need to settle an estate.

- ❏ The owner may owe the IRS money.

- ❏ The owner may need to sell the property for an emotional reason—for example, if someone has died.

- ❏ The owner may have decided to downsize because the property requires too much upkeep, the children are grown and gone, and the owner wants to live in something smaller or something more manageable.

- ❏ A family member is getting married, and the owner needs to raise money from the sale to pay for the wedding.

- ❏ College expenses.

- ❏ A growing family, where the owner is in a starter home and has a contingency on another property. The owners are buying a larger home or building a home, and they need to sell their existing home in order to quality for the loan on a new home.

Getting the Seller to Talk to You

When you're negotiating, it's important to see what the seller's motivation is. To find that out, you've got to get that seller talking. Once you've identified the seller's motivation to sell, it is easy for you to sit down and assess what you can and cannot do to solve his or her problem.

The first thing you want to do when you look at a property, whatever the source—whether you find it through the newspaper, an open house, a property manager, or the financial advisor of a seller who happens to call you because she knows you're looking for property—is to find out what the seller's story is, why he or she wants to sell this particular property. And you do that by asking *open-ended questions* that will get the seller talking: the who, what, where, how, why questions. Start by telling the owner, "You have a beautiful home." Then simply ask, "How did you arrive at this price?" and "Why are you selling the property?"

To encourage the seller to talk to you, be *empathetic*. For example, if the seller tells you that the reason she's selling is because of a bad personal situation in her life, you should respond with something like, "Gee, I'm sorry to hear that; that's too bad." This type of response encourages the seller to continue talking about the property. This isn't manipulative; it's a kindness to listen to the seller's story. Selling a property (or just having to leave it, especially if it's been the seller's home) is often an emotional decision for many people, and most people will be more than happy to talk to you and tell you their story.

Recall the story that I told in Chapter 1 of the couple who wanted to move to the wine country. I learned the couple's true motivation to sell—which was *not* financial; it was emotional. I talked with the wife *and listened to her* tell how she and her husband wanted to live in a more peaceful place. She already saw herself living there. In another case, I bought a property from a widow because I was nonthreatening to her. You will have greater success if you're quiet and considerate. Ask open-ended questions to get a person to open up. Don't ask questions like, "What do you want?" Instead, encourage an owner to talk by saying something like, "Tell me a little bit about your home." Make it personal; people like that. People feel comfortable doing business with individuals who they believe will, in the end, be people they can envision seeing in the property they're selling.

Don't come off as a know-it-all . . . or you are going to turn the seller off. People like doing business with people they feel they can trust.

Here's another example of how I did this on one of my own deals. I looked at a property owned by a woman whom I'll call Jessica, who is from Argentina. I met Jessica at a seminar that was put on by a "for sale by owner" company. I had gone to the seminar to learn what properties were available. Jessica needed to move back to Argentina to take care of her mother, so she was selling her property in New Mexico, and she was selling it on her own. She needed to sell this property because she didn't know if she was ever going to return to New Mexico. In other words, renting her property to someone else wasn't an option for Jessica.

Before Jessica had her open house, I made an appointment with her to view her property. I got a head start on Jessica's property, and then she held her open house in conjunction with my visit. I went through her property, and I told her it was a very nice home. I told her that I was a real estate investor and that I was interested in purchasing her property, then I asked whether she had a few minutes to give me some information and answer a few questions about the property, which she did. People will take the time to answer your questions about the property if they are motivated to sell.

Jessica asked me what I wanted to know; my questions were assessment or fact-finding questions. "How did you arrive at your price?" She told me that two neighbors had sold property within the last six months, and she had come up with the number by averaging what those neighbors had sold their property for.

My next question was, "How flexible are you on this number, since you're not using a real estate agent?" Jessica went on to tell me that if she doesn't have to sell through a real estate agent, she could discount the property a little bit, because she had factored that into her price. However, if she didn't sell the property within two weeks, she would have to list it with an agent because she needs to get to Argentina.

Then I asked her, "Why are you moving to Argentina?" This question led to a half-hour conversation, in which she told me that her mother has Alzheimer's, there's no one else to take care of her, and Jessica didn't want to put her mother into a facility. She was the oldest child, and her siblings did not have the resources and didn't know what else to do. She was living in the United States, but she said she was ready to go back to Argentina. Jessica got very upset, and the more she talked about her situation, the more upset she became. I sat and listened to her, and I said, "That has got to be very, very difficult, trying to manage a parent from so far away," and she just continued her conversation. This wasn't fake empathy; it's listening to someone, knowing that she's a person with a story, and expressing, whether through facial expressions or body language, feeling for that person.

When you do that, when you sit and listen to someone talk, and you ask questions ("How did you arrive at your price?" "Why are you moving or selling?"), you are getting their story, firsthand. Let them talk. The more they talk, the better they're going to feel about you. The key in most negotiations is to keep your mouth shut, because if you continually interrupt—which a lot of people do—then you have lost the rapport with this person.

That is a major mistake. Don't come off as a know-it-all—that's another major mistake people make—or you are going to turn the seller off. People like doing business with people they feel they can trust, in their heart of hearts.

Regardless of what business you are in, this strategy of building rapport with people works. Ask open-ended questions like those listed in Checklist 7-2—not questions with yes or no answers.

Checklist 7-2   Open-Ended Questions to Ask a Seller of a Property You're Considering Buying

❏   How did you arrive at this price?

❏   Why are you selling this property?

❏   How much do you need? (Here, you should clarify that you're not asking what the person needs necessarily from a financial standpoint—i.e., how much cash the person needs—but what is the person's real need for selling.)

❏   When were you planning on moving?

❏   How are you planning on getting there? (Here, I am looking to see whether there is something else I could use when making an offer. For example, could I help offset some of the seller's moving expenses? If she needs six weeks, could I close on the property earlier and let her live there for six weeks as part of the deal, and build that into my purchase price?

When I am negotiating with a seller, I'm looking for creative strategies so that I can come back and make an offer that turns out to be a win-win offer that the seller feels comfortable with. The seller will understand how I arrived at this price, and why it benefits him or her.

In Jessica's case, I bought her house. I let her stay in the house for six weeks until she was able to move her things. I got the property at about a 15 percent discount from the price she had originally mentioned, and then I turned around and leased the property for two years before selling it. She sold it to me for a 15 percent discount because I let her stay in the property for six weeks free, plus she no longer had to make mortgage payments and didn't have to pay a real estate commission. This was a good deal for her.

The seller's motivation **is not always financial—and this** *is a very important thing to keep in mind.*

It was also a good deal for her emotionally. She was very nervous because she had to get to Argentina, so she wanted to wrap up this deal as quickly as possible. I made her an offer before she listed her house with a Realtor. She still had her open house, but nobody came in with an offer that day, and that made her nervous. She started thinking about what we had talked about, about how long she needed to stay there, and about when she would be ready to move. I worked with her so that she was able to move when she wanted to. I even said to her, "If you need longer than six weeks, we can work something out." So, she knew that I had flexibility, that I wasn't going anywhere, and that there was no urgency for me that would mean that I would have to get her out of the property. All of that gave her peace of mind.

Be Flexible to Meet the Owner's Need to Sell

Here's another example. A year ago, I bought a property in Phoenix, Arizona, from Monica, who is an attorney. Monica told me that she had grown up in the sticks, flat broke, but that she had become a physical therapist and put herself through college. Eventually, she decided to become a lawyer. In the meantime, she had married someone who became an alcoholic, and was supporting the family. Monica and her husband had built a home for about $200,000, maybe a little bit less, a year and a half before I bought it from her. Then they got a divorce. Monica could no longer afford to make the mortgage payments on the home. However, she did not want to leave and uproot her three children. One of her girls was old enough that she had friends in the community and was having an emotional crisis over the fact that the family was going to move.

Monica's need was to try to stay in the property, even though she needed to sell it. I bought the property from her, and she now rents that property from me. I offered her $223,000. She had had a better offer (financially) of $237,000, but she sold to me because I let her stay in the property on a long-term lease. Her story illustrates that the seller's motivation *is not always financial*— this is a very important thing to keep in mind. This is what makes us successful real estate investors. I think we do a better job of being able to sit down one-on-one with people, have a cup of coffee, and just talk.

Both Jessica's and Monica's stories are good examples of why it's not always the money that motivates a seller to sell a property—and why they do not always sell it for the highest price offered. Obviously, sellers want to get top dollar for property when they sell it. In general, people want to get top dollar for everything and to make as much money as they possibly can. Nevertheless, sometimes there are considerations that are more important than money.

Here's another example. I had hired David, the son of a Realtor, to look for property for me. (This is a strategy some people call *bird-dogging*, as mentioned in Chapter 6.) David was going to real estate school; he had not gotten his license yet, but he was very aggressive when it came to looking for property: he would walk the streets, knock on doors of "for sale by owner" properties, and ask the owners if they would be interested in having him show their properties; he told them he was not currently licensed, but that he was working with an investor (me). When I work with bird-doggers, I have certain guidelines for properties that I'm looking for: usually (as in this case) three bedrooms and two bathrooms, one of which has to be a master bathroom. I provide these guidelines so that the people who are trying to find property for me know what I'm looking for, in which communities, and any other considerations.

David had met a couple living in Colorado who had an autistic child and needed to move to North Carolina, where there was a center for autistic children. The child was getting to the point of being unmanageable. The couple loved their home: it was 1,200 square feet, with three bedrooms and two baths, in a good school district. It was not in an area that I would normally go into—but it was a lovely little home, clean and neat.

David said to the owners, "I know an investor; I don't know if she would really be interested in this property, but I can certainly have her come over and take a look at it and see if there is anything she could do for you." So I went over and visited with the couple. I could see that their child was in very bad shape. He was running back and forth in the fenced back yard; they must have had to repair the fence 15 times because he would run into the fence, get up, run back and forth, and run into the fence again; he didn't stop. And I could see the parents' concern: their son was only seven years old, and his parents knew that they were at a crossroads, that they needed to do something. The husband had an excellent job, but it wasn't a job that was transferable. Still, they wanted to move to North Carolina, even though they didn't have jobs or anywhere to move to there.

> *Property managers can be great resources . . . , because they often know landlords who are . . . sick and tired of renting properties, and who just want to get out.*

I listened to their story, I hooked them up with another investor in North Carolina who found them a property that they could lease until the husband found a job, and I bought their Colorado property from them, solving their cash crisis and helping them make a smooth transition, without hassles and without having to worry about whether they had enough money to move to North Carolina.

Obviously, the money from the sale of their Colorado property was not the most important factor in this sale. What made the deal was that the owners needed a place to go. They had no connections in North Carolina, but they knew that the school was outstanding and they wanted to put their child in this facility, and they needed to sell their Colorado house in order to do that. They felt comfortable selling to me because I introduced them to a Realtor in North Carolina who could help them get settled. I just happened to know somebody where they were going, and I said, 'Well, why don't you work with my friend Linda? She's been an investor a long time. Perhaps she has something," and I hooked them up with Linda. I solved their problem, created a win-win situation, and they got the cash they needed to move forward.

I know some people would say, "Oh, you didn't have to do that. Why didn't you try to steal the deal?" It is solving the seller's real problem that helps your dealing and negotiations go smoothly. Clearly, these people were desperate. But I don't believe I need to take advantage of sellers: I offer a fair price, and the people I buy from appreciate that and thank me for that. In fact, after I complete a transaction, I send the seller a personalized letter that basically asks for a testimonial. Essentially, I ask whether the seller thinks I treated him or her right, and if there was anything I could have done to make the transaction better. I send just a brief letter that says something like the following:

You recently completed a financial transaction with our company. Please answer the following questions, so that we can improve our service for future customers. Thank you for your help.

And then I ask just a few simple questions:

- How would you rate us?
- Was the transaction satisfactory to you?
- Would you recommend our company to others who need our service?
- May we use this letter to show other potential clients?

And I ask them for their signature, so that I have a signed testimonial. This is similar to what a Realtor should do, but I do it for myself as an investor. I try to get these testimonials so that I can use them when I'm negotiating with a new seller, because one of the points I always try to negotiate on is financing. Testimonials help other sellers feel more comfortable doing business with me. They're essentially references from other satisfied customers that show that I did what I said I would do in completing the transaction.

Out-of-state owners offer great opportunities for owner-financed sales because they're getting payments and they already have the mentality of being a landlord.

How to Find Property Owners Who Are Motivated to Sell

How can you find motivated sellers? Here are just a few ways.

Look in the Newspaper. Many motivated sellers put ads in the newspapers to try to sell their houses on their own. "For sale by owner" has become a very, very popular method of selling property. Many people don't want to pay a real estate commission to a broker or agent. Instead, they want top dollar for their property. However, 80 percent of the time, these sellers are not as flexible as people who work with a Realtor—though as time passes, if they can't sell their property or if they really want to sell the property, they'll lower their price.

Keep in mind, too, that some people put their properties on the market just to see what they can get. If they can get top dollar, they'll sell. If they can't, they'll just let the properties sit there.

Check Online. Many owners also create their own Web sites or Web pages to sell their houses on their own, without a Realtor. You can find them simply by doing an online search for "properties for sale by owner in ____" (the area you're looking for), and these Web sites should be linked to that search.

Call Local Property Managers. Many sellers contact a "gatekeeper"—e.g., an attorney, a Realtor, a financial manager, a property manager, or someone else—to help them sell their property on their own. Property managers can be great resources because they often know landlords who are fed up, who are sick and tired of renting properties, and who just want to get out because they don't want to be landlords anymore. Chapter 8 covers working with property managers in more detail.

Look for Vacant Properties. Out-of-state owners make terrific motivated sellers because they're not there to baby-sit their property. Chapter 5 described how to find and contact such owners: simply look for what appears to be vacant property, find out who the owner is by checking courthouse records, and write the owner a letter asking if the owner is interested in selling—or at least discussing the possibility of selling to you. Set up an appointment by phone to get into the property and look around and to discuss the reasons why the owner may want to sell it.

Out-of-state owners offer great opportunities for owner-financed sales because they're getting payments and they already have the mentality of being a landlord. The worst that can happen from their point of view is that if you don't make the payments on the loan, then they foreclose and take the property back; they've got some money out of you, and they can then sell the property again. Once you understand the risk to both parties, you will come across as a knowledgeable investor whom the seller will trust and feel that he or she is doing the right thing by dealing with you.

Network.   Keep in touch with your Real Estate Investor Associations, local apartment associations, and the Chamber of Commerce. These are all great ways to find motivated sellers. Some investors write letters to an entire community that they're interested in, along the lines of, "If you know somebody in your neighborhood who's getting ready to sell, call me." That's another good way to find motivated sellers.

Look for Recurring Newspaper Ads Offering Property for Rent. Landlords who are trying to rent a particular property and have ads in the newspaper for a month or longer might be very motivated sellers because at that point they may just want to get out, and you might be able to get them to accept an offer to "rent to own" that property. This approach requires little or no money down, and you can create a win-win situation for yourself and the landlord who's having a difficult time finding a suitable tenant.

Find Out Everything You Can about a Property before You Make an Offer

The previous suggestions are just a few of the many tips and techniques you can use to help you find motivated sellers. The idea is, you want to find a property, learn what the seller's motivation is, negotiate, and create a win-win solution that you both can live with— you want to find that person the quickest, easiest way, in places where other investors aren't looking or in ways that others aren't using. Again, to find *motivated* sellers, use the following strategies:

- Ask open-ended questions to encourage a seller to talk.
- Get the seller's story. Find out what his or her motivation to sell is. Do this in stages: you don't want to just do it during the first visit and make an offer. Instead, you should try to get to know the seller, and then come back as soon as possible to see what kind of win-win offer you can put together.

The next step in the negotiation process (after you've found out how much the property is, of course) is to ask the seller all of the questions listed in Checklist 7-3. You need to ask these questions so that you can assess the property and the deal for yourself and make an offer that's going to make sense for both you and the seller. The worst thing you can do is low-ball your offer; this will offend the seller and destroy the credibility that you have worked to develop and the relationship you've established with the seller, who has taken the time to sit down with you and tell you his or her story.

Checklist 7-3   Questions to Ask
a Seller During Negotiation

- ❏ Do you have any outstanding loans or mortgages on the property?
- ❏ What are the balances of your outstanding mortgages?
- ❏ What's your real estate tax payment?
- ❏ What's your average utility bill? Do you have copies of the utility bills that I could look at so that I can make an assessment of what my costs would be on this property?
- ❏ Have you ever rented the property?
- ❏ Why do you need to sell?
- ❏ When do you need to close?
- ❏ Where are you going (i.e., where are you moving to)?
- ❏ How much cash do you really need?
- ❏ Are you in a position to carry an owner-financed loan?

Tips on Making People Comfortable During Negotiations

This section gives some general rules of etiquette for dealing with other people—and these are important in encouraging sellers to open up to you.

Always Look People in the Eye When Speaking to Them

Have you ever had a meeting with someone whose eyes were shifting all around? One where the person isn't looking directly at you or is looking down at you—at your chest, for example? People don't feel comfortable if you can't look them in the eye. They feel that they can't trust you. On the other hand, if you have the ability to look someone in the eye, that shows respect and consideration for the person you're talking to.

Shake Hands upon Your Initial Meeting with the Seller

You want to feel warm and friendly, and you want the seller to feel warm and friendly about you. You want to enter into a situation in the belief that it's going to be a positive event. You don't want to be a nervous wreck. Don't just stand there. Instead, walk up to the seller and introduce yourself with a simple but cordial opener: "Hi, I'm Lisa Bromma, how are you? Thank you for making the time today so that I can view your property. It is nice to meet you." Show some consideration for the fact that the seller has taken the time to show you his or her property.

Do not become the seller's best friend, in case a problem develops during the due diligence: becoming overly friendly could make your negotiation uncomfortable.

Never, Ever Interrupt When the Seller Is Speaking

As mentioned throughout this book, you can learn so much about a property and the owner's motivation to sell *if you listen* and ask open-ended questions. Once you have asked a question, *don't interrupt*. Your turn to talk will come. Sit there and listen. I know this is often the most difficult thing for people, myself included, to do, but it's not only polite but also extremely helpful to you in finding out about the property so that you can make an offer that will solve a problem for the seller and create a win for you.

Make Sure Your Cell Phone Is Off

When you walk into a negotiation or even into an initial meeting with the seller, turn off your cell phone. The rudest thing you can do is to have your cell phone ring—even if you don't answer it—when you're trying to talk one on one with somebody. You will lose your train of thought if you take the call (which you absolutely should not do!), and the seller will lose theirs which is more important. It's natural to think about who's looking for you, what does the caller want, and so on, and you could lose your focus on what you're trying to accomplish with this meeting. The seller will also be interrupted and may lose *her* train of thought—and she may have been in the process of telling you something very important about her motivation to sell or about the property itself. *So turn your cell phone off.*

Be Aware of Your Tone of Voice and Body Language

Your tone of voice and body language are also very important when you're trying to make a deal with someone. There are certain things that make people feel uncomfortable, and speaking too loudly is one of them. Be aware of the volume of your voice; many people don't realize how loudly they speak, and a seller may interpret your speaking loudly as yelling at him or her—which is obviously not a good negotiating strategy.

On the other hand, you want to make sure you're speaking loudly enough. Talking too softly so that you can't be heard is also a problem: if the seller can't hear you, he or she doesn't know what you're offering. If you're generally soft-spoken, practice trying to raise the volume of your voice a little bit so that people can hear you. When I can't hear somebody, I find that I have to concentrate so much on just *hearing* that person that I can't really follow what he or she is saying—and, believe it or not, that can kill a negotiation. Even if you're the nicest person in the world, don't be too loud, and be careful that you're not speaking too softly either.

Be Sure to Follow Up

If you say that you're going to follow up—and this is one of my big pet peeves—make sure you do. For example, if you say that you're going to call the seller back tomorrow night at 7:00, I don't care what you're doing, call that person back tomorrow night at 7:00. If you miss that call, you've lost the deal. That person will be sitting and waiting for you to call, and if you don't follow up when you say you will, you can count on that sale not happening. Don't make promises you can't keep.

Dress Appropriately

You want to make a good impression on the seller. You want to be neat and tidy. You don't have to look like Miss Rich. In fact, you don't want to look *too* rich because if you go to look at a property or meet with a seller, and you're wearing a Rolex watch or big fat diamonds, that seller will naturally think that you have a lot of money and that you're going to try to "steal" that property from him or her. Perceptions are everything, so dress appropriately. Just look neat; you don't need to look like a million bucks when you're negotiating to buy real estate.

Be Professional

When you're buying property, you are actually solving the seller's problem: the seller wants to sell. Of course, you, too, are going to benefit. Therefore, maintain a professional stance. Do not become the seller's best friend, in case a problem develops during the due diligence: becoming overly friendly could make your negotiation uncomfortable when you and the seller are discussing how to resolve that problem.

Instead, simply be polite. You want the seller to respect you. You never want to look like you're taking advantage of a situation. At the same time, you want to be very clear in your communication, while trying to help the owner get what he or she is looking for. As mentioned, successful women investors can make the people they are working with feel good about themselves and about the transaction.

Think before You Speak

Finally, before you say anything to a property owner with whom you are meeting, work out what you are going to say. Even if we don't try to judge, most of us, at one time or another, find ourselves in a situation where, unfortunately, we look at somebody and, whether we mean to or not, we get a poor first impression. Yet sometimes that first impression is wrong. Think it, don't say it.

For example, suppose you go to see a house, and the house is a mess. You are not going to say something like, "What a lovely home." If it's really a mess, that would be disingenuous. Instead, you can do one of two things: either you can say, "Thank you for your time today," and then leave the home very quietly, or, if you want more information and want to continue the negotiation, you can start building rapport with the seller.

Also, try to look past the mess to see what the property *really* looks like. This owner may happen to be a slob. But if you're simply looking at the owner's underwear all over the floor or some cosmetic problems (such as the house needs a coat of paint or there's a hole in the carpet), but *structurally* there's nothing wrong with the property, don't walk away.

Sometimes the owner will admit that the property needs some work—for example, she might say something like, "I know the house isn't in very good condition." In that case, your response should not be something like, "I'm not here to evaluate whether it needs a coat of paint." Instead, try, "Thanks for pointing this out to me. I am here to see if your home meets my needs." My personal investment strategy is to buy single-family homes in established neighborhoods. Therefore, I'm most interested in the floor plan: I look for homes that have at least three bedrooms and two baths, with one of them being a master bathroom. When I tell owners that I am looking for the right floor plan, not whether the seller is a great housekeeper, it helps the seller relax. For me, a coat of paint is not going to break the deal. What's going to break the deal is if there's no master bathroom in the master bedroom.

On the other hand, if you look at a property and it's a mess, you might wonder, "What else are they hiding?" That's what most people would think. After all, the owner should know you're coming to look at the property. You didn't just walk into the home unannounced; instead, you called and arranged an appointment. And therefore, you would expect the owner to at least clean up.

Let the seller talk; one of the most difficult things for people to do is to just keep their mouths shut.

Also, if the seller is a smoker, he or she should have tried to air out the property, because if you have asthma, for example, you probably won't survive the walkthrough of that property. This is nothing against smokers, but the smell and residue of smoke can become a financial issue, one that you should consider during your negotiation if you're interested in making an offer. For example, if I'm the buyer, and I don't smoke, and the particular property in question smells as if it's been on fire, the first thing I'm going to think is that I'm going to have to hire a heavy-duty cleaning company like SERVPRO.

These companies come in and professionally "soak" the house, clean the carpets, use fans to air the place out, and apply a chemical cleaning agent to the walls if need be. Carpets and drapes trap odor. If SERVPRO can't fix it, you can count on having to replace the window treatments and carpet and paint the place. This adds additional expense. It can cost up to $2,000 just to get rid of the smoke, which is especially important if I'm planning to re-sell or rent the property to somebody who *doesn't* smoke. Some property owners won't even rent to smokers because of the extent to which smoke residue clings to a building long after the tenant is gone. They make this a condition in their lease.

Here are some other types of inspections that investors will pay for:

- Termites
- Soil (in areas where there are sinkholes or shifting of foundations)
- Radon, mold, lead paint

What to Do If a Property Owner Won't Open Up to You

Earlier, I recommended not interrupting a seller and suggested that you just let the seller talk; one of the most difficult things for people to do is to just keep their mouths shut. You may also be faced with the opposite problem, however: some sellers may get defensive when you ask them questions about their property. For example, when you ask, "Why are you interested in selling?" a seller might get defensive and hostile and say something like, "Why do you care why I'm selling?" Or, the seller might simply be shy and reserved and may therefore respond with something vague, like, "Oh, you know, it's just time for a change." Let's look at how to handle some of these situations.

In general, you should continue to ask open-ended questions. But in the first scenario, if the seller seems defensive and says something like, "It's none of your business why I'm selling," my answer to that person would be, "I'm not trying to pry into your business. I'm trying to get an idea of what your motivation is, because I don't want to offend you with any offer." If the seller is really trying to sell that house, that should be an acceptable answer.

Also, "it's none of your business" is not a typical response from most sellers. A seller might say, "It's a personal matter. I'd rather not get into why I'm selling." In that case, my response would be, "I can understand that. Let me move on and ask you some questions about the property. Are you willing to give me some information on the property itself?" And then I would try to introduce a different subject that's still related to my trying to buy the property.

> *When you are dealing with objections from sellers, you need to realize that their objections are usually emotional as well as financial; they don't want to get burned on the sale of their property.*

How to Respond to Objections from the Owner to Deals You Propose

There are certain objections that a real estate investor will typically run into when someone is trying to sell a property. Let's look at how to respond to some of these.

"I Don't Want Tenants in My House." This is the number one objection that I hear from emotional sellers, especially when I tell them that I'm an investor. And whenever you're negotiating with someone, you should *always* disclose that you're a real estate investor. I never give anybody the impression that I'm buying the house for myself. I am always up front; I tell the seller, "I'm looking for nice properties in neighborhoods just like yours. I tend to rent to individuals who stay with me for years. I can show you many properties and pictures of these properties in your own area that I have held for years. You are welcome to check them out so that you feel satisfied with the way the properties have been taken care of."

Having pictures of the properties I rent out available has helped a lot in negotiations and overcoming objections. Obviously, however, if you're just getting started in buying real estate as an investment, you won't have pictures of properties. Therefore, you need to find another way to make the seller feel comfortable with you. One way to do this is to bring letters of recommendation from your banker, your CPA, an attorney, or other professionals who know you and would be willing to put in a good word on your behalf.

"What If You Don't Make the Mortgage Payment?" This is another common objection that you may encounter if you ask the seller to owner-finance the sale. Your response to this concern needs to be empathetic; you should say something like, "I understand your concern, but let's look at this objectively. If I'm buying your $200,000 house and I'm putting $20,000 down, you've already got $20,000 of my money. If I pay you $2,000 per month on the mortgage, and if I pay that for, let's say, two years, and then I stop paying, you will have received two years of monthly payments of $2,000 each—which is $48,000—plus the $20,000 down payment. The worst that can happen would be that you will have received $68,000 from me, and then you get to take the property back and sell it again to someone else. Moreover, there is the opportunity for the property to have gone up in value while I've been making payments (though, of course, none of us has a crystal ball), so your house could be worth maybe $210,000. You would be in a great position, with more security and the opportunity to end up with more money." When a seller can understand the simplicity of this, he or she will usually feel much more comfortable about doing an owner-financed deal with you if he or she is able to.

"Why Do You Need So Much Time to Close?" You may hear this if you're dealing with a seller who really wants to close tomorrow. One way to respond to this is to calmly remind the seller that you have to wait for the bank to do certain due diligence before it will authorize your loan. Let the seller know that as soon as you get a title commitment (which is the last piece in the closing process), you will be happy to close. That usually mollifies sellers, because it lets them know that it's not you who is holding up the deal; instead, there's a legal process that has to happen whether they sell the property you or to someone else.

When you are dealing with objections from sellers, you need to realize that their objections are usually emotional as well as financial; they don't want to get burned on the sale of their property. A general way to respond to any objection is to reiterate the objection—e.g., "Let me make sure I understand what your concern is"—and then respond to that objection face to face, head on, without making the other person feel threatened. In other words, try to build rapport with the seller while you're responding to his or her objection.

If the seller feels that you are honest, focused, and clear in answering his objections, he'll understand and be able to relate to *your* communications and concerns (if you have any) about his property. Most sellers want a positive outcome just as much as you do. The more you make someone feel comfortable about selling his property to you, the more willing the seller will be in your negotiating process. In contrast, if the seller feels that you're *not* honest, that you were doing something that made her feel uncomfortable, then she'll be wary of you. You've lost her trust, and you can forget about making a deal with that owner to buy her property.

If you follow these suggested techniques when talking with people, responding to any objections, and treating people right, your negotiations should be positive. I once worked briefly for a training company that taught its trainers the following:

1. Maintain and enhance self-esteem.
2. Listen and respond with empathy.
3. Ask for help in solving the problem.
4. Be responsive to the need.
5. Reach a positive outcome.

These five steps are the basis of your negotiation strategy.

When to Walk Away from a Seller

There are a few situations in which I would walk away from a negotiation with a seller. The most typical is when the seller is absolutely, completely inflexible: "His way or the highway." For example, suppose a seller says to me, "I *must* have $330,000 for this house," and I've done market research and found that it's worth only $300,000. No matter how much I talk to that owner, whether I get the seller to finance some of it or do anything else, if the person is just not willing to be flexible on his price or on other terms of the deal, then there's no point in my continuing the negotiation. In that case, I'm happy to walk away and wish the seller the best of luck. I'll usually tell the seller, "If your listing expires or if you don't sell the property and you're willing to consider selling it at a different price, I'll be happy to talk to you."

After all, I'm not a nonprofit organization—and neither are you. If you can't get the deal to break even or generate cash flow, you shouldn't be interested in doing that deal.

The worst thing you can do is low-ball your offer;
this will offend the seller and destroy the credibility
you have worked hard to develop.

Putting Your Offer Together

First, I find the property—in any of the ways mentioned earlier in this chapter—then I call the owner and ask if I can come see the property—whether they're having an open house or whether I can make an appointment to see it privately. I ask open-ended questions, so that the seller can feel comfortable with me and I can find out what his or her story is. Then, I have a checklist of what I'm looking for, and I try to put the numbers together to see what I can offer.

I go through the same steps in my negotiation/offer process as I want to make sure that I am comfortable and feel that I won't lose money on the deal.. To some extent, my offer will depend on the economy of the area where I'm buying the property. After I've gotten answers to my questions and calculated what I can offer, the next step before I make that offer is to evaluate the rental market—that is, if I'm going to keep the property for the long term. (Chapter 8 describes how to evaluate a rental market to determine whether or not it's a good market.) I do this evaluation before I write the offer because I need to know what kind of money I'm going to make on the property. I don't want to be in the hole on my investments.

My next step would be to put my contract together—i.e., my offer to purchase. Every state has a typical real estate contract for purchase, which you can get from a Realtor's office, from a property manager, or even from an office supply store. For example, in Colorado, Office Depot carries these purchase contracts, which you can modify to write your own offer. You do not need to hire an attorney or a Realtor to write an offer.

On the other hand, if you want to be protected, or if you think it's going to make the seller feel more comfortable, you could both agree to work through an attorney. But from a legal standpoint, your initial offer to purchase does not have to be made through an attorney, even though some people think it does.

Before You Close on a Property, Do Your Due Diligence

Time is of the essence when you're closing on a property. *How much* time is likely to be needed, though, seems to vary depending on whom I asked. Here are just a few of the responses I heard to the question, "How long should it take to get a property closed?":

- Realtor Anna Mills says that cash deals and contracts to buy land can often be done very quickly, but financed deals take longer. However, they typically don't take as long as they used to, which was four to six weeks or more. Now they can often be done in 30 days.
- Realtor Tami Spaulding confirms this; she says that if you either have cash or are preapproved, and the home is vacant, you can close in a couple of weeks; the typical time is 30 days.
- Owner-financing expert Tracy Rewey gives a wider time range: "If the transaction involves conventional bank financing, closing seems to average about 30 to 45 days. With owner financing, those averages can be reduced to 14 to 21 days. There are certainly ways to decrease those averages when working with a competent and responsive title company, lender, property inspector, real estate agent, closing agent, and appraiser. Of course, having cash on hand can reduce those closing times to just a few days!"

- Broker Jaime Raskulinecz agrees that a closing can happen in 30 days, but she says 60 to 90 days is typical.

Finally, broker and trainer Magi Bird cites an even greater range of times for closings:

[Closing time] *will depend on the type of property, the type of financing being sought, and market conditions. For instance, commercial properties may require an MAI narrative appraisal, which currently in our area would take five weeks to receive; therefore, a loan could not be funded, even if all conditions were perfect, in less than 7 weeks. [In contrast,] I have done residential escrows in as little as 48 hours, but this is by no means normal.*

Inspections are really important if you're buying an older building (i.e., one that was built before 1978), because you need to be aware of lead paint.

I recommend not rushing your closing: do your due diligence! Renee Falgout, the operations manager of a central Florida mortgage company, agrees:

More often than not, during the financing process, many challenges present themselves and need to be overcome. Therefore, when you're signing contracts, give yourself some time—30 days might seem like a long time, but a 45-day closing or more will save you some heartburn in case something does go wrong and you are in a crunch to get it done.

Lenders look at everything under a magnifying glass; they often request extra documentation, and they need to verify everything about a deal through their own resources. And sometimes they will look at a file only once a day, especially in a busy market. So give yourself time for things to go wrong, and try never to schedule a back-to-back closing, where one deal depends on another.

When you're going to buy property, there are certain aspects of due diligence that should happen before you close on that property. When you put in an offer to purchase a property and the seller accepts your offer, the first thing that happens in many states is that the title company opens an escrow account while you're working on getting your loan or, if you are paying cash, arranging for any funds transfer. People who act as escrow holders (i.e., when an escrow account is opened) include title companies, real estate attorneys, and escrow departments of lending institutions. The following sections describe what you should do in terms of due diligence.

Get an Inspection

First, get the property inspected. Inspections are really important if you're buying an older building (i.e., one that was built before 1978), because you need to be aware of lead paint. There are lead paint laws because lead paint is toxic, and if you rent out that property, and if it has lead paint and that paint is discovered, it is your responsibility to have the paint removed; if you do not, you could be involved in a lawsuit. Getting rid of lead paint can cost a fortune. (This applies to properties that were built before 1978, since lead paint has not been used since that date.) Debbie is an investor who bought starter homes in downtown Baltimore. Lead paint was discovered in one of her properties after she acquired the property. In order to fix the problem so that she could rent or sell the property, it cost her *$18,000 a room.*

Another thing that inspectors should be looking for is mold. Believe it or not, to abate mold also costs a fortune. Mold is seen more in some parts of the country. Don is an investor in Philadelphia who took every single real estate investor's class he could find, covering everything from rehabs to foreclosures to lease options to flips; he probably spent $20,000 on classes and training materials. Finally, he decided to buy an older building just outside of Philadelphia intended for soft commercial use (i.e., offices). The building cost around $400,000. Don borrowed part of money from a bank, and he used his retirement money for the rest of the building's price. Then he fixed up the building and decided he was going to sell it.

Unfortunately, Don didn't have this building inspected before he bought it. When he tried to sell it, he got an offer, and he would have been able to sell it at a profit, but the buyer, of course, made his offer subject to an inspection. The inspector found mold, and Don's buyer would not close on the building until Don removed the mold, which requires commercial bleach preparations and other chemicals. The mold removal cost Don more than $50,000—which was all of his savings—and he still hasn't been able to sell the building. Once a mold problem becomes known, it's very difficult to sell the property, because you need to disclose it to all potential buyers. Also, this particular building is located in a very slow-moving part of the country.

> *Title insurance ensures that there are no liens*
> *or encumbrances against the property . . . ,*
> *that everything has been paid off, and . . .*
> *that you're getting clear title to this property.*

So these inspections are very important. Poor Don has nothing now. He was hoping that this real estate investment would be his way out of the sales business (he had been selling securities), but now that his real estate investment has failed, he's back to selling securities. He has been able to get commercial tenants for the property, so he's been renting out the building, which does provide him with some rental income. He tried to put in his leases that if he finds any additional mold, it would be the responsibility of the tenant—which didn't fly with the courts, of course, because how can you make a tenant responsible for mold? It's really important that people get inspections on property.

Get Title Insurance

Besides getting a good appraisal, an inspection, and your loan commitment, it's also very important to get title insurance. Title insurance ensures that there are no liens or encumbrances against the property that you are not aware of, that everything has been paid off, and therefore that you're getting clear title to this property. Why is this important? The purpose of the insurance is to protect you in case the title company did not go far enough back and the property has a lien against it.

Generally, the seller pays for the title search and the title insurance policy. This can be expensive. Depending on where you are in the country, and depending on the policy itself, title insurance can cost $400 and up. The title company sends you a policy that basically guarantees that they've done the research on the property to determine that there are no mechanics' liens, IRS liens, or any other types of liens against the property; that the property you are getting is stable and free and clear; that you will be the rightful owner of the property; and that you're coming in clean.

Debbie signed an IOU (i.e., a promissory note) to the seller, Sue, and agreed to make monthly payments for 15 years, which was the time period that Debbie and Sue had agreed to. Six months later, Sue realized that she needed cash (to pay a big tax bill to the IRS), so she contacted Karen, who buys private mortgages (aka owner-financed loans). Karen bought the 15-year income stream that Debbie had agreed to pay. Sue sent a letter to Debbie informing her that Sue had sold Debbie's note to Karen; Karen also sent a letter to Debbie informing her that Karen had bought Debbie's note from Sue. Debbie then started making payments to Karen, based on the original terms of the note, the IOU. The mortgage (aka the deed of trust) is the security. If Debbie does not make her payments on time and gets behind, Karen can foreclose and take the property back, because Karen got the legal right to receive the payments when she bought the note from Sue.

Here's another example: I was in a seminar years ago, taught by a real pro who was teaching the owner-carried loan business and how to do private mortgages. He had 100 people in attendance. I was sitting next to Michael from Florida. On the other side of Michael was Jim from North Carolina. The three of us got to talking. And Jim said, "I just bought a note out of the *Wall Street Journal*." And Michael said, "Wow, that's weird; I've just bought a note out of the *Wall Street Journal*." So they were looking at each other because how coincidental was that? So Michael asked Jim, "Where was the property?" And Jim replied, "Dunedin, Florida." And Michael said, "My property was in Dunedin, Florida, too."

At this point, they both raced to pay phones (this was back in 1990, and cell phones weren't that big yet). They each called their staff to research when they bought their note and what was the name of the person who had sold them the note. They found out that Michael was in first position, and Jim was number 13. The note seller had "sold" that same note 20 times! The title company never came up with a multiple-sales cross-reference. Fortunately, the title insurance paid Michael back in full because he was the rightful owner. Jim also had title insurance, but because he wasn't the first (and therefore legal) buyer, he got back only the money he'd invested. He lost future potential income, but at least he got his investment back. Had Jim not had title insurance, he would have lost his entire investment.

Some real estate brokerage houses (especially the bigger ones) may also have an escrow department. Companies that handle money must be licensed and bonded to accept your deposit. Escrow accounts are maintained by a third party who is responsible for the disbursement of funds after all of the following conditions are met:

- Inspection
- The loan commitment
- Title research
- Appraisal and survey
- Homeowner's insurance on the property
- Seller's payoff
- Any other research deemed necessary to close the transaction

These are functions that the title company is responsible for. It coordinates the disbursement of the funds, real estate agent commissions, the documentation review at the closing for both seller and buyer, and review of the settlement statement showing what each party pays and receives, so that in the end the investor gets the property, the seller gets the proceeds, and the title company gets a fee for doing the closing.

If you're buying a property that is currently an investment property for someone else, make sure that your offer is subject to your reviewing the lease.

What You Should Include in Your Contract

You need to have clauses in the contract that protect you as well. The following discussion covers some of the contingencies that you may run into and have included in your contract. These contingencies are from the buyer's (i.e., the investor's) perspective.

Your Contract Should Be Subject to Your Getting Financing.
For instance, your contract should be subject to your getting financing at 7 percent for 30 years. If you can't qualify for the financing, that gives you an out.

Your Contract Should Be Subject to a Home Inspection. This clause protects you, because if there are any problems with the property, the inspection will reveal what those problems are, and then you can decide whether you want to buy the property or not.

If there is something major wrong with the property, and the seller is unwilling to fix it, then you have an out.

Clauses are inserted by mutual consent. You will not buy the property without an inspection unless your contract says that you're buying the property "as is." Many investors buy properties as is, although you need to be careful when doing so, because you can't see any hidden defects in the property—as Don in Philadelphia discovered when he acquired a building that had a mold problem. Still, many people buy houses in as-is condition, which means that if the property has problems, you've inherited those problems.

Your Contract Should Include a Clause That Says "Subject to Review of the Title" to Make Sure That There Are No Legal Problems with the Property. These problems could include liens or encumbrances against the property (as described earlier in the chapter).

Your Contract Should Include Reviewing All Leases, If the Property Has Been Rented to Tenants. If you're buying a property that is currently an investment property for someone else—i.e., if the seller has been renting it—you want to make sure that your offer is subject to your reviewing the lease. You want to know what the term of the lease is and when the lease expires. In fact, you should ask to see a payment history to prove that the tenant has been making the payments.

Also, there are cases where a seller says that he or she is renting out a property to someone else, but that's not true. The seller may be telling you this to entice you to buy the property, but having the rental history and a copy of the lease helps to verify that there is a tenant in the property. Include in your contract a clause that states that your offer is subject to your reviewing the existing lease for approval, as well as subject to a final inspection or walk-through. These are clauses that real estate professionals are familiar with.

Your Contract Should Be Assignable. It's also very important that you have an assignability clause, which allows you to assign the contract if you decide that you're not going to keep the property or if you have another buyer waiting for the property and you decide at some point that you want to resell it to that buyer. You want to have the words *and/or assigns* in that contract; most investors will buy property with their name and the words *and/or assigns*: e.g., "Lisa Bromma and/or assigns."

A seller [may say that] *he or she is renting out a property to someone else, but that's not true:* [your contract should require] *the rental history and a copy of the lease.*

Your Contract Should Protect *You*. Contingency clauses protect *you*. Make sure that they are included in your contracts. If in doubt, have an attorney review the contract before you sign it.

If you're *selling* a property, and for some reason your buyer doesn't go through with the deal, you also want to protect yourself. In this case, you should have a liquidated damages clause in the contract, so that if the deal doesn't go through, you at least get to keep the buyer's deposit.

If you're working with a Realtor (refer back to Chapter 6), you're usually protected from these problems. These are just some of the clauses that will be consentable clauses in your contract.

Take your time going through a contract. Read and understand it before you sign it. If you're uncomfortable with it, you should sit down with an attorney in your state and make sure you understand what you are signing, from a legal perspective, before you start buying real estate. Don't wait until you find a deal and then think about seeing a lawyer. Instead, meet with a lawyer first, do your due diligence, and make sure you understand what you're getting into. Investor Barbara O'Connell strongly recommends this: "Get a good real estate attorney to look over any contract before you sign it. Better yet, make the deal subject to your attorney's approval." (Chapter 13 discusses how to find a good attorney.)

In general, these contracts are not difficult. They basically state that you (the investor) are entering into an agreement with the seller (Jane Doe) to buy the said property at 123 East Main Street, subject to the following conditions (itemized, like those described earlier as the general "subject to" clauses). Examples might be "subject to a home inspection within seven days" and "subject to 7 percent financing over 30 years with the lender."

Sometimes you can avoid the financing requirement, if you want to facilitate a deal and make the seller feel better, by being preapproved by a lender. Having a preapproval letter from a lender is a good negotiating strategy. Some sellers feel more comfortable with that, because it makes them think that you're serious about buying property: you've already gone to the trouble of getting preapproved for a mortgage. The downside to the seller is a buyer who tries to stall the closing as long as possible, which is going to make the seller more nervous than somebody who says, "I can close this deal in three weeks." So the purchase contract must spell out the basics of what you and the seller are agreeing to do. The more you spell out, the more the seller is going to understand the offer, and the easier your transaction is going to be.

One final point about contingencies and home inspections: you don't want the deal to break down because the seller has a few small problems—for instance, a leaky faucet. That type of problem is something that can easily be fixed. If you are going to be a stickler and insist that the seller fix every single little thing that's wrong with the property, whether it's been disclosed to you or not, and you don't find out about it until the home inspection, you're going to have a seller who is not going to be very happy with you in that transaction. If there's a problem like a roof leaking or a crack in the foundation or a positive radon reading—i.e., something significant—you should expect to have those problems corrected. Just don't let something small be a deal breaker. Be as fair and flexible as you can, without it costing you a whole lot of money.

Conclusion: Always Leave
Negotiations on a Positive Note

Will you win in every negotiation you attempt? No. Will you get every deal you set out for? Absolutely not. Sometimes it's not meant to be. Don't let rejection stand in your way, however. Keep in mind that there's always another property and another opportunity. Thank each seller you meet for the time that he or she spent showing you the property and talking to you about it. Tell the seller you're sorry you weren't able to work things out to his or her satisfaction. And then move on. You should always leave a negotiation on a positive note, even if you don't get the deal.

8

Rental Property Management: What Every Investor Must Know

This chapter discusses why rental property is a good investment, how to find good rental properties, how to find good tenants, and what you should include in your lease in order to protect yourself. It also covers the pros and cons of being a do-it-yourself landlord vs. hiring a property manager to manage your rentals for you, if you acquire property for the long term. This is an important factor in the success or failure of real estate investors, so you should understand what's involved in property management. Finally, it discusses what you need to know about renting to particular types of tenants—e.g., students or individuals on a fixed income.

Why Rental Property Is a Good Investment

People who invest in real estate—especially those who invest in rental property—do so as a way to build wealth. When you have the opportunity to buy a property at the right price, and you have good tenants who maintain your property well and who pay on time, that's a good investment for you. Your tenants are paying off your loan for you (through the difference between what you're charging them in rent and what you owe on your mortgage to the bank or whomever you borrowed money from). You end up having a free-and-clear property, thanks to your tenants. In other words, someone else is helping you make the payments that will let you get ahead financially.

According to a report from the National Real Estate Investors Association, in 2004, 23 percent of all homes sold were for investment purposes, not owner-occupied. Although you can't use this information as a barometer for future success, still, the way real estate has surged recently, the prospect of doing well in the real estate market over time has become very attractive to many people. Therefore, buying and holding a property for the long term is a strategy that many investors utilize.

***In 2004, 23 percent of all homes sold were
for investment purposes, not owner-occupied.***

There has been much recent speculation regarding what the future of real estate will be. *Ignore it*. You need to look at each deal and see whether that deal is going to work for you. Determine whether you can generate cash flow from that deal, whether you can get income every month off of this investment, or whether the investment is going to meet whatever your needs are.

Keep in mind that in some states—e.g., California, Nevada, New York, and parts of New England—many people are better off renting than buying because the prices of property are so high. For example, if I were to go to Marin County, California, right now and buy a piece of real estate, I would be paying almost $1 million for that real estate. If I were to *rent* that same piece of real estate, I might be paying $3,000 a month. My mortgage on that million-dollar piece of real estate would be much, much higher—probably double what I would pay in rent. Obviously, it makes more sense to rent in that area.

Therefore, in certain parts of the country, you have a pool of tenants who are accustomed to renting because they cannot afford to buy a property. Average home rents right now are rising at about 4 percent per year, so there is a protection against inflation that you can capitalize on by building it into the rent you charge for your property.

Rental Property Management: What Every Investor Must Know

In marketplaces like these, it is becoming more difficult to have a property generate cash flow—interest rates have been down, so more people have been able to go out and buy property, and the mortgage payments (aka the PITI: principal, interest, taxes, and insurance) that they're making may equal or, in some markets, be less than what they would pay in rent on a property. So, a lot of times, landlording is market-driven.

That said, many landlords have done a phenomenal job over a period of time. The average landlord I know through the Real Estate Investors Association has been holding property longer than ten years. If a landlord bought properties for, say, $200,000 ten years ago, today those properties are worth $400,000, have a mortgage payment of $1,200 a month, and generate $1,800 a month in rent. You can see that the investor is making $600 a month in income, in addition to getting the appreciation of those properties.

Of course, *appreciation* is not *cash*. When you build equity in a property, that's a great thing, but if the market turns downward, your equity is not going to be worth as much in the future as it is today. For example, looking at the scenario just mentioned, where the property was purchased for $200,000 ten years ago, if the marketplace changes and your property, which at one time was worth $400,000, is now worth only $300,000, yes, you've still made $100,000, but you haven't made $200,000. Real estate is based on equity and on appreciation. That's why people buy property for the long term. They are looking for free-and-clear property that will enhance their incomes. That rental income is a way to supplement other possible retirement income. Realtor Tami Spaulding is an investor who views her own rental properties exactly that way; as she puts it, "I do practice what I preach. We now own 19 rentals, and over half are free and clear. I am on track for some really good wake-up money in the future."

Moreover, *retirement* doesn't necessarily mean when you reach 65 years of age. You could retire when you're *40* years old because you've accumulated so many rental properties and have so much positive cash flow that you can live off those payments.

Finally, keep in mind that you don't have to keep rental property for the long term. For example, broker Jaime Raskulinecz has a great success story that shows the benefits of rental property, even though she held this particular property for only a year:

*One of my most successful investments recently was a condo pur-
chased on the water in Fort Lauderdale. When I purchased the
property, it was in move-in condition, so I didn't have to invest in
any rehab. My plan was to hold the property and rent it and see
how the market behaved, to determine how long to hold it.*

*I purchased the property in the fall of 2004 and sold the prop-
erty in the fall of 2005. I had a renter for the year it was held. When
the property sold, my profit was about $100,000. It was sold at the
right time: it was the highest sale for a condo in the building. Also,
the market in Fort Lauderdale has softened quite a bit, so I got out
at the right time."*

---

*Selecting tenants is about 80 percent of the challenge . . .
in property management. You want to make sure
from the start that you're selecting the right
quality tenants for your property.*

Who Rents and Why

Why do people rent in the first place? Who rents and why? Some people are
just not ready—either financially or emotionally—to buy a home yet. Other
people can't afford to buy a home: they don't have the down payment, or they
have bad credit, a bankruptcy, or a low FICO score (refer back to Chapter 2
for details on these problems). Or they want to live in a nice community, but
they can't afford the cost of ownership in that community, and, as mentioned, sometimes renting is a better deal financially than owning a property.

So, people who rent don't always have bad credit or other financial
problems. Instead, here are just a few reasons why some people rent instead
of buying a home:

- They may be starting a business and need cash for that business. They
  can't have to make payments in any way, shape, or form because they
  need to keep their credit for borrowing for their business.
- They've relocated to a new area, and they want to look around and see
  where they want to live first.

- They may be planning to live in a place for only a short time—for example, some people relocate for a job for only two years, and know that at the end of that time, they'll be relocated again, to another city.
- They may be serving in the military and have only a short period of time to go before their time of service is over.

---

*Many successful investors . . . do Section 8 housing
because they like the fact that their payments
are guaranteed by the government.*

Of course, selecting tenants is about 80 percent of the challenge and work involved in property management. You want to make sure from the start that you're selecting the right quality tenants for your property.

If you're interested in buying property and managing it yourself, and you want some help and additional information, check out the National Association of Rental Property Managers. It offers professional courses and seminars and a community of people who are owners of single-family homes specifically or small residential properties. Its Web site is www.narpn.org.

Investing in and Renting Section 8 Properties

Section 8 is a government program, run through the Department of Housing and Urban Development (HUD), that assists low-income families with their rent. It's based on a voucher system: tenants are given housing vouchers, then they look for houses in the private marketplace. The local housing authority that gives them those vouchers must approve the unit before the tenant can rent it. Tenants pay a percentage of their income toward the rent, but the government pays the balance to the landlord (or to the owner of the property) through the vendor program. For example, if you're charging $1,000 a month rent, a Section 8 tenant might pay $300 toward the rent, with the government paying the other $700.

Therefore, if you own a property and are renting it out under Section 8, essentially, your rent is guaranteed by the government. And payments will continue to come to you as long as the tenant remains eligible for assistance. As an investor, you need to decide for yourself whether or not you want to buy Section 8 property. I know many successful investors who do Section 8 housing because they like the fact that their payments are guaranteed by the government. On the other hand, many investors do not like Section 8 because they feel that their tenants should be able to make their own payments—and that if the rest of the payment isn't made for some reason, having to go after the government for the rent can be a nightmare.

Most people who use Section 8 don't have a problem screening tenants because the tenants have been preapproved by the government. Whether this program is right for you depends on whether you want low-income tenants who are government subsidized. If you are buying apartment units in areas that are hard to rent to begin with, Section 8 could be for you.

Harriet owned Section 8 housing in New Orleans. She loved it because she believed that the program is a great resource for low-income families. She was helping people who couldn't get into housing without this program, and, by the same token, the government was guaranteeing her rent for this housing.

No matter what type of real estate you buy, there are fair housing laws that you need to be aware of. These laws prohibit any type of discrimination, including discrimination on the basis of religion, race, nationality, gender, sexual preference, marital status, age, weight, and family status (e.g., if a single mom with three small children wants to rent your two-bedroom house, you can't discriminate against her because of her family situation).

If you're buying a property for the long term,
you need to take into consideration all your
expenses and what your income will be,
then you can evaluate the bottom line.

Be aware that the government agencies may send what I like to call "mystery shoppers" because I don't have a better term for them—people who will look for rental properties and pretend to be interested prospective tenants. This happened to me at a property of mine: a mystery shopper came out and said, "I want to rent the house." Well, I had the house already under a rental contract, which I explained to this person, and I offered to show her the rental agreement, which proved that I had followed the protocol.

How to Find Good Rental Properties

If you decide that you want to find property to rent out, Checklist 8-1 offers eight ways to locate rental properties.

Checklist 8-1   Eight Ways to Locate Rental Properties

❏   Search through newspaper classified ads.

❏   Go on the Internet to find property.

❏   Look through real estate magazines, either for homes or for land.

❏   Work with Realtors; ask them if they know any landlords who need or want to sell.

❏   Work with "bird dogs" (people who will find property for you). Talk to people who are in the marketplace already: Realtors or other individuals who may find property that you may be interested in.

❏   Join professional associations—e.g., the National Real Estate Investors Association or local real estate investor clubs—where you may meet people who have property for sale.

❏   Visit FSBOs (for sale by owner properties) in your area.

❏   Write your own ad—e.g., "I'm looking for a nice three-bedroom, two-bath home in _____ community. Willing to pay $1,000 per month." Your strategy would be to sublease that property for $1,200 per month, giving you $200 per month positive cash flow.

Even if you are willing to accept a negative cash flow each month—and there are a lot of investors out there right now who are in a negative situation; they are paying more in mortgage payments than they are getting in rent—keep in mind that projections for the future are that rents will increase faster than they have in the past, so that you might be able to catch up. However, in general, you shouldn't base your investing philosophy on what statistical or economic forecasts are projecting. Instead, you should base your forecasts on *fact*:

- Calculate what you can afford to buy today.
- Estimate how much cash flow you can get from a property.
- Decide whether it makes sense for you to buy a particular property for the long term, and why.
- And then, if it's a negative situation, determine when you would be at a break-even point.

Use this information to assess whether or not buying a particular property as an investment for the long term makes sense.

Advantages and Disadvantages of Owning and Renting Out Property

So, what are some of the advantages and disadvantages of owning property for the long term and renting it out? Let's look at the advantages first:

- You get future appreciation potential.
- You get income tax write-offs for depreciation and other expenses.
- If you buy the property at the right price, you get monthly income and you're able to make some money on that property every month.
- You're building a portfolio of investment property.

The disadvantages are a bit more involved. First, tenants don't always pay you on time—you're waiting for your money, but you still need to make your mortgage payments. Just recently, I had to call one of my tenants because I hadn't received his rent payment, and it was already the tenth of the month. I offer my tenants a discount if they pay their rent by the first of the month; if they don't, they owe a late fee. When I called this particular tenant, his excuse for being late was, "Well, my car blew up, and I needed the money to repair it." Tenants forget that we as landlords also have expenses—in fact, most of us have mortgages on the properties our tenants are living in.

Well, it's not a free ride, so landlording can be a headache. If you don't have that kind of mentality (which I'll cover later in this chapter), you may want to consider hiring a property manager. Just because you don't want to be a do-it-yourself landlord doesn't mean that you should not consider buying property for the long term.

A second disadvantage is that if you have a maintenance situation that you need to handle—e.g., one related to the roof, the hot water heater, the plumbing, and so on—you have to react quickly to fix the problem with the property.

For example, Hugh owned a property in Ocala, Florida. Because he lives 3,000 miles away, he hired a property manager. Unfortunately, a problem developed: something was leaking behind a wall and was destroying the entire wall and the room—and there also were potential electrical problems. The property manager didn't notify Hugh because she "didn't want to bother him"; she felt that it wasn't a big deal. Hugh found out about the leak from another investor who was doing due diligence on property managers and looking at properties under this person's management. This investor saw the problem and called Hugh. So now Hugh had to handle the problem himself. Fortunately, Hugh is good in a crisis; he doesn't get emotional. He found a contractor through his investor friend, made sure that the contractor was licensed and bonded, and had the problem fixed.

Keeping cool and being practical is the best way to handle problems. If you get emotional or upset, this will delay your getting the problem solved. Try not to get emotional over any property problem.

A third disadvantage is that you need to do your own accounting, making sure that you record when income (i.e., rent) comes in and when money (i.e., mortgage payments) goes out, and that everything balances so that your accountant has the correct recordkeeping for your tax return.

Fourth, you need to make sure that the utility bills (for electricity, gas, water, and trash pickup) on your rental properties are paid promptly. In some areas of the country, if your tenants don't pay their utility bills, the utility company has the right to put a lien on the property. Therefore, you need to know how your local government handles utilities, and you need to make sure that those utility bills are paid.

Fifth, you need to make sure that the property taxes are paid. Taxes and insurance are not always escrowed in people's mortgage payments.

Finally, you need to make sure that all insurance and maintenance costs are being paid. For example, if your rental property is a town home, it may have homeowners' association dues, or if it's a condo, you may have condo association dues. Who pays these fees? Is your tenant paying them? If so, you need to make sure that the tenant pays the fees so that you don't have a lien put against your unit because the association dues weren't paid.

The best way I've found to get good tenants for long-term rentals is to hold open houses, just as Realtors do when they're selling properties.

How to Find Good Tenants

Hold Open Houses

How do you find the right people to rent your properties? Everybody has a different way of doing this; Checklist 8-2 lists the most common methods.

Checklist 8-2   Typical Ways to Advertise Rental Properties

- ❏ Put signs on the property that say, "houses for rent."
- ❏ Put up fliers on telephone poles.
- ❏ Advertise in the newspaper.
- ❏ Call property managers and Realtors in the community and ask if they know of anybody looking for a rental for *X* period of time, and go through a referral system.
- ❏ Create a Web site for each property and try to rent the property that way.
- ❏ Hold an open house.

In my years as a real estate investor, the best way to get good tenants for long-term rentals that I've found is to hold open houses, just as Realtors do when they're selling properties. I run an ad in the local newspaper that says something like: "cute, cozy, and clean, three-bedroom, two-bath, adorable home located in the Lopez Elementary section of Ft. Collins available for rent. Open Sunday, 2-4 p.m., 123 East Main Street, $1,395 discount rent; pets are negotiable."

That's all I put in the ad. Notice that I didn't include a telephone number, because I don't want people calling me on the phone wanting to learn more about the property. Instead, I want them to show up at the open house and see the property for themselves—which will be much more convincing than my describing it over the phone. With an ad like this, when I show up at the house on Sunday at a quarter to two, there are usually a number of people waiting to get in. There are two reasons that this type of ad attracts so many people.

The first reason is that I offer a discount on the rent. First, I look at what the fair market rent is. Recall that in Chapter 3, I discussed how to determine fair market rent: look in the newspaper and see what comparable rentals are going for; talk to property managers and find out the rent on the properties they're managing; and look at the situation of the individual tenant. Try not to make exceptions on this; keep in mind that you have to generate cash flow. Once I find out what the fair market rent is in a neighborhood—let's say it's $1,200 a month—if I can afford it, I rent the property at a discount, say for $1,095 a month. That way, the tenants will save $100 a month in rent if they do what is required of them in the lease (i.e., pay on time) in order to qualify for the discount. Discounted rent is one strong factor that attracts potential tenants to my open houses.

> *Every time a tenant leaves, you have maintenance issues . . . you need to take into account the work required, the time it takes to do it, and the loss of monthly cash flow while you are fixing the property.*

The second reason people come is that I allow pets. Many landlords do not agree with this, but I allow pets in properties, as long as they're not attack-trained dogs like Rottweilers or Doberman pinschers, and as long as I have a chance to "meet" the pet. I don't allow more than two pets, however. I also get a security deposit for the pets, and I charge an additional monthly rent as a pet fee. The tenant helps to determine what that monthly fee should be. For example, after I meet the pet and determine that it is not going to be a problem, I ask the tenant, "What do you think would be a fair amount per month in order to have Fido included in the lease?" This way, the tenant is involved and understands that pets can ruin carpets, screens on patio doors, and other items, so I need to be able to have an additional monthly fee to cover the wear and tear that animals create. I usually average $25 per month per pet. This is a good strategy if you are willing to rent property to people with pets and you can be more selective. I always mention in my ads that pets are negotiable, and that draws a lot of people.

I prefer to hold open houses because I believe I get a better selection of qualified tenants. I can see what kind of car prospective tenants drive and how well behaved their children are, so I can decide if they would make good tenants for my property—for example, if six people in tattered clothing get out of a 30-year-old car that looks like it's been in ten accidents, that would be a bit of a red flag that suggests that perhaps these tenants may have difficulty paying their rent. I can talk to them face to face and find out why they need to rent, how long they need to rent, and what they can afford. I tell everyone who comes to my open houses that I'm looking for a family or individuals who will live in this property on a long-term basis and who will take good care of the property and think of it as their home.

How long should it take to get a property rented? Property manager Dorrliss Cisy Ware says that you should be able to find a tenant within a month, depending on the amount of rent you're asking; some higher-priced properties may take a little longer to rent. Also, you may need more time if, for example, you refuse to allow pets (or if the restrictions on the property don't allow pets).

Rent for the Long Term

As mentioned, my strategy is always to rent for the long term, which for me is a minimum of a one-year lease. I do not do month-to-month rentals, because I don't want the turnover if I am managing the property myself. After all, every time a tenant leaves, you have maintenance issues: you need to clean the property, and you also may need to paint it and perhaps even replace the carpets or do more extensive renovation. If you're going to rent out your properties on less than a one-year lease, you need to take into account the work required, the time it takes to do it, and the loss of monthly cash flow while you are fixing the property. My preference is for long-term rentals to people who are going to take good care of the property.

A one-year lease might seem like a short-term lease to some people, but it's long enough for me. First, I try to have my leases expire in either June or July. Because of the type of properties I buy, I want to rent to families with children who are going to schools they can walk to. And most families will move in the summer months, so that they can get settled in before the school year starts. Second, if I were to have longer than a one-year lease, then I would have less freedom to raise the rent. With a one-year lease, I can look at the property once a year and decide if the rent is still appropriate for that property.

Keep in mind that you don't want to gouge people, because I believe you should try to attract long-term tenants for the properties you're renting out. There are some landlords, of course, who raise the rent significantly—10 percent or more—when they renew the lease. I don't do that. But I always raise the rent, and I encourage anyone who's going to be in the rental business to raise the rent. Even if the person's paid you like clockwork or even early, you should raise the rent, even if only by $5 a month, because you never know when *your* expenses are going to increase. For example, you don't know if taxes are going to increase, or if the roof is going to leak and you'll need to spend some maintenance money to repair it. You need to prepare yourself for these expenses by having your own "savings account" for each property you own, so that if something does happen that you weren't expecting, you have the money to pay for it.

In Florida, for example, right now it's very popular for people to ask for seven-month leases because they're building a home, and they need somewhere to live during the seven months until their home will be completed. If the rental market is tight, meaning I could not find a good long-term quality tenant due to overbuilding, inventory, or vacancy factors, I would consider a seven month rental. But I would prefer not to. The decision would be market driven.

Use a Step-by-Step Approach to Help You Manage the Property

Once you have found a qualified tenant (whether by holding an open house or by through some other means that you choose), if you're managing the property yourself, you should have a checklist to make sure you do everything you need to do.

Have Potential Tenants Fill Out an Application. The application for a rental is very important. It should include an authorization at the bottom to allow you to check the applicant's credit. Never check a prospective tenant's credit without his or her signed authorization. Caution: It is against the law for anyone to check anybody else's credit without that person's authorization. Make sure your application includes such an authorization. You can get standard application forms locally through property managers or real estate offices, or you can create your own, but make sure that an attorney reviews and approves it so that you know you're following all state laws.

Checklist 8-3 lists all the critical information that you should include on the application that prospective tenants will fill out for you. As a landlord, your primary concerns are whether the person has committed any crimes, whether he or she has declared bankruptcy, and whether he or she has the income to pay you.

I give out applications to everyone who comes to my open houses and tells me that he or she is interested in renting the property. I number the completed applications that people give back to me, so that I have a sequential record of who returned the application first.

Ask for an Application Fee. I get a $25 check from each person who is interested in renting the property. However, I do not cash the check until I'm ready to pull the person's credit history. Once I do cash the check, it's nonrefundable. Before a prospective tenant who is interested in renting the property leaves the open house, I sit down with that person and review his or her application. (Also, my application requires the prospective tenant to provide a driver's license number, and I look at the license to make sure it matches what they wrote.)

Checklist 8-3   Information to Include
on Applications from Prospective Tenants

- ❑ Name
- ❑ Address
- ❑ Social security number
- ❑ Driver's license number
- ❑ Spouse's name (if applicable)
- ❑ Children's names (if applicable)
- ❑ Children's ages (if they'll be living in the property)
- ❑ Bank references
- ❑ Personal references
- ❑ Employment information
- ❑ Whether the person has been arrested or convicted of a crime
- ❑ Whether the person has filed for bankruptcy within the last three years.

I strongly recommend that you check credit. You should get as much history as possible on anyone who will be living in one of your properties.

Ask Potential Tenants about Their Credit.   After talking to each person who is interested in renting the property and making sure that I have all the pertinent information I need, I ask them one last critical question: "Is there anything you want to tell me before I run your credit?" At that point, the person knows I'm going to run his or her credit, and this question usually reveals the person's whole credit history. For example, I've heard responses like, "I got a divorce 18 months ago, and my wife took me to the cleaners, and I owe a lot of money, so you're going to see judgments against me." Or, "I owe the gas company beaucoup bucks." Or, "I lost my job and I had to live on credit cards." Or even, "I bounced a check at Safeway three years ago."

What you are looking for when you ask this question is *not* the specific responses, but whether the person is telling you the truth—because the credit report will confirm the person's financial situation. And for myself, if I find out when I pull somebody's credit that that person hasn't been honest with me, I will not rent to him or her.

Do a Credit Check. Once you have all the completed applications (and the $25 application fee) from people who are interested in renting from you, you should check the credit of each of the applicants, in the order in which you received the applications—again, so that there is no discrimination. You can pull credit reports yourself if you belong to a credit reporting agency, as I do, or if you don't want to do this yourself, there are companies you can go to that will pull credit reports for you for a small fee. You can find these companies on the Internet—e.g., Tenantcheck is one.

I strongly recommend that you check credit. You should get as much history as possible on anyone who will be living in one of your properties.

Some landlords also conduct criminal background checks or civil background checks. That's your decision, and it's probably influenced by where you are buying your properties and what your general investment philosophy is. Everybody has his or her own way of handling a portfolio, and you need to be comfortable with your way of finding the right tenant for your property.

You should also verify that your prospective tenant is currently employed and at what salary, because the tenant should be paying no more than 40 percent of his or her gross income in rent. If your rent is more than that amount, that tenant can't really afford to rent your property.

Verify all the information on the rental application: call the applicant's employer, and call the personal references listed. If the applicant lists previous landlords as references, *don't* call the applicant's *current* landlord, because if that tenant is a problem, the current landlord will most likely want him or her to leave, so the landlord may give the tenant a *good* reference, even if that's not at all accurate. Instead, go back to the landlord *before* the current landlord to find out what type of tenant this person really was.

Renee Falgout confirms this advice:

When an applicant fills out your application to rent, have them sign an authorization for you to be able to verify their information. Run a credit report, verify employment duration and the potential of projected employment, and contact their prior landlords to confirm their payment history. It can be the difference between someone who sends in their rent checks the day before it's due and someone who sends in their rent check on the fifteenth that bounces anyway.

Finally, evaluate whether your prospective tenant is really suited to this particular property. For example, if I have a 1,000-square-foot house, I would not want to rent this property to a couple with five children, because they're going to take a greater toll on the property in terms of its maintenance, water, utilities, and even the building itself.

Verify all the information on the rental application: call the applicant's employer, and call the personal references listed.

Tell Other Interested Parties That You've Rented the Property.

Once you have confirmed that one of the interested people meets your criteria, set up an appointment to sit down and review your lease with your new tenant (I'll cover this in the next section). Send a letter to everyone else who filled out an application. *Never* call them on the phone and leave an answering machine message: "You didn't get this house because your credit stunk," or "You didn't tell me the truth, and you're one step from bankruptcy." Just send them a polite but brief rejection letter saying, "Thank you very much for your interest in this home. We have rented this to another family. I have enclosed your check (marked void). I wish you the best of luck in your future, sincerely yours."

You don't need to give a reason why you decided not to rent the property to a certain party—or even why you *did* decide to rent to the person you chose to be your tenant. You don't want to be accused of discriminating in any way. The real reason for your choice is that you believe that the person is going to make the payments and take good care of the property.

If one of my applicants calls and asks me, "Why didn't I get this apartment?" I'll be happy to sit down face-to-face and talk to that person. But again, I would simply say, "I had another applicant who was just as qualified as you, but who was a better fit for the property." Fortunately, in general, people won't ask why they weren't chosen.

Keep a Database of Information on Interested Prospective Tenants. If you get several qualified people who are interested in a property, but you have only one vacancy, you should keep the information on the others for future reference, in case other properties that you own become available. I simply ask everyone if I can keep them on a list, and if I have another vacancy, I will notify them. I keep those people in a database, because I never know when I may buy another property and need a tenant. If it's soon enough after I had an open house, people who came to that open house may not yet have found the right property; therefore, I may be able to find a tenant for another property without having to do anything. I recommend strongly that you keep a database of people who are willing to be contacted in the future.

Meet with Your New Tenant. Once you've chosen a qualified tenant, arrange a meeting in a neutral location. It's better if the location is neutral, because if you meet in your office, you will be in a control position, and the tenant may feel intimidated. On the other hand, for the same reason, you shouldn't meet in the tenant's home or office, because then your new tenant is in a control situation. Pick a neutral location, such as a coffee shop or a local restaurant. You do not want to meet at the property the tenant will be renting.

If the new tenant has pets, as mentioned earlier in the chapter, you should meet the pet. Therefore, you should insist on visiting the new tenant at his or her current property, and there's a good reason for that: you want to look at the property and see how the tenant has cared for that property and whether the pet in question has done any damage. If you simply allow your prospective tenant to *bring* the pet to you, the pet could be showered and groomed to make it look beautiful. But if you go into the tenant's home, that could be much more revealing of what you can expect from the pet on the property you're renting to its owner. Also, as mentioned, if you're getting a little additional monthly income from the pet, then it's worth your time to go look at it. Do not believe what anyone tells you.

Do not rent to tenants who have trained attack dogs, because they will pose a potential liability to you should the dog attack someone on your property. Even with property managers controlling the rental of my income property, I want to know what type of pet will be living in the house before the manager rents it. The liability is just not worth it.

Most states are pro-tenant. They are not pro-landlord. Keep this in mind if you have a problem with your tenant later on.

Specify How the Rent Is to Be Paid.   At your meeting with your new tenant, he or she should bring *certified funds* for one month's security deposit and the first month's rent. After this initial payment in certified funds, you can allow your tenant to make payments using a regular checking account. You might also consider including in your lease that if the tenant bounces a check, he or she will need to pay an additional fee to make the check good—and may need to pay you by money order or some sort of certified funds thereafter. That's very important to me, as I am not in the collections business.

Get a Late Fee If the Rent Is Late.   As mentioned, my leases offer a *discounted* rent if my tenant pays me *before* the first of the month. If, however, the tenant pays me *after* the first of the month, I have a built-in late fee. If you're going to structure your rent payments this way, check your state law to see what the limitations on the late fee are. A ballpark figure might be 5 percent, but check your state law to make sure you are not violating any laws pertaining to fees. A local attorney can answer this question.

I am very careful about when payments are due. All my tenants' rents are due at the same time. Tenants should realize that they mail their checks at their own risk. If I don't receive the check when it's supposed to be received, the tenant will be hit with a late fee. I go by the postmark that's on the envelope; I can't be any fairer than that.

Write Your Own Lease–but Have a Lawyer Approve It. I personally prefer to have my own customized lease for the properties I manage, rather than using a standard lease For the properties I own out of state, it's obviously not a good idea for me to try to manage those properties myself (especially if, for example, I might be 2,000 miles away), so I work with a property manager (discussed later in this chapter), and the property manager typically has his or her own lease, which I of course approve. If you're going to create your own lease, you can choose whatever terms and requirements you want to include, but please get it approved by a real estate lawyer before you present it to a tenant.

Review the Terms of Your Lease with Your New Tenant

Most states are pro-tenant. They are *not* pro-landlord. Keep this in mind if you have a problem with your tenant later on. One way to avoid problems is to review the terms of your lease carefully with your tenant before he or she moves in. This usually takes me about an hour and a half, because my lease has 35 clauses. Verify that all the conditions of the lease are terms you can live with and that you're protected. Following are some of the things you want to discuss with your new tenant.

Verify Who's Going to Live in Your Property. This important clause is a verification of who is going to live in the property. It further specifies that if an additional person moves in (i.e., in addition to the tenant signing the lease—for example, a roommate, boyfriend, girlfriend, adult child, or parent), that arrangement must be subject to my written approval. If your tenant gets pregnant and has another child, that's fine; however, this clause protects you. If your tenant's mother gets sick and she wants to move her mom into the property, that requires my written approval. The reason for this is that an additional person living in the premises will increase wear and tear on the property. Of course, you need to understand that family situations change, and you should be understanding and accommodating— but you should also charge a small additional fee (for example, $75 a month) if an additional person moves into the property.

In some parts of the country, property owners who are renting have to be very concerned about this issue, because some tenants may have families of 12 siblings or cousins, and after the tenant gets into the house, the entire family moves in. And even if you have a lease, if your lease doesn't address that particular issue, you are not protected.

Set the Term of Your Lease. As mentioned, all of my leases expire at the end of June or July, because for my real estate strategy, I prefer to rent to families with children going to local schools, and summer is when families are most likely to move. This schedule works for me because it limits the time I need to be around to re-rent those properties should I have a vacancy: it's only two months of the year.

Make Sure You're Noted as the Agent for the Property. You want to make sure that you are listed as the agent on all records pertaining to the property—such as the utilities—and indicate that you should be notified if your tenants don't make payments on their utility bills. This is very important, because some cities will be happy to notify the landlord of a delinquency in payment before they put a lien on your property. Also, more important, the utility can simply shut off the electricity, which could cause problems (for example, if your tenant has a refrigerator full of food, and the electric company shuts off the electricity because the tenant hasn't paid the bill, that can require quite a cleanup). Make sure you're notified if the tenant doesn't pay his or her bills.

Require the Tenant to Pay for Minor Repairs. Make sure you include a clause in your lease that specifies that the tenant pays up to a certain amount for expenses. For example, I use $75. It's the tenant's responsibility to take care of those minor items like leaky faucets. Also, you should be able to refer your tenants to a handyman who can do minor repairs. (And if you do refer someone, make sure that person is licensed. Never hire somebody who is not licensed and bonded to do work on your rental property, because if that person trips and falls or has an accident, you're liable. You want to make sure that all workers are licensed.)

Keep a Key to the Property. Finally, most landlords require that they keep a key to the property in case there's some emergency and they have to get into that property.

Inspect the Property with Each New Tenant

After you and your new tenant have reviewed and signed the lease, and after you've received certified funds, you should inspect the property *with your tenant*. Use an inspection checklist that covers the entire property from roof to cellar, inside and out: gutters, roofs, floors, ceilings, wallboards, walls, kitchens, bathrooms, every single inch of the house. Walk through the house and mark off together any existing problems with the property. I also take digital photos of my properties, inside and out, with the tenants in front of the property.

I leave the inspection sheet for three business days so that the tenant has additional time to see if we missed anything. This inspection checklist and the pictures protect me, because when the tenant vacates the property (whether at the end of the term of the lease or beforehand), I have pictures of what the property looked like, with the tenant standing in front of it, before the tenant moved in. Then, when the tenant leaves, we do another walkthrough. If there's simple wear and tear, that's expected. However, if there's damage to the property, you should draw on the tenant's security deposit to cover the repairs of that damage. Therefore, it's important that you have pictures of the property with the tenant in front of it, and that you have the pictures dated, to protect yourself in case you ever need to go to court (which, unfortunately, does happen; I have had to go to court to dispute damage situations in the past).

If you take the time to identify and get the right tenant in the first place, that tenant should take good care of your property.

During the inspection, I also review with my tenant what maintenance I expect the tenant to handle, and how I will handle more significant maintenance problems. For example, I expect my tenants to take care of minor problems, such as a leaky faucet. On the other hand, if the roof is leaking, I expect the tenant to call me, and I'll have it repaired at my expense.

You don't want to come across as hostile during this inspection. Be conscious of how you present yourself; for example, I tell my tenants at the outset, "I'm really looking for someone who will take good care of this property. I hope you'll stay for a long time. I'm not the type of landlord who's going to 'baby-sit' you; I'm not going to come over and check up on you constantly. In turn, I expect you to treat this property with respect, and for that, there's a certain give and take." Some of that give and take includes the discount on their rent that I offer my tenants if they pay early.

I also tell my tenants that the inspection protects *them*, because whatever issues or problems we find during the initial inspection are obviously preexisting. Therefore, when I do a final inspection when that tenant moves out, I'll know that those problems aren't that tenant's responsibility. Most tenants are very cool about inspections; I've never had anybody object to doing one.

The inspection sheet is *really important*. Make sure the tenant signs and dates it; you should also sign it, and you both should agree on the condition of the property when the tenant moves in. You should also make sure that your tenant has rental insurance for the property. Finally, it's also very important for you to make sure that the tenant does not have any hazardous materials or substances in your building that could be a problem environmentally or cause fire or other hazards.

Getting the Right Tenant Prevents Problems Down the Line

Finding good tenants isn't difficult, especially if you follow the guidelines provided in this chapter. It may be a bit time-consuming at first, but if you take the time to identify and get the right tenant in the first place, that tenant should take good care of your property. The tenant should call you when there's a problem with the building, but, as mentioned, the tenant should not call you for small, minuscule fix-ups. You and the tenant should agree on what constitutes minor fix-ups, and this should be included in the lease.

I rarely bother my tenants. Because my strategy is to rent property in areas that I know, I have had situations where a neighbor has called me to tell me that there's a problem with my building. For example, one Fourth of July, a relatively new tenant's kids were sitting on the roof of the house they were renting from me, shooting off sparklers. A neighbor called me and told me what the kids were doing, and I had to call the police to get the kids down. I told the tenants that if that happened again, they would be evicted.

There are code violations and city government ordinances that the tenants need to comply with, and if they don't abide by those ordinances, that's grounds for me to evict them. I've found that when I follow my checklist for finding good tenants, my tenants understand from the get-go what I expect of them and what they can expect of me in return. Also, it's a win-win situation, because my tenants are renting my property at a discount, and they know that I'm not looking to boot them out; instead, I want them to stay for the long term. Other landlords may sell their properties after owning them for only a short time; in contrast, I tell my tenants that I keep my properties for the long term. Therefore, my tenants don't have to worry about going anywhere. If they take good care of my property, I'm going to take good care of them.

I also do a little extra for my tenants. For example, at Christmas, I send my tenants gift certificates to local restaurants: $25 if they've been with me for a year, $50 if they've been with me for two years, and $75 if they've been with me longer. Also, in the springtime, I give all my tenants gift certificates to a nursery so that they can plant something—which, of course, beautifies the property, but it also makes them feel good. I recommend doing small things that are a little bit outside the box to foster goodwill with your tenants, instead of simply being a typical landlord who doesn't do anything except collect the rent.

Do everything possible to avoid evicting your tenants. . . .
There are other ways to terminate your
relationship with a tenant.

Maintaining Your Rental Properties

If you're going to manage your own properties (actually, even if you're dealing with a property manager), I strongly recommend that you do regular maintenance on your properties. Have your heaters/furnaces and air-conditioning units serviced every year to ensure that everything's in workable order. Also, I strongly recommend that you send your tenants batteries for smoke detectors and remind them that they need to change the batteries so that you—and they—are in compliance with your insurance. There's no excuse for their smoke detectors not to be working.

If you feel that you want to do a yearly (or more frequent) inspection of the property, be considerate enough to give your tenants sufficient notice. This should be in your lease, so that your tenants will expect it. Some landlords like to give written notice, and others simply call; either way, you need to let your tenants know. Don't just pop in. Again, if you treat your tenants well, they'll treat your property well.

Try to Avoid Evicting Your Tenants: Alternative Strategies

The previous section touched briefly on the subject of eviction, but the topic merits a bit more discussion. Do everything possible to avoid evicting your tenants, because it's an ugly, time-consuming, and difficult process. There are other ways to terminate your relationship with a tenant: you can let the tenant out of the lease, and you can even pay the tenant to go.

I had a tenant who met her future husband and wanted to marry him and move to Arizona. She still had six months left on her lease; it was December, and the lease did not expire until June. I would have had to take her to court to collect, which is time-consuming and expensive. My other option was to simply find another qualified tenant just like her, and then let her out of her lease. I chose the second option and discussed it with my tenant. She understood that she was still liable for making payments on her lease until I could find a new tenant.

I put an ad in the newspaper and held open houses. It took me about six weeks to find somebody, because it was right around the holidays and it was freezing cold, so most people weren't looking to move. This turned into a win-win situation for everyone: my tenant could move to Arizona, she didn't have to pay six months of rent on a property that she was no longer living in, and I found a new tenant.

If you have a tenant who's not paying the rent, start by sending the tenant a late letter that lets the tenant know that the rent is late, reminds the tenant how much of a late fee the tenant now owes, and includes a date by which you expect payment. Then, if you don't get a check by the date you specified, you should send a demand letter that says, "You are in violation of your lease. If you do not bring your lease current, I will take legal action." Usually, that's enough of a warning to get tenants to pay.

Personally, I've been fortunate to have had only a couple of tenants over the years who still did not pay even after I sent them a demand letter. I think the reason for this is that I make sure that my tenants are financially qualified before I rent to them. Also, I work hard to maintain good relationships with my tenants. I stay in touch with them and ask them how things are going from time to time. Therefore, I usually know when a tenant is in trouble.

The time required to evict a tenant varies, depending on where the property is. In some states—for example, Nevada—you can get somebody out of a property in three weeks, but it takes a lot longer in other states—for example, New York.

No one is going to take better care of your property than you are. . . . If you turn over [property management] responsibility to someone else, . . . learn as much as possible about a property manager before you hire that manager.

Wrap-up: If You Decide to Be a Do-It-Yourself Landlord

To summarize, if you decide you want to be a do-it-yourself landlord, it's a good choice for all of the following reasons:

- You don't pay a property manager's fee.
- You control your own investment.
- You identify who your tenants are. You are responsible for making sure that you've got the right tenants in your properties.

- You do have a bit of legwork to do, but once you've got a system in place, being a landlord is not a full-time job. Instead, once a year, you have to do a bit of accounting, and every month, you need to make sure that you receive your rent payments. If there are any problems with the property, you need to have a network of different contractors; roofers, and other repair people whom you know you can call and who are reliable and skilled.

Property Managers: Are They Right for You?

If you decide you *don't* want to manage your rentals yourself, or if you decide to have someone else manage your rentals for you, you need to find the right property manager. This is somewhat similar to finding a good Realtor (refer back to Chapter 6): you need to have some sort of job description in your mind.

Questions to Ask a Property Manager before You Hire

Keep in mind that *no one is going to take better care of your property than you are*. I do use property managers because I own out-of-state property, so it isn't feasible for me to manage those properties myself. If you're going to turn over this responsibility to someone else, you should try to learn as much as possible about a property manager before you hire that manager. Following are some questions you should ask.

"Do You Have a Current License?"   In most states, property managers need to be licensed. Make sure that the property manager's license is current, and make sure that the property manager is bonded.

Some Realtors will offer to do property management for you, but property management is not something that should be done part-time— i.e., "on the side," in addition to the Realtor's primary work. That Realtor may be well intentioned but may not really be able to handle the demands of the job.

For example, I know an investor I'll call Patricia who hired a Realtor from a very large real estate brokerage company to handle her property management. The Realtor did absolutely nothing. The tenants had a lot of problems with the property, including electrical malfunctions. Unfortunately, the property manager never notified Patricia. Now the tenants are leaving because nothing has been done to repair the problems with the property. Patricia is losing money because no rent is coming in on her investment property. When Patricia asked her property manager why he didn't contact her, he replied, "If you don't like the way I manage property, you are welcome to find someone else." That type of "protection" didn't help Patricia; she's out $1,300 a month—and she still has the electrical problem that the property manager didn't tell her about!

"Do You Yourself Own Investment Property?"   Personally, I prefer to work with property managers who are investors themselves. If a manager you are talking to does own investment property, find out how long he or she has owned property and ask if you can see some of the properties that he or she owns or manages directly. Keep in mind that many property managers will not tell you how much investment property they own, but you need to at least get some idea of their experience.

"How Do You Find and Screen Potential Tenants?"   What process does the manager use? Does the manager require an application? What are some of the ways the manager finds quality tenants? Or, does the manager just put an ad in the newspaper and rent to the first person who comes along? Some property managers just don't take the time and trouble to find good tenants. On the other hand, some are terrific: property manager Dorrliss Cisy Ware says that she does a credit check and criminal background check on each individual 18 years and older (all of whom are also required to sign the lease); she also verifies their employment and their rental history.

"How Would You Increase Rents?"   For example, suppose you have a property that you're renting for $1,400 a month. You need to pay your property manager 10 percent of that off the top, so your net isn't $1,400, it's $1,260. Therefore, at the end of the first year, if the tenant wants to renew the lease, you need to know whether the property manager has included an inflationary clause.

"How Many Properties Do You Currently Manage for Others?"

You might also ask how long the property manager has been in business. This is a very important question. Personally, I prefer not to hire someone who is not managing properties for anyone else. I want someone who has some experience already, who knows what he or she is doing.

One exception to this is in Florida, where attorneys are allowed to be property managers. In that case, I would consider hiring an attorney as a property manager because I know that lawyers are, in general, tenacious—and that they usually have an office and staff, so that they can probably handle a couple of properties. Try to find somebody who's in the business and has a track record—*and do your due diligence* on anyone you are considering doing business with.

That said, there is no minimum or maximum number of properties that you can use as guidelines. You simply want to make sure that the property manager you hire has experience managing other properties, so that yours is not the first one he or she has handled. For example, on the maximum end of the spectrum, I know very successful property managers who can manage 400 properties and do a great job. They have a terrific system in place, they have staff helping out in different roles, and they have their own contractors and handymen whom they send out to handle maintenance, because they're managing so much property.

"How Do You Interact with Tenants, and How Will They Keep You Informed?"

I want a tough person who can't be pushed around. Yet I also want somebody who's pleasant, who's going to be able to deal with potential tenants, and who will be fair. Also, I want a detail-oriented person who will keep me informed of any expenses or any additional money that is needed.

"What Is Your Fee?"

The average property manager gets about 10 percent of the gross monthly revenue, although in some areas—for example, in Florida—they get as much as 18 percent. These fees are for long-term rentals. For seasonal rentals—i.e., if you're renting property in ski resorts or beach areas—where you're working through a short-term property manager for the season, the manager is going to get a much higher property management fee, sometimes as much as 50 percent.

You can negotiate with some property managers—especially if you have enough property—and get the fee down to 5 percent. But be cautious: as mentioned, make sure that your property manager is really going to represent you well and do a good job of finding the right quality tenant. This is another reason it's important to hire someone with experience, because if your property manager has never worked with other property owners or landlords before, he or she may not know how to deal with tenants and still be professional.

In addition to their fee, some property managers have a built-in 15 percent renewal clause in their property management agreements with property owners. That is, in addition to the 10 percent of the monthly rent from the tenant that the manager receives (let's say $150 a month if the rent is $1,500 a month), these managers also receive an additional 15 percent if the tenant renews the lease. In that case, the property manager would get, say, another $240 (flat fee) if the rent is increased to $1,600 a month for the next year. I think this additional fee is outrageous: after all, anybody can renew a lease! So be careful of this when you're reading your property management agreements. In fact, you may want to have a third party look at the property management agreement before you sign on the dotted line.

How to Find a Qualified Property Manager

You shouldn't feel locked into working with a particular property manager; there should be more than enough people in your community who are working as property managers that there's no need to get stuck with one who's not working hard enough for you. The National Association of Residential Property Managers (NARPM) has enough members that it should be able to refer you to property managers in your area. Find somebody you feel comfortable working with. Ask around—here are some other suggestions for how to get good recommendations:

- Call several real estate offices to see if they know of a good property manager.
- Call a few CPAs in the area who do taxes and bookkeeping for people; they may have clients who are property managers or landlords working with property managers.

- Contact your local property manager association.
- Contact the National Apartment Association (www.naahq.org), which has chapters in just about every local area.
- Find out if your area has an independent rental owners' council—for example, in Arizona, you can contact the Arizona Multihousing Authority's Independent Rental Owners Council (www.azama.org/iroc).

Do your due diligence: ask the questions listed earlier, which describe what you should be looking for and the qualities of a good property manager. It's important that you find the right person. After all, as the owner of the property, you are the client, not the tenant. Your property manager is providing a service, and for that service, he or she is getting 10 percent of the monthly rent, on average. Therefore, your manager should represent you properly, and you should do follow-up to ensure that this happens. Your property manager should be organized, and should have the necessary skills to manage multiple properties professionally. He or she should keep normal business hours and have someone who answers the phone.

There are some positives to renting to college students, but . . . I recommend working through a property manager and not trying to handle [this niche] *on your own.*

If You're Renting to Students

Hiring a property manager is especially desirable and recommended for certain types of properties and certain types of tenants. Student housing is one of these. If you live or own property in a university town, there are students who will want to get together and rent private property instead of living in the dorms. Students can be challenging as tenants.

If you're *not* going to work with a property manager when renting to students, or if you prefer to be a landlord, you should have the parents of the students cosign the lease for the students, especially if a student has no income. That way, you're guaranteed to get your rent if the student can't pay it.

For some real estate investors, student housing is their strategy; after all, if there's a large university, there will also be a lot of people who need to rent. Moreover, if it's a tight real estate market, students will often sign a full year's lease to keep the rental—which means that even if the property is vacant in the summer, you're still getting rental payments. So there are some positives to renting to college students, but again, I recommend working through a property manager and not trying to handle it on your own.

If You're Renting to Individuals on a Fixed Income or in Over-55 Housing

Another strategy that some investors use is to provide housing for the elderly—not in assisted-living facilities, but by buying a building and renting rooms or space to individuals who have retired and are living on a fixed income. Such tenants are generally excellent payers because they're getting social security, Medicaid, and whatever retirement income they have (e.g., from pensions or other retirement funds). Here again, however, if you're interested in buying that type of property, I recommend working with a property manager. You won't want to get into the middle of a situation that could turn emotional. Having a third party involved is sometimes a good way to operate and makes paying the property management fee worthwhile.

What Your Property Manager Should Do for You

Once you've found a property manager who you think is qualified and experienced and who is someone you feel you can work with, get down to the specifics on what the manager's responsibilities will be. In general, your property manager should do all of the tasks listed in Checklist 8-4.

Property manager Dorrliss Cisy Ware is even more emphatic about what property managers can do for owners of rental property:

> *The property management company keeps the perspective in focus. Your property is your investment. We take care of it for you. A possible scenario: your tenant calls you and says, "I don't have all the money to pay the rent; I had to spend it for the kids. I only have $200. I'll give you the other $600 in a couple of weeks." Do you, as the owner, say, "That's O.K., honey, I've had to do that before. Don't worry about it, just give me the $200; you can pay the rest when*

you get it"? This is a very typical thing we run into when someone finally gives up on trying to rent it themselves.

The answer is no, *you do not take a partial rent. The rent is due on the first day of the month. It is late at 5 p.m. on the third. On the fourth (unless it falls on a weekend), they are posted with a late notice, which says, "The rent amount, plus a posting fee and a late fee, is due before 5 p.m. on the ninth." That gives them an extra five days. On the tenth, eviction papers will be prepared. This is something we don't have to do often.*

What I'm trying to get at is, we do the work:

- *We find the tenant and do all the screening.*
- *We order the lease from our attorney.*
- *We do the inspections when they are required. We take a full battery of photos before a tenant moves in, and we do an inspection at three and nine months.*
- *We know at this time if we want to keep them on for a second lease or not.*
- *We order the new lease.*
- *We do drive-bys at least once a month to view the exterior.*
- *If the exterior needs attention, we post them with a notice to take care of it (mow the lawn, trim the shrubs, remove any trash from the exterior, and so on).*
- *Also, when you are an absentee landlord, you can't keep an eye on the home and what is happening to it. We have contact with the tenants each month when they come in to pay their rent (no cash or personal checks; money orders or bank-issued cashier's checks only).*
- [We give tenants] *a repair request form, if anything needs to be done. If it is an emergency, they call the office. If it isn't, they fill out the form and either drop it off, mail it, or fax it to us.*
- *We then schedule the repair, first asking for an estimate. We then call you* [the owner] *with the amount. If the repair is over $200, we have to get your permission to have the work done, unless it is an emergency situation.*

- *Being here in Florida, if we have damage from hurricanes, lightning, high winds, or tornadoes, we contact your insurance company and make the home available for their inspection and repair.*
- [We send you] *a monthly statement with your rent check and a yearly statement. In January, our accountant sends you a W-9.*

This is a great list of services that property managers perform to protect the client (you) and your investment.

Checklist 8-4   What Your Property Manager Should Do for You

❑ Make sure the property is kept clean and is safe.

❑ Oversee immediately any issues or problems with the property.

❑ Have all repairs done that are necessary to keep the property up to code and habitable.

❑ Comply with the city's health and safety codes.

❑ Make sure that tenants are fulfilling their obligations in terms of:

   ❑ Keeping the property clean

   ❑ Making sure that garbage isn't outside constantly, but only on appropriate pickup days

   ❑ Using the fixtures and appliances properly

   ❑ Adhering to any city codes on noise

   ❑ Conducting themselves in a proper manner

❑ When a tenant leaves the property, at the end of a lease, make sure that the property is in good, clean working order.

So Should You Hire a Property Manager or Do It Yourself?

Here's a short "test" that you can take to see if you're the type of person who would be a good landlord or if you should be working with a property manager:

1. *Do you like handling crises?* How do you feel about people contacting you after regular business hours? You need to be tolerant of that, because even if you put it in your lease that your tenants can contact you "between the hours of 8:30 and 5:00, Monday through Friday," if your tenants have a problem, they're not going to hesitate to call you in the evenings or on weekends or even late at night.

2. *Do you have a network of people you can depend on who can come in at a moment's notice to fix any type of problem with the property?* This is important, because if your tenant has a problem with the property and you're not able to get it fixed fairly quickly, you're going to have a problem with that tenant. Therefore, you need to have a list of resources in your area that you can depend on to come in and make repairs.

3. *Are you available on a routine basis?* Do you have the type of job, profession, career, or life where you can handle making on-site visits, renting the property out, and doing all the necessary tasks to find and keep good tenants?

4. *If you're hiring a property management company, does it have those kinds of mechanisms in place?* Does the manager have a staff and personnel in place, such as a handyman, to help maintain property and fix it in an emergency? Has the property manager assured you, through her references, that she will do what she says she'll do? If not, and if you still want to pursue buying investment property to rent out, then you should be your own landlord.

Keep in mind that landlording is not for everyone. If you decide to work with a property manager, you should realize the downside of this arrangement:

- *You are giving up control.* You're allowing someone else to manage your investment, and this is something you need to consider when you're buying a property that you want to rent out. If you're a control freak, you shouldn't hire a property manager; you yourself should be the landlord.

- *No one is going to take as good care of your property as you are.* If you understand that you're giving up control, and you can live with that, and you feel that a property manager will do a good job of finding the right quality tenant, then using a property manager can be great.

Improving Your Investment Properties to Maximize the Rent You Can Charge

Whether you decide to be your own landlord or to hire a property manager, here are some improvements you can make that will let you increase your rents:

- Make sure the overall appearance is neat and clean. The property needs to make a good first impression.
- Use a flattering, neutral color for the interior walls, and install carpets or wood floors.
- Install good lighting, but not bright lighting.
- Make sure the kitchens and baths are spotlessly clean. Also, if the kitchen has older appliances, you may need to update them.
- Remember that if the landscaping looks good, believe it or not, you're going to get more rent. Make sure the lawn is mowed and the leaves are removed if your property is in a suburban area. Also, if possible, plant flowers in front of the property and outside any rooms that have views of the outside, so that prospective tenants will look out at a pretty garden.
- Consider adding a fence. Some tenants request a fence because they have children or pets (provided, of course, that your subdivision restrictions allow for a fence). Adding a fence also increases the value of your property.
- If you do put in a fence, make sure you put in high-quality fencing. Do not put in an old-fashioned cyclone fence. Put in either a wood fence or, in some areas, a vinyl fence; people prefer those types because they look nicer than metal fencing. Also, try to tie in the look of the fence with the look of the property overall.
- Invest a few hundred dollars and put a storage unit or shed in the backyard, where your tenants can put their lawn mower, hoses, and fertilizer or gardening tools and supplies. In fact, I've not only bought

a shed for some properties but also stocked it with all those supplies. This makes a great impression on tenants—and it's to your benefit as well, because you want your tenants to keep your property looking good. I included this, free of charge, with the property, and I encouraged my tenants to feel free to use this equipment.

- Some investors also increase their rental income by charging by the month for the use of washers and dryers, which are generally an option in a property; they're not something that usually comes with a rental. For example, many tenants will ask if the property owner will provide a washer and dryer, and this is very easy to do. Simply go to a consignment shop, buy a used washer and dryer, put it into the property, and rent that washer and dryer for $25 a month. That's additional money coming in from your rental, and although $25 may not seem like a lot of money, if what you owe to the bank on the mortgage is very close to what you're receiving in rent, that $25 could make a difference.

None of the things just listed should cost any significant amount of money; they're all inexpensive things that you can do to increase your rental income.

How to Reduce Some of Your Costs and Expenses

I also have some suggestions for how you can *save* money on your rental property. First, appeal your taxes. Every year, in most areas, the county assessors or local tax department usually tries to increase taxes on property. *You should appeal your real estate taxes every year.* See what has sold in the area near your property, then bring those comps with you and appeal the tax increase by simply asking, "Can you justify how and why you increased the taxes on this property?" In my experience, the county government has overturned the increase *more than 50 percent of the time.*

Georgia is an investor who has property in Florida. In one year, her property taxes nearly tripled. The reason given was that there were new houses going up in the neighborhood that were more expensive than hers. Georgia appealed the tax increase on the grounds that her house was smaller and older than these new large houses. She appealed the taxes and got them lowered. It's always worthwhile to appeal the taxes and save some money.

Finally, contact different insurance companies to get quotes before you insure your properties. Insurance is very tricky, depending on where you buy; for example, with all the problems from the hurricanes over the last couple of years, it's very difficult to get good insurance in some states, and insurance can be very expensive. So you want to let your fingers do the walking and prepare.

Some Final Tips on Renting out Property

Finally, here are some general issues to keep in mind when you're renting out your investment property. I recently made a presentation to a group of real estate investors on this topic, and as I went through my presentation, the naysayers (i.e., people who don't believe that real estate investors should be in the rental business), challenged me with questions like these:

- "What do you do about tenants who trash properties?"
- "How can you handle tenants who are always late with the rent?"
- "What about neighbors complaining about noise or junk in the yard?"

The general answer to all these questions is to find the right tenants in the first place so that these problems never arise. Real estate investing is a business. However you run your business—whether it's to buy and sell or buy and hold—your objective should be future income and wealth accumulation. If you decide to buy properties to rent, it is important that you manage your properties properly—that makes all the difference to your bottom line and to your sanity. Therefore, as a result of that presentation, I have a few final guidelines.

1. Don't Rent to Friends

Years ago, we had friends who were renting in our neighborhood. Their landlord kept raising their rent $50 every six months, and it got to the point where they could no longer afford the monthly payment. It just so happened that I had a vacancy coming up in one of my rental properties in a neighborhood nearby. This seemed like the perfect solution, because their children could continue in the same school district. They rented from me for seven years; then they finally bought their own home.

Unfortunately, when they moved out, the property was in terrible condition. There were holes in the walls and fixtures missing from the ceiling. They had even disconnected the washer and dryer (which they had bought from me on a payment plan) and left the hoses squirting water all over the family room. The cost of fixing that alone was more than their original deposit.

The tenants felt that they had left the property in good condition. I did not, and I refused to give them their deposit back. I took pictures of the property in case I needed them in court. Ultimately, we ended up splitting the deposit 50/50, but it was a difficult situation that became unpleasant and affected not only our investment property but our friendship. Never rent to friends.

2. Know the Landlord/Tenant Laws for Your State

Make sure you know the landlord/tenant laws for your state. Knowing the laws governing eviction proceedings, late-fee charges, and your rights as a landlord are important to the success of your business. You can obtain a copy of the law through the state government agency that issues licenses to property managers, or the reference section of your local library may be able to help you.

3. Make Sure Your Lease Protects You If a Tenant Breaks It before the Termination Date

As described earlier in the chapter, you should screen prospective tenants thoroughly at the very beginning of your application process. Still, even when you screen them properly, you may have problems later. I have a clause in my lease that deals with sudden vacancies in the winter months, when it's almost impossible to find suitable tenants for a vacant property. This is especially valuable if you are renting in cold climates.

4. Never Accept Partial Rental Payments

I have a friend who owns a lot of duplexes and four-unit buildings. He let his tenants make partial payments occasionally when money was tight. One month, he really needed full payment from every tenant. He threatened eviction if he did not get paid in full on the first of the month. He ended up in court—and he lost, because the judge determined that because he had accepted partial payments from his tenants in the past, he had established a precedent that this was acceptable. Don't do this.

5. Rent for Less

Finally, as I've mentioned, I've found renting at a discount to be a successful strategy. Your tenants know that they are getting a deal, and that gives you a variety of good prospects to choose from. They also tend to stay longer, so you shouldn't have the normal turnover problems that other landlords do.

Conclusion

This chapter provides an enormous amount of information on the do's and don'ts of managing rental properties, whether you decide to do it yourself or to hire a property manager. These basic rules have helped me grow my business and have made me a better landlord, which has also freed up my time to do other things—including finding more properties. Don't be afraid to be a landlord; if you have the right lease and are prepared, everyone wins.

Finally, broker and property manager Dorrliss Cisy Ware recommends that investors buy investment properties in a variety of rental areas: "Remember that not everyone can afford a high rental price; the lower and moderate rents stay rented for longer periods than the higher price range."

9

Mortgage Financing and Tax Strategies

This chapter covers the many different types of financing strategies. Most of us have a mortgage on our home. However, there are different types of mortgages and financing strategies that you may not be aware of. I want to cover several financing options that could be deemed "outside the box." This knowledge will help you get your offer not only accepted but funded. Did you know that you can use your IRA or 401(k) to buy real estate? I will cover this as another source of capital that most of us don't think about.

Mortgaging Property

First, let's look at your financial picture. Many people borrow money from the bank to buy their home so that they can take advantage of the interest expense deduction on their taxes. For investors, any type of tax advantage from owning real estate is even more valuable. However, in order to take advantage of the tax benefits that having a mortgage on an investment property can give, you need to be in a position to secure financing in the first place. If you don't have good enough credit to be able to borrow, you're obviously not going to be able to leverage, and you will lose this advantage of trying to pick up a property at below market value.

There are two schools of thought about financing. On the one hand, there are a lot of people who buy property and get it financed—either through conventional financing, seller financing, hard-money lending, going into partnership with someone else or doing an equity-share arrangement—with the intention of paying off the loan as quickly as possible because their strategy is income over the long term. On the other hand, there are a lot of people who shy away from any type of financing because they don't want to be in debt. Therefore, you need to decide first what strategy you're most comfortable with.

Suppose you're looking at investing in real estate as a way to get positive cash flow. For example, you could buy a property for $200,000, make mortgage payments of $1,200 a month, and rent out that property for $1,500 a month. Therefore, you would be making $300 a month off of leveraged property, which is what the majority of real estate investors try to achieve. If that's your strategy, there are certain things you need to know about financing in general, where to go to find good financing, what costs are associated with the loan, and so on.

For example, here's Barbara O'Connell's advice, based on her own real estate investing strategy:

Generally, it's a good idea to put as little of your own cash into a deal as possible and still be able to (1) obtain financing for the deal and (2) hold the property for a long period of time, if necessary, without a negative cash flow. However, in a very competitive seller's market, it may be necessary to put more cash into the deal than usual, just to get the seller to accept your offer!

Basically, I usually put the least amount of money down that I can and still have the property "break even" or have a positive cash flow. This formula is totally different for different areas of the country. Currently, I live an a city in Colorado where you can still put together a no-money-down deal and make a positive cash flow on a single-family home almost any day of the year. The catch is that there is very little appreciation in prices compared to other, hotter markets. On the other hand, you could put 50 percent down in cash on a property in California and still have a negative cash flow. However, in California, you can very often resell the property the day you close on it and make a substantial profit when prices are moving up fast and you are not at the top of the current market cycle.

A lot of people . . . shy away from any type of financing because they don't want to be in debt. . . . You need to decide what strategy you're most comfortable with.

Renee Falgout has an additional word of caution regarding borrowing money:

Investment financing has higher rates and tougher guidelines than financing that will be used for a buyer's primary residence. Lenders statistically show that if a buyer has financial problems, they will default on payments on an investment property before their primary residence. However, lenders do allow for buyers to have second homes or vacation properties, as long as they are more than 50 miles away from the buyer's primary residence. I see many investors take advantage of second home financing that down the road becomes a rental property.

Understanding the Components of Your Mortgage Payment—aka PITI

Most Americans use a mortgage when they purchase a property. Very few people are in a position to pay cash. The pieces of that mortgage payment—which you pay to the bank or mortgage company that's making the loan—are the principal, interest, taxes, and insurance (PITI). If you've bought your own home, you should already know these terms, but in case you haven't and you're just getting started in real estate, or in case you simply need a refresher, let's look at each of these components in more detail.

Principal. The principal is the amount of money that you borrow. For example, if you buy a house for $200,000 and you put 10 percent down, you've paid $20,000, so you're going to need financing for the remaining $180,000. That's the principal amount that you're financing.

Many investors would rather not have their mortgage companies escrow their taxes . . . ; instead, they would rather pay their taxes directly, because the lender is making money on their escrow account.

Interest. The interest is what the lender charges on the money it lends you—in the previous example, on the $180,000. The rate of interest being charged to the borrower is specified in the note that you and the lender have agreed on. For example, as of this writing, interest rates are in the neighborhood of 6.5 percent for a 30-year fixed-rate loan. Thus, you would be paying back the $180,000 at 6.5 percent interest.

Taxes. Every piece of property is taxed every year by the local assessor's office. As a convenience, most mortgage companies will escrow your taxes, or include them in the mortgage payment you're making every month, so that you don't have to pay out-of-pocket taxes on top of your mortgage payment. Many investors would rather not have their mortgage companies escrow their taxes (or insurance, described next); instead, they would rather pay their taxes directly, because the lender is making money on their escrow accounts—the bank gets the use of the cash for up to a year before the tax is due and makes money by getting interest on your escrow account. Personally, I believe that savvy investors should have their taxes and insurance escrowed, because that way they don't have to worry about making out-of-pocket tax and insurance payments, and many people do not have the discipline to save the difference each month without the escrow amount.

Also, keep in mind that the amount of your escrow can change when tax rates change. Mortgage operations manager Renee Falgout warns about this risk, which new investors especially should be aware of:

It always amazes me when I get a call from an investor who had closed on a property within the last four or five months, telling me that their rate changed, when I've secured a fixed mortgage for them. Increasing property taxes, changing flood zones, and increasing insurance premiums seem to be a given in areas of attractive investments. Escrows can and frequently do increase. Make sure to have room in your budget for increasing escrows.

Insurance.   Homeowner's insurance protects your property against fire, flood, or other hazards. Like taxes, your insurance payments are usually escrowed by the lender (though, again, there are investors who prefer *not* to have their lender make these payments, but rather pay the insurance premiums directly to the insurance company).

Read your documents before you sign them to be sure that they do not include a prepayment penalty.

Definitions of Key Financing Terms

To demystify some of the financial jargon you may encounter when you're seeking a loan, here are some definitions that you should know.

Straight Loans, aka Term Loans.   If you get a straight loan, also called a term loan, that's an amortized loan with a fixed maturity date and a fixed interest rate. In other words, you know what you're going to pay each month for the next X number of years, whether it's 10, 15, 20, or 30 years. Some types of loans—commercial loans, for example—may be shorter term than loans on residential property because the lender is only willing to go for the shorter term (say 10 years, which is standard).

Prepayment Penalty.   Read your loan documentation very carefully to see whether or not there's a prepayment penalty. A prepayment penalty is a penalty for paying off the loan early—in other words, if your loan specified that you would make payments for 30 years, and then you won the lottery or you got a terrific new job or a fantastic raise or your Aunt Harriet left you all her money, and you decided to pay off your entire mortgage in year 5. The bank would be, in effect, cheated of the interest payments that you agreed to pay over the next 25 years, so it imposes a prepayment penalty.

For example, Nicole is an investor who bought a property in France because she wanted to diversify her investments. She got a 15-year loan at a 3½ percent fixed interest rate; however, that loan included a prepayment penalty. The bank will charge her a 3 percent penalty if she makes additional principal payments. There is no ballpark figure for penalties; in Nicole's case, her lender would charge her a 3 percent penalty if she tried to pay the loan off early, and that's 3 percent of the loan amount, which in her case was $300,000.

Therefore, you need to read your documents before you sign them to be sure that they do not include a prepayment penalty. This is especially important if you are going to try to pay off your loan early or make double mortgage payments. For example, many people will make extra principal payments every month, or they'll pay twice a month (which is a strategy to help reduce the number of years of paying on the loan), then get the extra payments credited to them at year end. But if your loan has a prepayment penalty, paying off the loan early may not be worth it. *Read your documentation*. I can't emphasize that enough.

Adjustable-Rate Loans, Also Called Adjustable-Rate Mortgages, or ARMs. This type of loan has an interest rate that can be adjusted any time during the term of the loan. Those rates are generally tied to the federal funds rate, the Treasury rate, or the prime interest rate. Therefore, if rates go up, so do your mortgage payments, in accordance with the terms specified in your loan documentation. Therefore, with this type of loan, you need to read the documents to make sure you understand what you are committing to before you sign the loan docs.

Conforming Loans and Nonconforming Loans. If you're obtaining a government-type loan—such as one from the FHA (Federal Housing Administration) or the VA (Veterans' Administration)—it's a *conforming loan* if it's less than a certain amount; at this writing, the amount is approximately $322,000. If the loan is for more than that amount, it's considered to be a *nonconforming loan*, also known as a *jumbo loan*.

The best loan terms are offered to people with conforming loans. In other words, the interest rate will be lower on a conforming loan, one with an amount under $322,000. If you're borrowing more than $322,000, you will probably pay a higher interest rate because you're in a jumbo loan situation, so your cost of funds may go up.

If you can get a good rate and you plan to be a long-term investor in this particular property, . . . go with a fixed-rate mortgage.

Fixed-Rate vs. Adjustable-Rate Mortgages

There are different ways of financing loans; in particular, you can choose between fixed-rate loans and adjustable-rate mortgages. As interest rates are still going up, if you originate a new loan, this would not be the time to do a variable-rate loan. If you can afford it, you would be better off fixing your payments, because the Federal Reserve is still talking about raising interest rates further. If the Fed continues to raise interest rates, people who have adjustable-rate loans will have to make higher payments. The payment on a fixed-rate loan (with the exception of the tax and insurance portion) doesn't change. You signed a contract with the lender to pay back the loan at a set interest rate for a set period of time.

With a variable- or adjustable-rate loan, your payments are fixed for at least some period of time, depending on when you got the loan and the particulars of the loan. However, after that period, when rates go up, your lender will readjust your payment to keep pace with whatever your contract says. Therefore, again, in the current fiscal environment, you should be very, very careful, and I strongly recommend that you shop around for a fixed-rate loan. You can use ARMs for short-term financing; however, I would still watch the market before I signed an ARM.

I get a fixed-rate mortgage on any property that I purchase for the long term. I also bought two properties that I sold within two years; I got ARMs on them because I knew I would not keep them. Finally, I bought one small commercial property that I'm not sure what I'll do with (or what the market will do); although I intend to sell it, I'm not sure when, so I got a fixed-rate mortgage on that property.

When is the best time to use an ARM or an interest-only mortgage, or negative amortization? Renee Falgout, president of Windsor Capital Mortgage Corp in Palm Harbor, Florida, sums this up nicely and describes the five basic types of mortgages available. (For more information on Renee's experience, see Appendix B.)

1. Fixed-Rate Mortgages.   The fixed-rate mortgage is a good strategy for conservative investors:

- If you plan on keeping a property for a long time
- If you don't foresee the need to refinance in the near future to pull cash out
- If you have good credit
- If you can get competitive financing

Buyers will also opt for a fixed-rate mortgage when they think the market might be getting ready to go through some changes and interest rates will be rising. If you can get a good rate and you plan to be a long-term investor in this particular property, Renee recommends that you go with a fixed-rate mortgage. Today, the market has expanded amortization options to include a 40-year term, which makes housing a little more affordable.

Use an ARM only when you're . . . going to either
sell or refinance the property you're buying
before the change date, because the new payments
could put you in a difficult financial position.

---

2. ARMs.   On the other hand, if you're planning to hold on to a property for just a short time, such as a few years, then a two-, three-, five-, or seven-year ARM is typically more attractive because the initial interest rates on an ARM are usually lower than those on with a fixed-rate mortgage. The lower interest rate can improve your cash flow because the difference between your incoming rent (if you're planning to rent out this property) and your outgoing mortgage payment is greater. With an ARM, your payment is fixed for the first portion of the term (again, two, three, five, or seven years), and then it will start to adjust according to a predetermined index and margin.

For example, suppose the interest rate on a 5 percent, two-year, LIBOR ARM with a 3 percent margin is fixed at 5 percent for the first two years. (*LIBOR* is the London Interbank Offered Rate, which is the rate of interest at which banks offer to lend money to one another in the wholesale money markets in London. It's a standard financial index used in U.S. capital markets; also, in general, its changes have been smaller than changes in the prime rate.) On the twenty-fifth payment (i.e., the first payment in the third year), the payment will change from 5 percent to reflect whatever the six-month LIBOR is on that date, plus 3 percent added to it. As of this writing, the six-month LIBOR is 5.263 percent; therefore, this payment would change to reflect a new rate of 8.263 percent. This payment will change every six months to reflect the LIBOR at that time.

You should use an ARM only when you know you're going to either sell or refinance the property you're buying before the change date, because the new payments could put you in a difficult financial position. You can also use ARMs when you do not have good enough credit to get a competitive rate on a fixed-rate mortgage. In that case, you should refinance to a better rate when you have had time to improve your credit standing, and that should take no more than two years.

[Negative amortization mortgages offer] *great cash flow if you're in a tight spot when you buy, but* **[they can]** *be a disaster when you're ready to sell if the market softens.*

---

3. Interest-Only Mortgages. Lenders also make interest-only payment options available on both fixed-rate mortgages and ARMs. If you are in a position where you can use an ARM and the property is likely to appreciate, then paying only the interest on the mortgage will enhance your cash flow. You will still be able to get out of that loan by either selling the property or refinancing to pull cash out or get a better rate.

However, if you, as a buyer, take the option of making interest-only payments on a fixed-rate loan, you need to understand that once the interest-only period is over, you will need to make larger payments during the remaining time on the loan in order to catch up on the principal that you chose not to pay during the interest-only period. This can be either the first

10 or 15 years of the term. Therefore, Renee recommends that the only time you, as a buyer, should choose this option is if your cash flow is tight and you just need a little wiggle room from time to time. It's best to pay the full principal and interest payment if you are planning to keep the property and want to pay off the mortgage.

4. Negative-Amortization (Neg-Am) Mortgages. A negative-amortization mortgage is a different animal altogether: it allows you, the buyer, to make a minimum payment that is much less than what is actually due, with the difference being added to the existing balance; therefore, the balance actually *increases* during the term of your loan. (Neg-ams are also called deferred payments.) Renee recommends that buyers use such loans only in a situation where they will be either refinancing or selling within a very short time period and the property is in an area where there is solid appreciation.

Some lenders will allow the balance to grow to only 15 percent higher than the original balance, then they throw the buyer into a schedule where the interest rate is constantly being adjusting to an index and a fixed margin *plus* the payments that were deferred in the beginning. You may see this advertised as a "1 percent rate, 40-year term." This is what the minimum payment is calculated at; however, the *actual* rate could be as high as 8 percent, and the difference will be added to your existing mortgage every month. This offers great cash flow if you're in a tight spot, but it could be a disaster when you're ready to sell if the market softens.

5. Home Equity Lines of Credit (HELOCs). Finally, home equity lines of credit (HELOCs) are usually used for accessing a small portion of the equity from an existing investment or as a second mortgage while purchasing to avoid lenders' mortgage insurance. Lenders will require private mortgage insurance (PMI) if you have little or no down payment. This protects the lender should you default on your payments.

Mortgage brokers can be a tremendous resource for investors because they have avenues for lending that investors may not necessarily be able to find directly.

Working with a Mortgage Broker

Mortgage brokers are individuals who generally represent several lenders; they present your financial picture to their lenders and find the best fit for a loan. Shemane had some credit problems and could not afford to purchase real estate from a local builder. So she went to a mortgage broker and told her story: her credit score was in the low 500s; she had been divorced; she really wanted to buy this property. In the meantime, another buyer, an investor, came along who had an interest in the same property. The builder sold the property to the investor, who turned around and leased the property to Shemane with a two-year option to buy for $5,000 more than the investor had paid.

For about a year, Shemane worked on improving her credit. In the end, her mortgage broker was able to find a lender who would make her a loan based on her still low but improved credit score. Shemane bought the property for $290,000 instead of $285,000, but by that time the property was appraised for $300,000, so she was still within the fair market value.

The investor got a $5,000 bump after a year and rent payments that provided an additional $250 positive cash flow. Shemane paid all closing costs, as negotiated in their agreement, so the seller netted $8,000 on a one-year investment. Not bad!

Mortgage brokers can be a tremendous resource for investors because they have avenues for lending that investors may not necessarily be able to find directly.

Interviewing Mortgage Brokers

If you're going to work with a mortgage broker, you should ask certain questions because you want to know what he or she can offer you:

- "Do you offer programs other than what banks and lenders currently offer?"
- "Do you handle government programs, such as FHA, VA, or certain government-type programs where money might be more available?" For instance, if you are buying a property as an owner-occupant, and this is the first time you have ever bought a home that you were going

to live in, depending on what your income is, there are special loans available for first-time home buyers. The mortgage broker you work with should know about those. Therefore, if you're looking to buy a property to live in, you want to ask that question: what kind of government programs does the broker represent?

- "Do you do subprime lending?" *Sub-prime lending* is lending to people with credit scores that are below normal. (See Chapter 2 for a discussion of credit scoring.) The mortgage broker will pull your credit report and will know your score, so if the broker represents subprime lenders, he or she will know who to go through.
- Finally, "Do you do hard-money loans?" A *hard-money loan* is one where the lender charges points and fees and a higher interest rate for short-term financing. For example, many rehabbers who buy fix-up property and know that they're going to resell it quickly will use a hard-money lender, so that they can get the cash that they need to renovate the property.

These four questions should help you, as an investor, identify whether a particular mortgage broker is right for you.

Where to Find a Qualified Mortgage Broker

In my opinion, the best way to find a good mortgage broker is to ask around for a referral. Ask Realtors. Ask builders. Ask contractors. Whom would they recommend? What brokers have they worked with who have been really flexible, efficient, and quick? If you ask enough people, you'll usually hear the same person recommended over and over again. For example, I found Renee Falgout, a mortgage broker in Florida, when I was interested in buying a brand-new property that was being built in Northport, Florida. I asked the builder to recommend a mortgage broker, and I asked a local property manager, and both of them, independently, recommended Renee. I met with her, and I was very comfortable with her from that first meeting: she knew her stuff. Since then, if I buy any properties in Florida, I work through her.

In general, I suggest getting two or three recommendations, and then going with the mortgage broker you feel the most comfortable with.

Using Conventional Financing Strategies

There are the typical ways in which people go about financing property: either they go to the bank and borrow, or they work through a mortgage broker, who finds them a lender. Then there are crazy methods, like buying properties on credit cards, for example. If you watch late-night TV, you may see a variety of different ideas and strategies advertised on infomercials, claiming that you can "put nothing down—buy your house on credit cards!" More recently, there are many companies advertising on TV how you can get a loan online.

Have your financing in place before you start buying property because you want to be able to take advantage of whatever deals come your way.

But if you think about these ideas realistically, you know that most normal investors, who are just trying to get ahead and increase their portfolios, should stick to strategies that make sense, that they can afford, and that they feel comfortable with and can manage. Therefore, my recommendation is that you not pay attention to slick salespeople; instead, focus on your strategy, your portfolio, and your financial picture (what you can manage). If you live above your means, and you use some of those strategies like putting a property on a credit card, you may find yourself in financial trouble.

Get your financial house in order: review and adjust your spending, borrowing, and saving habits so that you feel comfortable before you go out and start dealing with bankers to get a loan, get a home equity line, or do whatever it is you're going to do to get your financing in place to buy property.

You should have your financing in place before you start buying property because you want to be able to take advantage of whatever deals come your way. Lenders want to know the answers to the following questions before they will lend you money to buy property:

- Who are you?
- How much money do you need?
- What will this loan be secured by?
- And the most important question: how are you going to pay me back?

People who are employed—i.e., who have a guaranteed source of income—are going to have a better chance of getting a loan because, from the lender's perspective, they are stable.

Banks are typically not willing to give unsecured loans unless you already have a banking relationship.

Some lenders are nonportfolio lenders, who may sell your loan to another bank or to Fannie Mae—in other words, they're wholesaling your loan by selling it after three or six months. If you've financed a property through Countrywide (which is the nation's largest home lender), your loan will probably stay with that company. If you started out with a small mortgage brokerage company or a small bank, that bank may have sold your loan to Countrywide or Wells Fargo, Citicorp, or Washington Mutual.

From the bank's perspective, the best loans are those made to people with good credit scores and stable employment, because the bank always wants to be sure that the person it's lending money to has the ability to pay back the loan. Therefore, from the get-go, when you're looking at your financial picture, keep in mind that lenders are going to ask you the four questions listed previously. If you can satisfy the lender, you'll get the loan.

Most investors develop a relationship with an individual banker or mortgage broker, and work with that person whenever they buy property. For example, earlier in the chapter, I mentioned Renee Falgout, a Florida-based mortgage broker whom I've worked with on my last several transactions—all of which were properties I bought in Florida. We've met face-to-face only twice. I worked with her because I was buying from out of state. Once I got approved by Renee, it was easy for me to work with her because she knows exactly what my credit score is, she knows where to look for the best loan based on my criteria, and she knows other things about me, such as that I am a fixed-rate investor—I do not want an adjustable-rate mortgage or interest-only payments. She knows my mentality. She knows what percentage I will put down on a property, so all I need to do is e-mail her and say, "I'm putting a contract on 123 Main Street," and she handles the transaction from there.

I do the entire closing out of state, get my documents notarized, overnight the package back to her or to the title company that has instructions, and the deal closes. Therefore, even though I could go online to one of the many companies that does online loans, and I'm sure that company would do a good job, I'm more comfortable dealing with Renee—even if I have to pay a little more in origination fees (which I don't believe I do; Renee is as flexible as any online lender, which I know because I've checked). I simply prefer to work with Renee because I've developed a good relationship with her, which wouldn't be the case if I bought another property through an online lender. If I did that, I'd have to start over from scratch.

Finally, keep in mind that there are limits on the number and amount of loans that an investor can do on a conventional basis. Renee provides the following information:

> *Conventional guidelines allow ten investment properties, with a combination of up to $1.2 million in liens. However, some lenders offer in-house investor products that have rates very close to conventional rates. In these instances, some lenders don't care how many mortgages an investor has, as long as they do not have more than $1.2 million in mortgages on investment properties. Other lenders allow up to six investment properties with a $2 million limit in liens through their in-house products. In-house products have varied guidelines and can be very close to conventional rates.*

Questions to Ask a Bank When Seeking Financing for Real Estate

If you're going to talk to a bank and you're going to use conventional means to get financing, here are some questions to ask your banker.

- *"What is my personal spending limit, both secured and unsecured?"* Essentially, you're asking the bank how much money it will lend you. A *secured* loan is secured by a piece of real estate or some other collateral (e.g., a car or a mobile home); in the event that you don't repay your loan, the bank can take that real estate or other collateral away from you. *Unsecured* means that there's no collateral whatsoever; the loan is secured only by your signature on the loan documents. Banks are typically not willing to give unsecured loans unless you already have a banking relationship.

- *"What do I have to do to get approval?"* You need to know what the bank will require from you up front. Do you need a written verification of income? If you have passive investments, such as dividends from stocks, is the bank going to look at your bank receipts? Is the bank going to want to talk about any other property you may own? Will the bank want to look at the other property? If the property you are trying to purchase is intended for a rental, the bank will need to know what the vacancy rate is in the area or will base it on a 75 percent occupancy rate as a general rule of thumb. In other words, you need to know what factors the bank takes into consideration and what information the bank wants you to provide in order for you to get approval for that loan.

- *"Do you pool your loans?"* Is the bank a branch-based lender? There are *nonportfolio lenders*, who will pool, and *portfolio lenders*, who don't pool. Here's what this means: a portfolio lender tends to keep its loans in-house, meaning that the bank will collect the payments every month. In contrast, a nonportfolio lender will pool the loans and sell those loans to others. Portfolio lenders have more flexibility in their decision-making process.

- *"What are the bank's requirements on investor loans?"* Is the bank making investor loans right now, or has it slowed down? Are its loan requirements stricter? You want to know this because if you're trying to develop a relationship with a banker, you want to choose a bank that's still in a lending mode. If the bank is *not* in a lending mode, you'll just be beating your head against the wall trying to get a decent deal from that lender. And you need to know what your deal from the lender is going to be before you put in an offer to buy a piece of real estate, so that you'll know what your costs will be.

What a Bank Requires from You When It Lends You Money

After you've asked the questions discussed in the previous section, the next step in working with a bank involves providing the documents the bank needs in order to give you a loan. First, you'll fill out an application. Then the bank will want to see the information listed in Checklist 9-1.

Checklist 9-1 Information and Documentation Required by a Bank before It Will Lend Money

❑ The contract—i.e., the purchase agreement you have with the seller of the property.

❑ A financial statement that shows your personal assets and whether you own any other real estate. Here, the bank is essentially looking at a balance sheet (i.e., your personal balance sheet) to see what your assets are, what your liabilities are, and what your net worth is in order to determine whether you're a good financial risk.

❑ Verification of cash for the down payment on the property.

❑ Savings accounts and bank statements, as well as any type of retirement information.

❑ Your credit report, to see what your FICO score is.

The bank will also do other due diligence:

- It will look at the property itself to see if it's going to be appraised for the amount borrowed; if the appraisal is lower than the amount that you're paying for the property, the bank will not make the loan.
- In addition to doing an appraisal, the bank will usually also want a survey of the property done, to make sure it knows where the property lines are.
- The bank will verify any leases.
- The bank will verify the property taxes.
- The bank will make sure that there is an insurance binder—i.e., that there is homeowners' insurance on the property.

These are typical procedures for lenders, so don't be surprised when your bank requests this information from you and takes these steps before it agrees to make a loan to you.

Find Out in Advance What the
Bank's Fees Are for Making Loans

When you get a loan from a lender (that is, from a conventional lender, not via owner financing), several fees are required; these are listed in Checklist 9-2. You need to take all fees into account. Get an estimate of what those fees will be, so that you have your costs covered.

Renee Falgout mentions an additional cost on some loans:

Lenders will impose mortgage insurance (MI) on loans where the loan amount is over 80 percent of the purchase price. This averages $119 a month on a $150,000 purchase. If you are going to finance more than 80 percent of the purchase price, it's almost always better to get a second loan to cover anything over 80 percent and have two mortgage payments rather than pay for MI because the lender feels the loan is risky. Secure a first loan of 80 percent and then a second loan for the rest. While your first loan of 80 percent of the purchase price might be at 6 percent and your second loan of the remaining 20 percent might be at 7.5 percent, your total monthly payment will still be less than the payment on the single loan of 100 percent with the MI.

Lines of Credit to Finance
Real Estate Investments

In addition to mortgages, there are other ways to finance real estate investments. For example, some investors will use credit lines: they will get an equity line of credit, either by putting a home equity loan on a property they currently own or by getting an individual line of credit that they can tap into when they need the money to go out and buy a property.

Ask the seller . . . to finance the sale for you, or to do a second mortgage . . . so that you don't need to have as much to qualify on the first mortgage.

Checklist 9-2 Bank Fees Required for All Mortgages

❑ An application fee, which varies from lender to lender and by type of loan.

❑ A fee for the appraisal. This is typically between $250 and $400 on residential real estate.

❑ The cost of getting a loan, which is known as the origination fee. Costs can depend on the type of loan you're getting. Occasionally, you might see advertised "0 points origination fees." Most often, however, if someone is advertising no origination fees, the cost of the loan (the interest rate) is going to be higher. Nothing in life is free!

❑ Recording fees, due to the land recorder's office for the recording of the deed. Costs are determined by the recorder's office.

❑ The escrow costs for title. Title costs more in some states than in others, so check with a local title company if you are interested in knowing what you will pay for title and escrow costs.

There's a difference between owner-occupied lending and non-owner-occupied financing: for investment properties—i.e., non-owner-occupied property—you *usually* need to make a larger down payment. This is determined by the loan-to-value (LTV) ratio, which is the loan amount divided by the fair market value of the property. This is why, when you refinance property, the lender will require a new appraisal. The lender wants to see the LTV.

The required LTV will be lower (generally around 80 percent LTV or less) in a non-owner-occupied property, because with an owner-occupied property—i.e., a property that you're living in—the lender is assuming that you will do everything in your power to make your loan payments, because if you don't, the lender will foreclose on the property and take it back, and you will be forcibly evicted from what you thought was your home. In contrast, with a non-owner-occupied property, the lender's perception is that it's easier for you as an investor to walk away from that property if you're not able to afford your loan repayment.

Owner Financing

In many cases, a sharp investor will ask if the seller of the property has equity in the property. If so, you should ask the seller if he or she would be willing to finance the sale for you, or to do a second mortgage on the property so that you don't have to have as much to qualify for the first mortgage. With this approach to financing, you can buy more property and use it as either a long-term investment, to generate cash flow, or to meet whatever financial goal you have.

Wendy had a property in Sedona, Arizona. She worked for a high-tech firm and made an excellent income. She saved 25 percent of her entire salary each year for 10 years and amassed over $500,000 in savings. She wanted to quit her day job and open a bed-and-breakfast accommodation in an artists' community not far from her home.

Wendy bought her home 10 years ago for $347,000. She decided to sell it so that she could have more money to put into her new business. The home was appraised for $975,000. Diane and her husband were relocating to Arizona. They fell in love with the property. Diane had been an investor in real estate for 10 years. She and her husband wanted to buy Wendy's house as a home for them to live in. Diane asked Wendy if she would consider taking a second mortgage. Diane would get a first loan from the bank to pay off Wendy's mortgage plus some.

Wendy decided that some income might not be a bad idea. She and Diane negotiated a full-price offer of $975,000. Diane got a conventional mortgage for $575,000 and put $100,000 down, and Wendy took back a second mortgage for $300,000. Wendy was able to pay off her previous mortgage and still have $300,000 cash, plus she receives monthly payments on the other $300,000.

This is a win-win for both parties. Diane has more borrowing power to buy investment properties; since Wendy's second mortgage is not a conventional loan, it is not part of the credit reporting system and would not show up as debt to a lender. Between her savings and the cash she got from selling her property to Diane, Wendy got cash to infuse into her B&B and a decent monthly income.

From a tax standpoint, you should hold the property—if you can afford to—for at least a year because of the tax write-offs (which will be covered later in this chapter). When you hold the property for a year or longer and then sell it, you are taxed at a lower capital gains tax rate; if you hold it for one year or less, your gains are taxed as ordinary income. Savvy investors try to hold property for at least a year, if not longer.

Wrap-Around Mortgages

Wrap-around mortgages are a popular financing strategy, but you need to be careful with this approach. Under this arrangement, the seller retains the title to the property and "wraps" it. What this means is, if the seller has a $50,000 mortgage on a property and she sells that property to you for $200,000, then you will be making payments to her on a $200,000 seller-financed mortgage. Then the seller takes part of your mortgage payment to her and uses it to make her mortgage payment to her lender. She then pockets the difference every month between your mortgage payment to her and her mortgage payment to the lender, which generates a monthly cash flow for her.

> *Be cautious* [when doing wrap-around mortgages] . . .
> *read your documents and your contracts and look*
> *out for a due-on-sale clause.*

In other words, she's wrapped her mortgage around the new mortgage—*your* mortgage. When you use this arrangement, you must be cautious; you must read your documents and your contracts and look out for a due-on-sale clause, because that could have an impact on your financing. If there *is* a due-on-sale clause, that means that the seller should have sold the property, paid the bank back what she owed it, and had a clear sale. And if the lender finds out that the original property owner has wrapped the mortgage, the lender has the right to call the loan due and payable.

> *If you can convince a seller to owner-finance the*
> *sale for you, you will increase your borrowing*
> *ability on the next transaction.*

Wrap-around mortgages differ from owner financing in that the latter generally involves a free-and-clear property; nine times out of ten, the owner is creating a whole new loan with a note and deed of trust. In contrast, with a wrap-around arrangement, the seller basically retains title to the property and continues to make mortgage payments to the lender, and the new owner, in turn, makes mortgage payments to the seller.

Why is this important? Because up until recently, interest rates have been at a 40-year low. Now that rates are rising, the bank would be taking "a loss" if it allowed the sale while retaining the lower interest rate. Therefore, if the original loan was a low-interest-rate loan, the bank could be making more money from a new loan to somebody else than from a wrap-around mortgage. The bank may or may not call the loan, but there have been plenty of cases where banks have called their loans, so the new owner is required to pay off the loan, and that can run into a real cash flow problem. Again, if you're going to use this approach to financing your property, proceed with caution and understand up front that this could happen to you.

People who are tired of being landlords . . .
will consider seller financing because
they understand real estate and money.

Private Financing

If your strategy is to buy only one property a year, then working with a bank is the easiest way to do that, provided you can establish a good relationship with a particular bank. In general, I don't advocate trying to be too creative when it comes to financing real estate with a bank.

If you can convince a seller to owner-finance the sale for you, you will increase your borrowing ability on the next transaction; furthermore, if you are not able to get conventional financing, you can still get into the property thanks to the seller who financed the transaction for you. From the *seller's* perspective, owner financing makes sense if the seller has equity in the property and doesn't need all cash. The seller can charge the buyer a higher rate of interest than the seller could typically make on other investments.

For example, suppose money market accounts are offering 5 percent interest. If you own a property that you're interested in selling, you could offer a mortgage on that property and charge 7 percent interest—plus, you would have collateral on that loan (the property itself). Is 7 percent better than 5 percent? You bet it is. So the seller gets a down payment on the property, plus monthly payments from the buyer, which include interest. The worst that can happen is that the buyer doesn't pay—in which case, the seller can take the property back and resell it. Chances are the property will have gone up in value, so the seller will not be out any money.

Suppose you're buying a $200,000 property with a 10 percent down payment of $20,000, and you financed the $180,000 at 7 percent interest for 15 years. The seller is getting principal and interest payments. If, after two years, you can no longer make your payments, the seller has still had that income stream for two years, plus the seller gets to keep your $20,000 down payment. Therefore, the seller is in a good position to resell the property and make more money. Personally, I love doing owner-financed mortgages, and a lot of investors would rather buy mortgages from sellers than buy real estate.

For clarification, seller financing means that the seller carries the loan on the property that he or she sold to they buyer. Private financing can mean a private loan, either secured by the real estate the borrower is purchasing or unsecured. A good source of sellers who are willing to finance is people who are tired of being landlords and want to get out of renting property. They will consider seller financing because they understand real estate and money. They build equity, get income, and have security because they have collateral, as the mortgage has been recorded. In the event that the buyer doesn't pay, the ex-landlord turned seller has something to fall back on. The seller will make more money from seller financing than he or she would have by buying an insurance annuity (for example), because the interest on this loan is going to be higher than the interest on an annuity.

Therefore, someone with money, somebody with a lot of equity in a property, an older property owner who may be interested in downsizing, or someone who's just looking for an opportunity to increase his or her monthly income is a good candidate for seller finance or lending money.

In the late 1980s, seller financing was a popular investment strategy because sellers could get as much as 12 to 12½ percent interest. Today, these rates have dropped because interest rates in general have dropped, so the benefits of owner financing do follow the real estate market. Nevertheless, you will generally pay a higher interest rate in a seller-financed sale than you would pay a lender unless you are working with someone who does not charge a higher-than-market interest rate.

If you are out looking for property, and you end up negotiating with a seller, one of the questions you should ask the seller is, "What type of mortgage do you currently have on your home?" If the seller tells you that the property is free and clear (i.e., the seller has completely paid off her mortgage), then you should ask the seller if she would consider financing the sale. And you should make your pitch for why that would be a good opportunity for her to make money. The seller can then make that decision for herself; she can check with her financial advisor, and I always recommend that. Personally, I'm happy to sit down with someone's financial advisor and discuss the merits of owner financing so that the advisor understands it and can better advise his or her client.

> *As interest rates are increasing, more people will*
> *be interested in seller financing . . . this . . . will create*
> *an inventory of seller-financed mortgages for sale.*

People should not feel they're being taken advantage of or scammed when this type of investment is proposed; in contrast, this is something that people do all the time—the private-money mortgage industry is definitely alive and well. In certain parts of the country, it's one of the top ways to finance property; for example, in Texas, private financing is almost as popular as bank financing. Sellers are happy about creating seller-financed notes and receiving a higher interest rate than they would in another investment. Plus, this is a safe investment. From the buyer's standpoint, the buyer is being financed by the owner and doesn't have to worry about getting a loan from the bank, You can save that line of credit or your banking relationship for when you want to buy a property that you can't get seller financing on.

Once someone understands how to make a loan, he or she is often more comfortable with lending money than with buying property to fix up or rehab or to flip. This is primarily because, in the latter case, those investors have to deal with landlord or maintenance issues.

For example, Gail is a very successful real estate investor in Tennessee. Gail makes loans to rehabbers: she makes short-term (e.g., six-month) loans and is willing to extend a loan for another three months, and she receives 1 percent per month on that loan. She's not directly involved in the rehab; all she does is lend money to someone else who wants to buy a property. That buyer doesn't go to a bank for financing; the buyer comes to Gail instead. That person then buys a property for an average of $35,000 to $40,000, spends another $5,000 or $6,000 (about 20 percent of the purchase price) on fix-up costs, and then sells that property for a price in the high $50,000s. Gail gets paid back with interest at the time of the sale, which is usually within six months after the purchase. She rolls her profit into the next loan. Gail has been successful building capital from making loans.

If You're Considering Investing in Mortgage Notes

Another way to invest in real estate is to buy mortgage notes. Buying seller-financed notes is a business to many people. You are buying an income stream from a party who created an owner-financed note on a property that person sold. Now, for whatever reason, that person needs cash. You can buy the income stream for cash at a discount to solve this person's problem. You receive the rest of the income stream at face value (i.e., 100 cents on the dollar), which is where you profit. The difference between the discount you paid and the income you receive is your profit.

For example, a property seller who has owner-financed a sale of property for a buyer may find that she needs cash. She finds you from local ad in the local newspaper that says, "We buy notes!" You negotiate with the seller and come up with an amount that the seller is willing to take today for the future income, which is worth less than the total face value of the future payments. This is called the time value of money. Money today is more valuable than money 30 years down the road.

Suppose Ann made a $10,000 loan at 10 percent interest to Beth. Ann is receiving a payment of $132.15 a month at 10 percent interest for 10 years. Now suppose Ann needs cash to pay off a debt. Ann could sell that $132 income stream for 10 years to Cindy—except that Cindy isn't going to pay Ann $10,000 for it because Cindy knows the time value of money and knows that the future payments are worth less than what cash is worth today. Cindy explains this to Ann and asks Ann how much she needs for the note.

Cindy pays Ann only $7,500 for the note. As a result, Cindy will now receive the next 10 years of payments from Beth at $132.15, or 10 percent interest on the original $10,000 loan. That's what Cindy is going to get back on her investment, even though she paid only $7,500 for it. So Cindy's effective yield on her investment is 18 percent. Essentially, Cindy bought a promissory note at a discount from the remaining balance on the note.

Beth promised to make payments to the lender (Ann) over 10 years, in this example. Beth will now make her payments to Cindy. Both Cindy and Ann will send Beth a letter to this effect.

Why should you consider investing in real estate notes?

- There are no tenants in the note business, only payers. Any problems with improvements, the property itself, or neighbors must be dealt with by the payer on the note, not by you.
- Notes are, by definition, set up as income streams over time. Notes can be short- or long-term: the longer the term of the note, the larger the discount that the seller of the note will have to take.
- Holding a note defers some taxable profits over the same long term. Notes generate taxable interest income similar to taxable rent. If a property is sold on installments instead of for cash, some of the profit often can be deferred. Because principal is received one payment at a time, the percentage of it that represents profit is taxed, but the profit is spread out over multiple tax years.
- If the payer defaults, you keep the down payment and all the payments made to date. You can foreclose and resell the property to generate another down payment and a new note, all over again.

When you're buying mortgage notes, there are
four elements to consider: the total amount of the loan,
the interest rate, the monthly payment, and
the term in which the loan will be repaid.

Mortgage Financing and Tax Strategies

Finding discounted notes to buy can be difficult and competitive. However, there are people who do this as a business; they market and advertise for what they're interested in. Here are some marketing ideas note buyers have used to find notes:

- Put an ad in the obituary section of the newspaper with the heading "money to lend." This attracts people who have inherited notes from someone who has recently passed away. Heirs read ads in the obituary section.
- Buy mailing lists of people who may want to sell their mortgage note.
- Search courthouse records and get information on sellers who have financed sales of property and are receiving payments.

You can also search on the Internet under "private mortgages" or "seller-financed mortgages for sale."

There are so many ways to go out and find paper (i.e., discounted notes) that many investors have turned their hobby into a business—and it's a business that's becoming increasingly popular. When interest rates were low, buying notes was not as popular, because just about anybody could get a loan when interest rates were 6 percent or lower. Now, as interest rates are increasing, more people will be interested in seller financing, as this may become a more affordable option for the buyer and will create an inventory of seller-financed mortgages for sale.

When you're buying mortgage notes, there are four elements to consider: the total amount of the loan, the interest rate, the monthly payment, and the term in which the loan will be repaid. Also, you need to consider the safety of this investment, so you should look at the property. Where is the property? Has the value of the property gone up or down? You need to see what the note is worth *at the time you're considering buying it*.

If you're buying or selling seller-financed discounted mortgage notes, you have to watch out for usury laws in the state in which the note was created.

There are national institutional note buyers who pay a fee for seller- or owner-financed notes You can find such lenders on the Internet simply by searching under "private mortgages" or "discounted paper," either of which should give you a list of potential note buyers.

There are two good newsletters that cover the cash flow industry and buying notes at a discount: *Noteworthy* and *The Paper Source*. Both are written for investors, and in the back of each, there are ads placed by institutional buyers of mortgage notes. If you're interested in getting into this business, I recommend that you study *Noteworthy* and *The Paper Source*. Tell them I recommended that you contact them, and ask for a free issue, not only to check out the ads in the back, but to learn more and educate yourself on the note business, on regulatory issues, and on how other investors buy mortgages.

If you want to and are willing to work hard enough at it, you can actually make a living buying mortgages and selling them to institutional investors. In some states, you need to be licensed to do this, so check your state's licensing laws. If you're buying notes yourself as an investor, you don't need a license, because it's your money. But if you're going to broker notes, certain states consider that to be like being a mortgage broker, so you need a license.

[Doing a 1031 exchange is a very popular strategy because] *investors can . . .* **[defer]** *the taxes on their investments until they're ready to cash out altogether.*

The note business is fascinating because it offers you the opportunity to invest in real estate and diversify your portfolio without having to own any real estate directly. You can make loans from your personal accounts or from your individual retirement account—either an IRA or your 401(k) (a method covered later in this chapter). Realtors also use this approach to financing.

One word of caution: if you're buying or selling seller-financed discounted mortgage notes, you have to watch out for usury laws in the state where the note was created. This is very important, because each state has usury limits. Usury is the maximum interest rate that a lender can charge for making a loan. For example, in Florida, the limit is 18 percent. Private lenders are subject to usury laws, so you need to be careful that you're not going above the usury limits if you decide to make a loan, because if you do, you will have a problem with the state.

The Benefits of Tax Write-offs

When you own property, there are some wonderful tax benefits. For instance, you can depreciate your property over a period of time, which provides a tax advantage—while the property itself increases in value. Of course, when you sell that property, you must recapture the depreciation.

Tax benefits are one of the top reasons that investors buy real estate. If you hold a property for a year or longer, when you sell that property, you will pay only capital gains tax on your profit, instead of having to pay at your current tax rate on ordinary income. For example, at this writing, the capital gains rate is 15 percent; if you're in the highest tax bracket—i.e., the 30 to 35 percent rate—and you hold a property for a year or longer, you can pay only 15 percent in taxes instead of 30 to 35 percent when you sell that property. That's a substantial tax benefit.

Also, if you have a principal residence and you are living in that principal residence right now, you can exclude up to $250,000 from capital gains if you are single and up to $500,000 if you're married. Therefore, a lot of people will buy a property, live in it for a couple of years, then turn around and sell it and move up to a nicer property, without paying capital gains tax. This is another financial strategy that people utilize, especially if they're simply buying property to live in.

Doing a 1031 Exchange to Defer Capital Gains Tax

Another financial strategy is the 1031 exchange. Instead of selling a property and taking the cash from the sale, you can do a 1031 exchange (1031 is the section of the Internal Revenue Code that covers exchanges). The IRS allows you to exchange (or trade) like-kind property for other like-kind property. For example, suppose you own a three-bedroom, two-bath house in Colorado, and you decide you don't want to invest in Colorado anymore. You have $100,000 in equity in the property. Suppose the tenant you're renting this property to wants to buy the property. You could sell the property outright and make $100,000 on the deal. In this case, you would pay the tax on the gain. Or you could do a 1031 exchange: you can trade that property for another like-kind property anywhere in the United States where you get to defer the tax. No tax would be due at the point of sale or in the current year the property was exchanged.

Also, the IRS definition of "like-kind" doesn't mean that you have to exchange your three-bedroom, two-bath house in Colorado for another three-bedroom, two-bath house in Colorado. Instead, the definition is much broader than that.

- You can trade your property for two or three properties (three is the IRS maximum).
- You can trade it for property anywhere in the United States.
- You can exchange your property for land, for a commercial property, or for another residential investment property. The IRS requires only that the trade be for *another investment property*, meaning that it's not for your personal use—you can't live in any of the properties you acquire through a 1031 exchange.

Investors can keep building their portfolios and deferring the taxes on their investments until they're ready to cash out altogether. At that point, they will probably be in a lower tax bracket and not interested in managing real estate.

The rules of the 1031: once you've sold a property, you can't touch the funds. A third party has to hold the funds for you, and that's where the qualified intermediary (QI) comes in. The QI holds your money in a bonded escrow account to help facilitate the 1031 exchange for you. You select the QI, who acts as an agent.

When you sell a property to a buyer, you tell your title company that you're going to do a 1031 exchange. You have your QI work with the title company so that it knows not to distribute the funds to you. Once you've closed on the sale of your property, the title company will send the proceeds to the QI. You have 45 days from the day of closing to identify replacement property and six months to close. If you go beyond the 45 days, you cannot exchange the property; *you have only 45 days* to find the like-kind property. This may sound like a long time, but for most investors, it's not. Therefore, you should be looking for new property before your sale. A good time to look would be when you're under contract but before the closing; you should be out pounding the streets looking for property during that period.

Also, you can trade your property for as many as three new pieces of property. Therefore, if you have a lot of equity in the property that you're selling, the 1031 exchange is a great way to leverage it into multiple properties with one exchange.

Once you find the new property you want, you put a purchase offer together and put the property under contract. The QI is listed in the contract, which indicates that you're going to do a 1031 exchange. Then the QI goes ahead and does all the work to make sure the exchange is done legally and doesn't violate any IRS rules. You've got to be careful, because you want to make sure you exchange all the proceeds you received from the sale of your old property for the new property (or properties). If you don't use *all* the money you received from the sale, you'll be subject to tax (called *boot*) on any money that you did not use. It's almost like taking that money out and having to pay tax on it.

A 1031 exchange is a very good tool to utilize, although obviously you won't be in a position to do a 1031 until you've acquired some real estate so that you have a property you can sell and exchange. The tax benefits are great because you're deferring the tax until you're at a stage in your life when you're ready to pay those taxes.

To invest in real estate through a retirement fund, you need to have a truly "self-directed" IRA or 401(k).

Tax-Deferred Real Estate Investing: Using Your IRA or 401(k)

Most people are not aware that you can use your Individual Retirement Account (IRA) or, in some cases (but not all), your 401(k) to buy real estate, make loans, and buy leases. In fact, there are more than 47 different types of assets that you can invest in through your IRA or 401(k); real estate is only one of these. If you have a 403(b) retirement plan, you *cannot* use this to invest in real estate.

To invest in real estate through a retirement fund, you need to have a truly "self-directed" IRA or 401(k). For example, Hewlett-Packard's 401(k) plan is just one example of a plan that is *not* self-directed, because this company does corporate matches with HP stock; also, some investment advisors (including Charles Schwab and Fidelity) will say that they offer self-directed retirement accounts, but they don't; instead, they direct your money into their mutual funds.

What's important about self-directed retirement funds is that *you are in control.* You are identifying your investments. You are putting those investments—in this case, real estate—under contract. You are making sure that your investments are being followed through, and although you are not managing your investments directly (because you need to work through a third party, as discussed in the next section), you are managing the process because the fund is truly self-directed. You need to understand that this is not like buying mutual funds, stocks, bonds, equities, CDs, or Treasuries; it's not conventional investing. Investing through an IRA or 401(k) is not for everyone, but it is another approach you might want to consider, because it's almost like having another bank account to tap, and you're able to use money that you've set aside for your future.

For example, last year, I used my IRA to make a loan to a friend for $55,000 at a 12½ percent interest rate for one year. That loan was not secured. At the end of one year, my friend paid back the principal plus 12½ percent interest to my IRA. That interest amounted to about $6,000, and I did not have to pay tax on it. If I had made that loan personally—in other words, *not* using my IRA—then I would have to pay tax on that interest. By lending through my IRA, I got to defer the tax. If you have a Roth IRA and use that to lend money, then the return on your investment is tax-free.

To find out if your 401(k) is self-directed and will allow you to use your retirement funds to invest in real estate, read your retirement plan documents or talk to your 401(k) administrator *before* you try to buy any real estate through your 401(k) if you are currently employed by the company that is contributing to your 401(k). Once you have separated from that company (e.g., quit or retired), you can roll the 401(k) into an IRA to invest in real estate. In smaller companies (e.g., those with fewer than 10 employees), your plan probably has more flexibility.

---

*If you're going to work with a custodian, make sure
the custodian deposits the cash in your
retirement account in an FDIC-insured account.*

When you leave the company where you have a retirement account, you can take your 401(k) funds and roll them into an IRA, and you can use that IRA to invest in real estate (or anything else you want to invest in). There are no tax ramifications to doing that as long as you roll the funds into a traditional IRA. If you roll your 401(k) into a Roth IRA, you pay taxes on the funds in the 401(k), because the Roth is an after-tax investment, but any profits you make from this Roth IRA in the future will come to you tax-free. If you don't want to pay the tax, you can roll your 401(k) funds into a traditional IRA and then use that traditional IRA to invest in real estate. One final point: if you're going to use your IRA to invest in real estate, the lender must issue you a *nonrecourse loan* because the IRA is guaranteeing the payments, not you personally.

Working with a Custodian

There are a few companies that will act as either a third-party record keeper, administrator, or custodial bank to hold your funds. As you know, you are not allowed to hold your own retirement funds, but you can indeed buy real estate (or other investments) with your retirement dollars as long as you go through a third-party administrator or record keeper. A third-party administrator does all of the IRS recordkeeping on behalf of your IRA or 401(k). I recommend the Entrust Group (www.theentrustgroup.com), which is the nation's largest administrator of truly self-directed individual retirement accounts. Truly self-directed means that you, the IRA owner, identify (find) the investments. You instruct the administrator that you are buying ABC property with your retirement plan. The administrator double-checks to make sure that everything is titled correctly and that the documents are correct. The administrator follows your instructions. A good administrator should never give you investment advice and should not even recommend financial advisors, but it should be able to tell you that the transactions that you want to do are legal and are not prohibited by the IRS.

Entrust has more than 30 offices around the country, so you have the opportunity to do business with someone in your local marketplace. This is a unique advantage and also an opportunity to visit one of Entrust's specialists and learn more about this subject. Entrust employees are trained to know the local marketplace and to work with individual investors in each area.

In contrast, all other custodian companies simply have an 800 phone number (and in some cases, they don't even have *that*, so you need to make a long-distance phone call); either way, when you call a central number, you'll be talking to people who won't understand or know your *local* market. In addition, Entrust employees are specially trained to help investors know what they're doing and see that you have some education on how acquiring investments in your retirement plan works. This is important, because when you truly self-direct your retirement funds, you will find your own investment properties and put them under contract.

If you're going to work with a custodian, make sure the custodian deposits the cash in an FDIC-insured account. Not all custodians do this. I would personally recommend that your cash be with a FDIC institution. For more information on this subject, visit www.theentrustgroup.com and take a look at the Virtual Tour; it is an easy step-by-step process that you can follow.

Finding a Lender That's Right for You

One last point: if you're more comfortable working with women professionals, there are subsets of the Mortgage Bankers Association and the National Association of Mortgage Brokers. You can network to find a female banker, who might spend more time trying to understand what you want to accomplish as a women business owner and as a woman investor.

Conclusion

In the end, you are responsible for your own financial picture. Utilize the financial strategies described in this chapter and the information presented here as just what it is: information. Here are some final tips:

Mortgage Financing and Tax Strategies

- Get the best lender or mortgage broker you can find.
- Try to stick with fixed-rate loans if you're going to leverage yourself and borrow money.
- Utilize some of the techniques described, like investing through your IRA or 401(k).
- When you're calculating and estimating what your profitability will be, realize that there are wonderful tax breaks for investing in real estate: you get depreciation, leverage (if you desire), and tax benefits. Also, you have the opportunity for appreciation.

Financing property—i.e., borrowing money to buy real estate—is not a bad thing. On the other hand, if your strategy is to be free and clear, then you need to set yourself up to do that by getting the shortest-term loan available, making extra payments each month, making two payments a month instead of one, or not spending your tenant payments, but reinvesting them in the property. Just stick to your plan of action. Utilize these skills, and you will get ahead financially.

10

When and How to Sell and How to Stage a Property for Resale

This chapter discusses the best *time* to sell a property and the best way to *sell* a property. There are many easy and inexpensive ways to make your property look more marketable, which should bring you more money and increase your profit on your real estate investment. Clean up the property, do simple repairs and minor fix-ups, decorate it nicely, and you're good to go. Let's take a look at some of these great ideas that can bring you more opportunity, help your property sell faster, and make more profit.

The Best Time to Sell a Property

The best time to sell a property is when you don't have to. You want to get top dollar for a property, so you don't want to be in a position where you have to settle for a lower price because you need the money right now.

Having said that, the best time to sell a property is in the spring because people are accustomed to looking for properties in the spring. Therefore, the stream of people who will be looking for real estate is going to be stronger in the spring, up to the early summer months. That's a time frame that many real estate professionals have used for years.

Generally, real estate investors will not sell property unless they're going to make a profit. They view their properties as opportunities: they buy a property; they may then fix it up to sell, lease it for a while (as discussed in Chapter 8), or just flip it (as discussed in Chapter 5), depending on their particular strategy. In any case, the best time to sell a property is definitely when you don't have to.

The best time to sell a property is when you don't have to.

Before you need to sell, do a market analysis of the area around your property to determine what the market is really doing, how quickly properties are selling, and at what price they are selling, full price or having to drop the price in order to sell. If you're not motivated to sell, is this the best time? You can determine that by finding out how quickly properties have gone up in value over the past year. Many real estate offices can provide you with this information. You can also research this online.

When you're selling a property, you want to begin with your goal in mind. Know when you plan to sell the property, how much you plan to sell it for, and what you plan to do with the proceeds. If you are purchasing another investment property, you might want to consider doing a 1031 exchange into that property and deferring the tax. If you are cashing out altogether, you will be paying tax on any profits at whatever the capital gains rate is at the time of the sale. You must hold the property for at least one year to be eligible for the capital gains tax rate rather than the tax rate on ordinary income, which is much higher.

The Best Way to Sell a Property

You want to maximize your exposure; therefore, you should use classified ads, real estate publications, and the MLS (multiple listing service). Also, consider working with a Realtor (as discussed in Chapter 6), who will list your property for sale, make referrals, create handouts, and do the promotion to try to sell the property for the amount you have listed.

Finally, tell everyone you know that you have a property that you're getting ready to sell.

Ideally, you should try to sell your property on your own rather than listing it with a Realtor. If you can sell it on your own, you won't have to pay a real estate commission, and this gives you a little bit more flexibility in the price if a buyer wants to negotiate with you.

That said, if you decide to go ahead and work with a Realtor in selling your property, make sure you give the Realtor the names of parties who have looked at your property before it was listed. The Realtor is not entitled to a commission if the party who purchases the real estate came through prior to the signing of your listing agreement.

How do you know what buyers really want? . . . Visit a couple of model homes. Look at the floor plan. Look at the list of options that are standard.

You want to sell what the buyer wants. Buyers have certain guidelines in mind. You do not want to have a bright green house with blue and pink walls or some other color scheme of that type that *you* might find attractive. Instead, you want to try to have the property look as neat and tidy and spacious as possible. Use neutral colors for reselling.

How do you know what buyers really want? The best research you can do is to visit a couple of model homes. Look at the floor plan. Look at the list of options that are standard—e.g., the refrigerator, a microwave, a dishwasher. Evaluate how your property compares with new homes on the market. Will the seller get more value with your property for the same price as another? What are the unique selling points of your home? Think of new homes as an opportunity to do research for ideas to make your property more marketable. As mentioned throughout this book, but especially in Chapter 3, you make money when you buy—for the right price and on the right terms. Therefore, you need to factor in all the costs discussed in previous chapters (refer back to Chapter 3 and Chapter 5 for costs of flipping or rehabbing): loan origination fees, closing costs associated with the property, taxes, and so on. All of that needs to be factored into your profitability. What are you going to net in the end? That is really the question.

Putting in the right furnishings, adding plants,
[and] *making the investment property look like a home*
[makes it more marketable].

If you want to be able to get top dollar for a property, you need to make the property as desirable as possible. Sometimes, if you try to sell a property too quickly, you will not be able to recoup all the expenses you've incurred in buying the property in the first place. In that case, you may be better off with a lease option (described in detail in Chapter 11), or you may be better off holding the property for some period of time before you try to sell it because you're capitalizing on the fact that it will have appreciated in value.

How to Stage a Property So That It Will Sell

Let's look at some quick fixes, cleanups, and repairs that you can do to make your property marketable—to make it something that a buyer would want to buy.

Consider Hiring a Staging Company

First, let's look at decorating the property. In general, women are great decorators. For example, I know three different women right now who have done such a great job of decorating their own properties for sale that they are now in the business of staging properties for sale. These entrepreneurial women help sell a property quickly by putting in the right furnishings, adding plants, and making the investment property look like a home—that is, warm, comfortable, and desirable.

All three of these women started out just buying homes. For example, Colleen bought her own home, fixed it up, and made the landscaping beautiful, with little flower boxes—in essence, she made her home look like a dollhouse. Then she got bored; she didn't work outside the home, so she spent all her time making her home look beautiful, and once it did, she wanted a new project. She sold that house and bought another. She lived in each of her homes for two or three years, and she fixed each of them up. When she sold each house, she got top dollar just from making those cosmetic changes to the property. That's a great strategy.

When and How to Sell and How to Stage a Property

Colleen has been so successful at decorating homes and selling them at a profit that she recently started a staging business. She comes in, looks at the property, determines what it needs in order to show well and be attractive to buyers, and puts in furnishings and decorations that the seller rents from her—i.e., these furnishings are sort of property props. Once the property is sold, she removes her furnishings, wall hangings, flowers, and everything else that she's provided, and she gets a nice fee.

She has a flair for this. She even does different themes to match the outside construction. The furnishings match the style. For example, Colleen had a southwestern-style home complete with a stucco body and a tile roof. All of the furniture she used in her interior was southwestern: furnishings, decorations, and the right style of paintings or other artwork to match that southwestern style. Realtors in the area use Colleen to fix existing homes, adding the sparkle that they need in order to go from plain to pretty. The seller rents her services, which include putting in all this furniture, and Colleen earns somewhere in the neighborhood of $750 per month per house (while it is on the market) for doing this.

> *The number one way to improve the way a property looks is to start with a simple cleanup.*

Moreover, she doesn't even have to store those props—she doesn't own them. Instead, she borrows them from various local furniture companies and puts out cards out that say "supplied by" or "compliments of" XYZ Furniture Company or Jane Doe, Painter. She makes deals with all the local furniture companies and different amenity-type companies (for things like canisters and other cute decorations for kitchens, bathrooms, and so on). And she gets the use of these materials for free from the companies that give her the furniture; those companies benefit because she's essentially advertising their products, and they get business from the people who see their products actually installed in a real home.

Staging properties is a phenomenal business opportunity. Colleen has been a successful investor, living in the homes she's bought, fixing them up, then trading up to another property or selling them and buying another property, and doing the same thing over and over again. She does a beautiful job, and the properties she stages sell very quickly.

There are staging companies around the country that an investor can go to, or you might consider doing this yourself. You can find staging companies through local real estate offices, although if you're not working with a Realtor to sell your property, some agencies may not be willing to recommend staging companies to you because you're not a client. You can also find staging companies through local property managers, who will occasionally refer individuals who are relocating for the short term and want to rent furnishings instead of buying them to a staging company. You can also call your local Chamber of Commerce or Better Business Bureau, or go online to look for staging companies in your area.

Simple Do-It-Yourself Decorating Ideas to Make Your Property Look Great

If you don't want to use a staging company, you can still, on your own, make a property more marketable so that buyers want it. The number one way to improve the way a property looks is to start with a simple cleanup. Here are some easy do-it-yourself decorating ideas.

Paint the Entire Interior of the House.   This makes the whole place look clean, new, and bright.

Install New Window Blinds.   You can get these at Home Depot, Sears, or other home-improvement discounters. You don't have to have customized draperies; you just need to make the property look cute and clean. In some regions, especially very sunny areas—for example, in Arizona—you might also consider installing window film. It's expensive, but it eliminates the heat problems.

Upgrade the Floor Registers and Heat Grates.   Typically, the vents in the floor that the heat or air conditioning comes out of are ugly, brownish-colored vents with striped openings, but you can install decorative brass or bronze registers with scroll designs that make the property look classy. Some people may think these are unimportant, but improving them can make a big difference in how the property looks.

If There's Paneling, Remove It. Paint the walls instead. Paneling dates a property (it's very 1970s), and it makes a room look smaller; painting makes a room look larger.

Update the Carpet. You should update the carpet, too, if it needs it—for example, if it shows a lot of wear. You don't want shag; it, too, dates from more than 30 years ago. Instead, you want something neutral—either Berber or a plush carpet—that is easy to maintain and that will be durable in case the buyer will have a number of people living in that property, because such buyers will take the durability of the carpet into consideration when they look at a property.

A lot of sellers will offer a buyer a $5,000 allowance toward new carpet or paint, but I don't recommend that. Instead, I recommend that you just paint and install carpet in a neutral color that's not offensive. If the buyer wants to change it at some point, she can do that at her own expense. But, in the end, you're going to be better off than you are if you give somebody an allowance, because allowances are negotiable—the buyer may come back and say to you, "I want a *$10,000* allowance instead of the $5,000 allowance you offered." If the project is completed, there is no room to negotiate. Instead, try to do the cosmetic fix-ups that I've described.

Install New Light Switches. Give the dimmer switches in the dining room and the switchplates and plate covers throughout the interior a fresh look. Buy something new. Even if they're just cheap white plastic, get new plates that look clean.

If There's Wall Damage, Repair and Paint the Walls. These are easy fixes, and they're things any woman can do. You don't have to hire a contractor to do these simple fixes.

Check for–and Replace–Any Rotting Wood. For instance, some parts of the country have termites, so you want to make sure that there are no termites in the property before you put it on the market. And if, for example, you have rotting wood on the windowsills, get that fixed—it's as easy as nailing a strip of wood over the windowsill and painting it.

Remember, anything that even looks like a problem is going to turn off potential buyers. Therefore, I recommend that you do easy, cheap, quick fixes that make the property look better and more marketable.

Your goal is to make [your] property something you can be proud of, so that potential buyers will fall in love with the property and see themselves living there.

Make Sure the Property Is Clean

When you're trying to sell a property, your goal is to make that property something you can be proud of, so that potential buyers will fall in love with the property and see themselves living there. You want them to walk in and be wowed, so that they'll say, "Hey, this is worth a little bit extra." Make sure the property is clean inside and out, especially if it has been a rental. If you don't want to clean it yourself, hire a professional cleaning company. Just make sure the property is spic and span; you do not want dirt in the house.

Here's a great example of how dirt can influence a buying decision. A couple of years ago, I looked at a property to buy. There were dead bugs—specifically, spiders—in all the corners. The place also needed a thorough paint job. There probably wasn't anything structurally wrong with this property, but it just turned me off. I didn't want to touch anything.

A clean, attractive property will bring you more dollars in the long run.

Many studies have shown that you can get more money for a clean house, whether you are renting it or selling it, than you will get if it's even just dusty. If you are the buyer, you may be able to capitalize on a property that does not show well.

Here's another example: one buyer bought a home on a corner property for herself and her husband. The place was filthy, but there was nothing structurally wrong with the property. She got it at a good price (probably because the house was so dirty and *looked* to be in such poor condition), and, of course, she cleaned it thoroughly because she was going to live there. It was so dirty that every time she ran a rag over a surface and rinsed the rag, the water in the bucket turned black, and she had to keep changing the water. Sure enough, just a couple of years later, when she sold that house to relocate to another state, she was able to resell it for $30,000 more than she paid for it.

Moreover, all these suggestions for making a property look nice are things that women can do *easily*—and most of us enjoy doing this type of decorating. Of course, few people enjoy cleaning, but everyone likes looking at a nice, clean property, and if a place needs to be cleaned, either clean it yourself or hire someone to clean it for you. A clean, attractive property will bring you more dollars in the long run. Checklist 10-1 offers some simple staging suggestions for do-it-yourselfers.

Checklist 10-1   Do-It-Yourself Staging
Tips for Home Sellers

DOs:

- ❏ Do pick up recent home decorating magazines to find low-cost fix-up ideas that will make the home more up-to-date.

- ❏ Do have a third party look at your home and give you her opinion on what cosmetic changes she would make to help the home sell.

- ❏ Do dedicate an area (preferably a bedroom, if the house is big enough) to a home office, because so many professionals work from home. Put in a computer, a desk, and a bookcase corner. Make sure this is near electrical and phone outlets.

- ❏ Do focus on the areas where the family congregates—the kitchen, the living room, or the great room. Add special touches, such as pictures on the refrigerator, area rugs that make the rooms look larger but have a cozy feel, and so on.

- ❏ Do clean out cabinets and closets. Don't have them loaded up. The closets should have a spacious feel to them.

❏ Do buy a new bedspread; it will make the room look fresh.

❏ Do install new lighting that is simple but adequate in wattage, and leave it on when showing the home.

DON'Ts:

❏ Don't use silk or fake flower arrangements. They gather dust and draw negative attention.

❏ Don't leave pet food in the dishes. If you have a pet, clean the water and food dishes. There is nothing worse than viewing a home and looking at old, caked food on a dog dish.

❏ Don't put in dark drapes. Instead, make everything as light and open as possible.

❏ Don't use wallpaper. Paint is fine, but wallpaper is trickier, because not everyone has the same tastes.

❏ Don't forget to make sure everything is clean and neatly arranged.

[Marketing] fliers really help sell properties. They're great take-aways that provide potential buyers with all the information they need about the property.

Advertising a Property for Sale

If you're going to try to sell the property on your own, put a sign in the front yard. The NAR (National Association of Realtors) has done countless studies on this, and it has found that *signs do sell property*.

What type of sign should you have on the property? Different people do different things. One approach is to work with for sale by owner companies. These are private companies that charge you a small fee to rent their signs or plastic boxes full of color fliers.

These one-page fliers describe your property and describe the features of the home. The flier also gives the price you're asking and often includes digital pictures showing various rooms in the house. These fliers really help sell properties. They're great take-aways that provide potential buyers with all the information they need about the property. Potential buyers simply take a flier out of the box on the lawn or at the edge of the property, and then they have a full information sheet to remind them about the property. The flier may give them something to think about, or it may answer some questions that they have about the property. Even people who may not consider themselves potential buyers but who are interested in local real estate may pick up a flier and then, once they have it to refer to at home, decide that they *are* seriously interested in looking at the property and potentially buying it.

You can also go to almost any lumber store or Home Depot–type store, which should have for-sale signs and plastic boxes. This is a very inexpensive way to advertise your property for sale.

Potential buyers really appreciate knowing the history of a building, so you want to include its age [on your marketing flier.]

One approach that I *don't* recommend is putting signs in the windows of the property that say "House For Sale." These look rather tacky, and I don't think people—i.e., potential buyers—pay as much attention to these signs as they do to larger signs outside the property. Be sure you have an outside sign, and make sure it's large enough so that people who are driving by can read the sign and write down the phone number, just as they would with a Realtor's sign. This type of advertising requires almost no work at all, and it's the same thing a Realtor would do initially.

Another inexpensive way to advertise your property is to create a Web page describing it, with pictures and detailed information about the property. This way, potential buyers who are looking online for property in your area will find your listing when they Google real estate in your area. An online description, with pictures, enables potential buyers to "look" at your property themselves to see if it's something that's of interest to them. Again, this is what a real estate agent would do, and you can do it yourself without paying a Realtor—keep in mind that the seller pays the real estate commission on the sale of a property.

Hold Open Houses to Entice Buyers

The next step in advertising your property is to consider holding at least three open houses before listing the property, so that you can get a good feel for the current market. You should advertise these in the newspaper; for example, "Open from 2 to 4 on Sunday," with the address of the property. When people arrive, have fliers on display in an inexpensive stand (which you can get at Office Depot or through Paper Direct at 1-800-APAPERS). Also, place a small basket for business cards, in case people want to leave their card to be contacted for other properties that you have.

Have a booklet on display—but not for take-away—that features the property. Take a picture of the property for the cover. Inside, have all the bills associated with the property so that people can see what it really costs to live there—i.e., utilities, taxes, insurance, trash collecting, and any other costs, such as homeowners' association fees or condo fees. Also, if possible, include information about the elementary, middle, and high schools in the area so that if families are viewing the property, they know what school district their children would attend. Checklist 10-2 lists other important information that should also be in your flier.

Checklist 10-2   Information to Include in Your Marketing Flier Describing a Property

❑ The square footage.

❑ The number of bedrooms and their size.

❑ The number of bathrooms and their size.

❑ The type of plumbing.

❑ How old the property is. Potential buyers really appreciate knowing the history of a building, so you want to include its age.

❑ How old the appliances are, and whether they're in good condition. This is something that many people really want to know. The National Family Opinion Survey publishes the average life span for various major appliances. For example, a cooktop should last about 21 years, whereas washing machines don't last as long. Therefore, if you list the ages of the appliances in your property and compare them to these average ages, that information can be very helpful to the potential buyer; plus you appear to be thorough, with nothing to hide.

❑ Whether there is an alarm system.

❑ What the window coverings look like; as mentioned, installing even inexpensive new window coverings can make a property look great.

❑ Whether there is a garage, and, if so, whether it has a garage door opener and whether it accommodates one car, two cars, or more.

❑ Whether there are fireplaces, and, if so, how many, and when was the last time the chimney was cleaned. Fireplaces really should be cleaned once a year, and that costs only about $75 (depending on where you live). Clearly, I'm not recommending doing things that cost a lot of money.

Most buyers really want to know what they're getting, so the information in your booklets should answer all potential questions. You can put together a few of these, but don't give them out to potential buyers; just have them available for people who are walking through. Keep in mind that most potential buyers will be looking at a lot of properties and going to many open houses, so yours may be only one of many houses that a potential buyer is viewing. Make sure you have a "take-home" flier.

Before you schedule your first open house, visit the property to make sure there are no major renovation problems.

If You Have Tenants Living in the Property When You Hold Your Open Houses

When you're planning your open houses, if you have tenants living in that property, you should arrange to have them go out while you're holding the open house. I've done that several times. If you need to show the property because your tenants have found a new place to live and are moving out, they will understand. Moreover, if you've been a good landlord to your tenants, they should be more than happy to help you.

If you're selling the property, but the tenants are going to continue to rent that property and live in it after the sale, you may need to be more flexible in showing the property. In that case, ask the tenants if you can arrange a time that would be mutually convenient to show the property and hold the open house. It may not necessarily be on a Sunday or a weekend.

A lot of investors sell properties with tenants in place. (This is why I advised, in Chapter 7, that when you're buying a property with a tenant already in residence, you review the lease so that you know what you're getting into.) If the tenant's still going to be living in the property when you sell it, you want to make sure you arrange with the tenant a time when you can show the property, you don't want to abuse this because the tenant really does not have to make time available for you to show the property. So be nice and arrange a time that works for both of you. If you've been fair to your tenants, they're going to be fair to you. I've never had a tenant give me a hard time about showing the property while they still occupy it.

To ensure that your property looks good when the tenant leaves for a couple of hours, you should arrive at the property at least half an hour before the start time for your open house. This way, if there's a problem, you will be aware of it, and if it is something simple, you can fix it before the open house begins. Doing a walkthrough before potential buyers come in is vital to the success of your open house. You obviously don't really have time to clean the property (nor should you do so), but you can at least tidy it up. However, again, if the tenant is going to stay on after the property is sold, the tenant probably wants to make a good impression on the new buyer, so most tenants usually make sure the place looks good before they leave.

If tenants are vacating at the time of sale and want their security deposit back, it is in their best interest to make sure the place looks good. Most tenants will make the property look as nice as possible because they know you're going to do a final walkthrough before they leave, and if the place looks bad on the day of the open house, you won't forget it. The final walkthrough you do when they leave may be more detailed.

Before you schedule your *first* open house, visit the property to make sure there are no major renovation problems. If there are, you should already know about them, because the terms of your lease should include a provision that your tenants should notify you if there's a major problem and spell out what needs to be done. Still, don't wait until the day of the open house to visit the property; do a walkthrough before you even schedule anything.

Whether it's a condo, townhouse, single-family home, or any other type of property, cleaning, decorating, and staging a property is important.

On the day of the open house, as mentioned, you should arrive 30 minutes early and do a complete walkthrough. Make sure that the bathrooms are clean, closet and cabinet doors are closed, lights are turned on, and the place looks light and airy. Make sure that there are no leaking faucets. Also, make sure that the property smells nice. Some property owners (and some Realtors, even) bake chocolate chip cookies or brownies in the house, because the smell is so enticing to many people. Other sellers will brew a pot of coffee, so that there's a coffee smell—although that doesn't always appeal to everyone.

I usually bring different potpourri air fresheners and place them strategically in different rooms. These give the property a homey feel—and if there are any odors (cooking or otherwise) in the home, they'll cover them up during the time of the open house. Most potpourri and air fresheners are strong enough to overcompensate for whatever other smells are in the house.

How Staging Can Increase the Value of Your Property

If you've made your property look like millions (which you can do without spending anywhere near that much) and you've fixed it up to get the largest return on your investment, you should be in a good position to get pretty close to your asking price—provided, of course, that you've priced the house correctly. After all, if a buyer is looking at property A, which is neat, has new carpet and a new coat of paint, and looks not necessarily staged, but cute, cozy, and clean, and then that same buyer looks at property B, which has the exact same floor plan but the seller didn't bother to paint it, redo the carpets, or make it look nice, that buyer is going to expect to see a significantly lower price for Property B.

As mentioned in Chapter 3, you make your money at the time you buy a property. Now, when you are trying to sell it, the profit you're going to be able to get depends on how the property looks, what the feel of it is, and whether a potential buyer falls in love with the floor plan. Whether it's a condo, townhouse, single-family home, or any other type of property, cleaning, decorating, and staging a property is important, as well as the economic factors and the local values in the real estate market. Women do a great job of staging property because we take the care and the initiative. That's not to say that men don't do that, but, generally speaking, women like to do interior decorating. And typically (or stereotypically), we do a better job of it, making sure that everything is in the right place. Potential buyers appreciate that.

Staging and minor renovations don't have to cost much, either. For example, Kathy was living in her own home in Colorado when she met a man that she wanted to marry. The two of them wanted to live in his home because it was larger than Kathy's, which was about 2,500 square feet. She needed to sell her home, which was in O.K. condition, but she really wanted to make it look sharp. She asked two Realtor friends of hers to come look at her house, and she asked them, "What would you do to this house to make it more marketable?" She wrote down their suggestions, she did exactly what they recommended, and she sold the home herself. Here's what she did.

Kathy had bought this property six years earlier for $190,000. Her total cost [for fixing it up to sell] *was about $13,500. She sold it in less than three weeks for $310,000.*

She painted the interior of her house, which cost her about $2,000. She didn't need to paint the exterior because the paint there was only six years old. To make the outside of her property look friendly and inviting, she planted irises and potentillas (which are yellow flowers native to Colorado); the plants cost only about $400, and she did all this work herself.

She also put down rugs. She had wood floors, but she wanted the house to look comfortable and lived in, so she bought some area rugs; this really didn't cost her much because when she sold the property and closed, she took the rugs with her.

She did a thorough cleaning. She resurfaced the Formica countertops in her kitchen with a more neutral color that really opened up the kitchen. That cost about $350 in material. Then she looked at her two bathrooms, and she had professional flooring laid because she thought that, in these heavily trafficked areas, nice floors would be something that people would appreciate. She didn't do the work on these, and reflooring the two bathrooms cost $10,000. Her total cost was about $13,500.

Kathy had bought this property six years earlier for $190,000. When she decided to sell, she did the fix up. She sold it in less than three weeks for $310,000. Obviously, she did very, very well. Also, she didn't have to pay the 6 percent real estate commission because she sold the property herself, and she got top dollar for her house.

What also helped the sale was the school system. The elementary school was literally less than a block away, so kids could walk to school. Her home was located in a nice family neighborhood. The house was only six years old, and she had been its only owner. She fixed it up, just simple little fix-ups. For example, the kitchen counter didn't need new Formica because it was in pretty good shape, but the color wouldn't have appealed to most people, so she changed it. All she did, on her own, was stage that property and do minor fix-ups.

Of course, one could argue that, in six years, the value of her property might have increased to that level anyway. In many parts of the country, real estate prices have doubled in the last five years. However, as of this writing, the market is flat in a lot of parts of the country. If she *hadn't* staged her property, she probably could have sold it for less. Still, for a $13,500 investment, she realized a nice profit.

Also, if she hadn't staged it, she probably would have had to sell through a Realtor and pay commissions. She wouldn't have had to spend the $13,500 she spent on minor fix-ups, but she would have had to pay 6 percent commission on \$300,000, which is \$18,000—nearly \$5,000 more than the \$13,500 that she put into her renovation. So she did a nice job of staging, renovating, and selling on her own.

[Cheryl] had paid \$160,000 for her condo two years
previously, and by changing only the back deck
[for a cost of only \$10,000], she was able to sell it in only
two weeks for \$210,000.

Here's another example: Cheryl bought a lovely condominium in Missoula, Montana. Two years later, she decided to move to California because there was no work for her in Missoula. She wanted to sell her condo, which was a unique property because it faced a golf course. A lot of people like golf courses, but a lot of people don't: if you're not a golfer and you don't like noise early in the morning, you're not going to buy a golf course property.

Moreover, Cheryl's condo didn't have a prime view of mountains; instead, it was on the golf course, near a tee. Therefore, what she decided to do to make her property as marketable as possible was to put up a fence. She got permission from the community association, and she installed an attractive, half-high (four-foot) wood fence that sheltered the property and provided some privacy, so that outsiders wouldn't be able to see in. Then she put in a hot tub, and she planted beautiful flowers, plants, and trees. She did all this over a weekend, with a group of friends pitching in to help her out. Because the fence was only four feet high, it kept the property's golf course flavor, but provided some privacy.

The only thing she changed about her condo was the back deck. For the entire project—the fence, the foliage, and the hot tub—she spent around \$10,000. She had paid \$160,000 for the condo two years previously, and by changing only the back deck, she was able to sell it in only two weeks for \$210,000.

According to Realtors in her community, Cheryl's staging strategy was what made the deal. Her condo was not marketable at the time she wanted to sell it without her doing something that made it look unique and different, which is what she did. The local Realtors believe that if Cheryl had not made these simple changes, her condo would have been on the market for three to four months, because the market there was flat.

Also, Missoula borders many resort communities, so if you're not selling property when everybody's there (which is in the summer months), you're not going to attract a bevy of buyers. That's the problem with resort communities. For example, in the wintertime, Missoula is quiet; in the summertime, for a short period of time, it's alive. But Cheryl wanted to sell in the spring, which is the rainy season and before people start coming up. Cheryl was very fortunate, and really, her landscaping helped her to seal the deal.

Conclusion

My assumption in this chapter is that women investors are looking to acquire properties, but don't necessarily want to hold them for the long term; instead, they want to fix up those properties to make them as marketable as possible, so that they get the largest return. The examples in this chapter illustrate that women have a good eye and can easily do the finishing touches that will to make property look good. When you assess a property, you should ask yourself, "What would *I* like if *I* lived here? What would *I* put in that would make *me* feel at home?" If you ask only those two questions, you'll do commonsense fixes that should appeal to everyone. And you'll have a better time selling that property.

Kitchens and bathrooms are obviously what most people fall in love with. Therefore, if you're limited financially and you have to concentrate your funds somewhere, you should concentrate on the kitchen because people always crowd around the kitchen. It's the hanging-out place. Also, concentrate on the bathrooms because they are the most utilized rooms in the house.

On the other hand, there are certain areas and aspects of a property that are not as important. A good example of this is the basement. You can finish it so that it can be utilized as additional square footage space if your evaluation of the cost of doing that renovation makes sense. If the cost turns out not to make sense, you may want to finish only a portion of that basement so that at least there's an additional room and some additional square footage of living space.

This extra space usually appeals to families with children. Of course, some empty nesters also buy larger homes, but if you're buying a property in family-type neighborhoods, you want to make that property as desirable as possible to families. Therefore, if you can increase the square footage without incurring a lot of expense, you should do so.

I've also seen some investors transform an unfinished concrete basement into a game room simply by putting down wall-to-wall indoor/outdoor carpet. If you're willing to spend a couple of thousand dollars to make the basement look like usable space, you will get some money back in return. Also, this simple "renovation" will make *your* property stand out from other properties that are being listed for sale.

Essentially, you want to fix up your property so that you get top dollar, and this chapter describes just a few strategies that you can use to help you sell your property quickly for the largest return you can get on your investment. And this is something that women are especially good at.

11

Buying Properties in a Down Market

This chapter covers how to invest if the real estate market turns and how to generate cash flow in a risky, down market. The focus is *not* on how to sell real estate in a down market, but rather on how to *buy* well, because volatility in the market presents terrific opportunities for investors to pick up property at prices below fair market value. As I've said throughout this book, *you make money when you buy*. And in a down market, sellers will need to have more flexibility in selling their properties because they can't sell them conventionally. This chapter covers:

- Buying real estate with a lease option to buy or a straight option to buy
- Doing "subject-to" deals
- Buying short sales
- Buying foreclosures

If these terms are foreign to you, read on: this chapter explains all these strategies in detail. Even in a volatile market, there are opportunities that you can capitalize on, and these are just some of the strategies you can use to either protect or advance yourself as an investor as the volatility continues.

Right now, volatility is a prime concern to a lot of real estate investors. For example, the National Association of Realtors just published a survey that was written up in the *Economist* and cited the following statistics:

- In 2004, 23 percent of all American houses bought were for investment—i.e., they were not owner-occupied. That's an *enormous* number.
- And another 13 percent were bought as second homes.

Clearly, real estate investors have been taking advantage of the heyday of low interest rates—which at one point hit a 40-year low. People have leveraged themselves to the hilt, and if they're wealthy and can afford it (which many of the second-home buyers probably can), they're not necessarily going to be adversely affected or care whether property values go up or down. They are not your typical motivated sellers.

Many . . . professional strategists are projecting doom and gloom: real estate prices will continue to fall; . . . and there will be even more volatility in the market.

However, there are also many people who are 100 percent leveraged, who don't have a lot of money, and who are living on a fixed income. And now that interest rates have gone up, if the 23 percent of properties that were bought for rental purposes become a problem for less wealthy investors, those people are going to be more motivated to sell—which means that buyers with cash or the means to get properties financed have an opportunity to buy. Also, there are investors who bought houses in preconstruction phases who, in the end, are not going to be able to obtain permanent financing because the finished property is worth less than the price in the original contract.

Therefore, the *Economist* and many other professional strategists are projecting doom and gloom: real estate prices will continue to fall; interest rates will go up; the price of oil will go to $100 a gallon, and there will be even more volatility in the market. No one has a crystal ball. No one can predict the future. Look at the stock market. If someone could predict the market, that person would be rich.

That said, how does an investor continue to be successful in real estate? And how can we identify opportunity, so that we can invest in property that will increase in value and make us money? There are a couple of different techniques in a volatile market situation, where the sellers don't have a whole lot of leverage, that you can focus on. One of them is doing options or lease options on real estate. There are some benefits to options that I'll discuss in the next section. And, of course, another option is buying properties in foreclosure, which I'll cover later in the chapter.

A Word of Caution about Foreclosures and Lease Options

Some states have recently passed laws dealing with lease options and foreclosures, so that if you use these techniques incorrectly, they can get you in a lot of trouble. In fact, in Texas, the law as it pertains to lease options was recently changed. Please check with your state government to see if any legislation has been or is being passed that affects this and other real estate investment strategies. Foreclosures are being scrutinized by state governments, so please do the research before you invest. If nothing else, a good real estate attorney would know what is happening in your state or can find out. There's been a lot of foul play, with people taking advantage of consumers, which has caused investigation.

Therefore, regardless of whether it's a buyer's or a seller's market, if you cannot do a win-win deal—if you know in advance, for example, that a potential buyer will never be able to get a mortgage—then don't take that person's money for an option consideration. If you're greedy and try to take advantage of a buyer, it's going to come back to haunt you.

That's not to say that lease options and foreclosures are scam techniques; they aren't—if you do them right, if you're honest, and if you treat the person right, many of the creative strategies investors do can create a win-win. It's when someone takes advantage of the person who wants to buy the property, knowing that he or she will never be able to afford the property in the first place, that there's a problem.

---

*[From the buyer's perspective, a lease option] gives
you the right to control [a] property, meaning that
you can either assign the option to another party . . .
or sublease that property to someone else.*

Some real estate investors believe these laws restricting lease options are excessive, however. Here's what three experts had to say about these:

- Realtor Anna Mills feels that

  Excessive laws and restrictions on subject-to, land contract, and lease options undermine affordable housing for all, not just investors. Such laws restrict free trade, smother affordable housing, and inhibit the "all-American dream." These are all creative finance methods for those who cannot use or have been turned down by the banking world. Often, it is a trade of "sweat equity" [for] the dream of owning and improving your own home. For investors, it is [a way of] making their own living and building their own retirement. It is never right to punish a whole profession or class because a few don't do things right. It is a hidden assault on the poor, the investor, affordable housing, and any entrepreneur who doesn't fit the [usual] mold.

- Rebecca McLean, executive director of the NREIA, agrees:

  My feeling [about laws restricting subject-tos and lease options] is that we are limiting the option of those who may either be in trouble or might not be eligible for conventional financing. Especially with the new bankruptcy laws, people need options in dealing with troubled finances. The new laws significantly limit their choices.

- Owner-financing expert Tracy Rewey had this to say:

  "Subject tos" and "lease options" have been useful and profitable investment strategies. Although not without risk, they can be an effective means of leveraging. Unfortunately, a few investors have

not used these techniques honorably, and some sellers have been treated unfairly. Trying to fix this with legislation sort of takes me back to kindergarten: remember when the whole class had to rest with their heads on their desks for the wrongdoing of one child? Why not just punish the wrongdoers and let the rest of us go about our business?

- Realtor and trainer Magi Bird says,

What concerns me most is the impact it would have on tenants. Every investor remembers the day they bought their first home. This is a day that such legislation would remove from the life experience of many families. In today's inflationary spiral, with both parents working, it is excruciatingly difficult to save and bank a down payment. For many families, being able to save in the form of monthly rent credits is the only way in which they will have a toehold on the housing market.

This will have the long-term effect of creating a stronger divide between the haves and have-nots and may, in fact, create a class of lifelong renters. . . . There are families that would end up on welfare after retirement, a price this country cannot afford to pay, even though an investor may look at families that rent for 10, 15, or 20 years as removing a good portion of their vacancy problems. Always remember that property values increase, in reality, only at the point of sale, and fewer buyers mean fewer sales, which means lower prices.

Another critical caution for investors using these strategies: do not promise somebody that you're going to do something if you don't intend to follow through on the transaction. That is the worst thing you can do. If you do it, you can count on that person contacting a consumer complaint department, filing a complaint against you, and having someone investigate the situation, because that person believes he or she has been taken advantage of.

Several years ago, a company in Denver was advertising a rent-to-own program in the newspapers. The company would do an option agreement with the "buyer" and inflate the property 10 percent over its fair market value. The buyer put up 5 percent of the purchase price as option consideration. If the buyer was able to finance the property in a year, that person could buy it. The rent (i.e., the lease part of the agreement) that was being charged over the year was well above fair market rents. This company allowed an additional $350 per month toward the down payment. But the consumer was paying several hundred dollars a month more than the fair market rent for that particular property.

If the borrower was unable to get a loan after the first year, the company would renew the agreement, inflating the price of the real estate yet another 10 percent and requiring additional dollars to keep the option agreement active. As you can see, this company knew that the buyer was not likely to be able to afford to exercise the option and buy the home. If somehow he or she did, and if somehow the property was appraised for the higher amount and a lender made a loan based on this appraisal, this company would walk away with a significant profit. Stories like this one are why state governments are clamping down on investors who take unfair advantage of consumers.

Finally, if you're serious about doing lease options, I recommend reading *Investing in Real Estate with Lease Options and Subject-To Deals: Powerful Strategies for Getting More When You Sell and Paying Less When You Buy*, by Wendy Patton; for other sources, see the "Recommended Resources" section (Appendix A) at the end of this book. The following sections provide a good overview of each investing strategy.

You definitely want to have an option agreement
that is separate from the lease agreement.

Buying Properties with a Lease Option

A lease option gives you the right to purchase or lease a property at an agreed-upon price and terms for a stated period of time. For example, suppose you're looking at a property that someone is selling for $200,000. The seller is financially sound and has a lot of equity in that particular property. You might ask the seller if, instead of selling the property to you today, could he give you the right to buy that property at any time over the next year, in return for a financial consideration (a deposit for the option to buy the property at a set price agreed by both parties over the next year that would be delivered as an up-front generally, non-refunded deposit)? This would give you an option to buy or not buy the property.

If the seller agrees to that arrangement, you have an option consideration agreement; this is a valid contract that gives you the right to buy that property from the seller for X amount within Y amount of time. The time period is especially important: the longer the option agreement you can negotiate, the better for you as the buyer. The option agreement also gives you the right to control that property, meaning that you can either assign the option to another party, allowing that person to buy the property for the price that you and the seller agreed to, or sublease that property to someone else (i.e., another buyer), in which case you would pocket the cash flow.

Therefore, your option agreement for this $200,000 property might state that you're going to pay the seller a $2,000 option consideration, and that you're going to pay the seller $1,200 a month. Then you could turn around and sublease the property to a tenant buyer for $1,500 a month. You would pocket the $300 a month cash flow for that period of time on the lease. You can also sell the option to the tenant or to another party for a fee. If you bought the option on the $200,000 property for $2,000 and the property rises to $220,000, you can sell your option for $10,000 to someone who wishes to buy the property. Your $2,000 investment is now $10,000; the new investor or buyer still buys a $220,000 property for $200,000, and everyone wins.

If you're interested in investing in markets where there's a lot of inventory or where rentals are slow, lease options are a particularly good strategy.

If you are the one selling a property on a lease option, you definitely want to have an option agreement that is separate from the lease agreement. Here's why. If someone is leasing property from you and those tenants don't pay you for leasing that property, you still want to have the right to evict them, which you can do if your lease agreement is separate from your option agreement. However, if you put those two agreements together, you're going to run into a major problem because the option agreement allows the tenant an option to buy the property at a fixed price within a fixed time period. If the tenant does not pay the rent, the tenant still has the option to buy. If you keep the contracts separate, you can evict and still continue to receive rent from someone else.

For example, the agreement might specify that at some period of time, your tenants can buy the property from you (for a higher price than you paid the original seller). You would then exercise your option with the seller to buy the property for $200,000, and you could sell the property to your tenant-buyer at $220,000. But how can you evict your tenants, if they're party to an option agreement saying that they can buy the property? Under that arrangement, eviction becomes much more difficult. Therefore, you want to have an option consideration agreement and you want to have a lease, and they should be two separate contracts.

An option gives you the positive right to purchase or lease a property at an agreed-upon price; this is the key point you need to remember. You want your option agreement to be a valid agreement, and you want it to be fair to the seller; otherwise, the seller has no incentive to do such a deal.

Benefits of Doing Lease Option Agreements

When you're in a real estate market that is flat or one in which sellers are starting to get nervous and prices are coming down (as we are at the time of this writing, in most parts of the country), you'll find that sellers are accustomed to being asked about lease options. Also, if you're interested in investing in markets where there's a lot of inventory or where rentals are slow, lease options can be a particularly good strategy.

The benefits for investors buying property utilizing lease options as a strategy are as follows:

You Don't Have to Put a Lot of Money Down. I've seen people put as little as $1,000 down. (Some guru real estate speakers may say they have put nothing down, but in the almost 30 years that I've been investing in real estate, I've never done that.) Because you can put down so much less of a down payment than you would if you were actually buying the property, this is a great strategy for investors who don't have a lot of money, but who want to control a property.

You're Dealing with the Owner Directly. You have the opportunity to sit down with the seller and explain how long you need to tie up the property before buying it and why. The seller needs to feel comfortable that you may or may not buy the property and understand that he or she is receiving income in the meantime.

> [With lease option agreements,] *you're protecting your cash, you're limiting your risk, you're controlling the property, and you're maintaining anonymity.*

Your Risk Is Not Very Large. The worst that can happen to you is that you can't exercise the option—i.e., you're unable to buy the property when the term of the option expires. Suppose you put down $1,000 (or whatever you and the seller agree to for the option consideration). Even if you can't buy the property, you've still generated cash flow for a year or two years, if you've been subleasing the property—you've already made your money back just from the cash flow. Or, even if you only broke even on the rent you received from the tenant, the worst that can happen is that you would have lost your initial investment. Finally, even in the worst-case scenario, your loss would still be *much* less than it would be if you actually bought a property, put out a lot of money, and had to get the right financing when you might not be ready to buy or comfortable with buying.

Your Monthly Payment Is Lower Than a Mortgage Payment. The amount that you're paying the owner is usually significantly less than a mortgage payment would be. For example, on this $200,000 house, if you're paying $1,200 a month, that would be a lower payment than if you went out and purchased the property with conventional financing in today's market (if you include the taxes and insurance payments that get made besides the principal and interest payments.) That's something to take into consideration if you're investing and you're looking to save money or you think that property prices will go up in the future.

You Don't Need to Qualify for a Mortgage. This is a particularly good benefit if you're just getting started in real estate, or if you've got spotty credit and you're trying to improve your financial status. Lease options give you time to improve your financial picture so that you're able to purchase investments later on.

You Get a Great Return on Your Investment. For example, if you're putting $1,000 down and you make $300/month cash flow every month from your tenant, you're making $3,600/year on only a $1,000 investment. That's not a bad return. Generating cash flow is a great benefit of lease options.

You Can Do Lease Options through Your IRA or 401(k). As discussed in Chapter 9, you can also use your IRA or 401(k)—if it's a self-directed 401(k)—so that the profit you get back on a monthly basis or the profit you'll make if you assign your contract (which is covered in the next section of this chapter) will come back into your retirement plan and will therefore be tax-deferred or tax-free.

You Maintain Privacy. Another benefit of doing a lease option agreement is that you're not going to be on public record as having bought a property. So you're protecting your cash, you're limiting your risk, you're controlling the property, and you're maintaining anonymity. Clearly, there are many benefits to having an option on a property and why that might work for you.

Make Sure You Can Assign Your Option Agreement

If you do an option agreement, make sure you have the right to assign it. What this means is that the contract should be in the name of, for example, "Lisa Moren-Bromma and/or assigns." That gives you the right, during the term of your option agreement, to assign that agreement to someone else.

Suppose you've lease-optioned that same $200,000 property, you have one year to buy that property for $200,000, and you're paying the seller $1,200 a month rent. If you find somebody who really falls in love with this property and wants to buy it for $220,000, you can assign your lease option contract to that person for $10,000; that person will then get to buy the property at a discount. In this scenario, you've still made $10,000 on your $2,000 option consideration by using this strategy. But to do so, you need to make sure that you always have the words "and/or assigns" in your original agreement.

The initial option agreement is between you and the seller and for that you pay an option fee, which is nonrefundable. If you decide not to exercise your option on this piece of real estate, you will lose your option consideration fee. Generally, that's an agreed-upon fee that you and the seller negotiate; it could be $1,000, $2,000, or $5,000 that you need to put down to get an option on a property.

The seller will typically want to have a shorter term on an option agreement. However, the longer the term is, the better for you (the investor) because if this property increases in value, you have a greater opportunity to profit.

Where to Find Lease Option Opportunities

So where can you find lease option opportunities? The following are just a few ways: you can run your own ad, let your fingers do the walking through other people's ads, or get on the phone and talk to referral sources who may be able to help you out.

Look in the Classified Ads. Some property owners will advertise property that they're willing to lease-option. If you look at your newspaper, especially the Sunday real estate section, you should see ads from owners who say that they will finance or do a lease option. Those ads are good opportunities.

Run Your Own Ad. You could run your own ad saying something like, "Looking for property, willing to pay $1,200/month and option consideration in ___ area of the city. Call Lisa." If someone is interested in selling a property on an option, that person will give you a call.

Keep an Eye Out for Landlords with Houses to Rent. When you're reading the real estate ads, if you keep seeing the same house listed for rent for, say, a month or more, call that landlord and ask if he or she is willing to sell the property on a lease option. If the owner is willing to rent it and can't do so, he or she may be willing to sell it. That's a great way to start talking to people about lease options; you never know what the seller will say until you ask.

For example, when I was living in North Carolina, I saw a recurring rental ad for a town home in New Jersey, where my children and I wanted to live for a year. I called the owner, Maureen, and offered to do a lease option, and she accepted my offer. I put down $1,500 in consideration for an option to buy the property for $150,000, and I paid a year's rent in advance. By paying $10,000 up front, I got the right to rent the property for $1,000 a month, which was less than the $1,200 a month payment that she originally wanted—I got a discount.

There's a significant downside to ["subject-to" deals]:
the bank may invoke the due-on-sale clause.

This was a good strategy for both me and the seller/landlord: Maureen got my option consideration of $1,500 plus $10,000 for a year's rent up front, so she received $11,500, which was profitable for her. In turn, I was able to rent the property and didn't pay any rent for a year because I had paid that money up front; also, as mentioned, I got a discount of $200 a month off the original $1,200 a month rent because I paid in advance, so that was a great strategy for me. If I had exercised the option to buy, I would have been able to buy that property at $150,000, and the property could have increased in value to, say, $160,000 or even $165,000. I decided not to buy it because I didn't want to stay in New Jersey; therefore, I lost my $1,500 down payment on the option, but in the end, I didn't really lose anything because my discounted rent saved me $2,400 for the year.

Work with Property Managers. Jeannie is an investor in Florida who finds lease option deals by working through property managers. She keeps in touch with different property managers whom she knows through her local Real Estate Investors Association in Jacksonville; she asks them if they know any landlords who are fed up with being landlords and would be willing to sell their properties on a lease with an option to buy. That's the only real estate investing strategy she uses, and she's been very successful.

Investing in "Subject-To" Properties

There's another strategy, called "subject-to," that can be confusing. "Subject-to" is a technique by which an investor gains title to a property but does not have a mortgage on the property. Instead, the seller keeps the mortgage in his or her name and *deeds* the property to the investor subject to the existing mortgage, which stays in place. The bank is usually not made aware of this change or asked about the change. The new owner simply starts making payments on the old owner's loan.

Obviously, there's a significant downside to this arrangement: the bank may invoke the due-on-sale clause. The bank has not been notified of the transfer of ownership of the property, so the bank assumes that the seller is still the legal owner of the property. If the bank finds out that the seller has deeded the property subject to the existing mortgage, the bank can call its mortgage loan due. If the bank calls its loan, someone will then have to pay off the loan—and, obviously, the person with the most incentive to do that is the buyer, because the buyer is the one who will lose the property if the loan isn't paid off.

For example, Mary Lou had a house in Texas. She decided to "sell" her property "subject to" to Jane, who then made payments to Mary Lou. Mary Lou continued making her mortgage payments to the bank. The bank didn't know about the arrangement between Mary Lou and Jane because the bank wasn't getting checks from Jane; instead, the bank continued to get checks from Mary Lou.

Property owners . . . do "subject-to" sales because they think that the lender will never find out, and doing a subject-to is a way to sell [the] *property.*

Unfortunately, seven months after Mary Lou and Jane made this deal, a third party did a search at the local courthouse, saw that there was a recorded transaction on this property, and notified the bank. The bank got in touch with Mary Lou and called the loan due and payable in full. The bank gave Mary Lou six 6 months to come up with the money.

Mary Lou didn't have the money to pay off the property. Jane was forced to find other funds to pay it off. The property ended up costing Jane more than it would have if she had gone to the bank and gotten a new loan. Had Jane not been able to come up with the funds, this situation could have turned ugly.

There are property owners who do "subject-to" sales because they think that the lender will never find out, and doing a subject-to is a way to sell a property and get out from under the mortgage. A property owner might do this type of deal if she can't sell the property through conventional means, or if a buyer convinces the seller to do this or pays her more money than she could have gotten in the open market.

Banks aren't happy about these deals because they can lose money. If interest rates are volatile and rates are going up, then the bank is losing money. If, for example, Mary Lou's interest rate on her loan was 5½ percent and interest rates had increased so that the rate would have been 7 percent if Mary Lou had done a real sale, then the bank is losing 1½ percent interest that it would have received if Mary Lou had just sold the property and the borrower had gotten conventional financing. Also, in "subject to" transactions, the lender hasn't verified the new owner; it hasn't been able to run a credit check, so the bank doesn't know if this person has the ability to pay the mortgage. Yet the seller went ahead and "sold" this property to someone else. But it was "sold" on a subject-to basis, and that is problematic for the bank.

Investing in Short Sales

Another interesting strategy that investors will use in volatile markets is short sales. When a bank is owed a certain amount of money on a home, and the owner is going into or already is in foreclosure, a *short sale* means that the bank will accept a significant discount on the mortgage balance to get rid of this property that isn't performing. Banks do not like bad loans; they're in the business of lending, not of owning real estate. They need to have money, not property, to be able to pay their depositors. Therefore, they want bad debt off their books quickly so that they can make new loans, and that's why they will accept an investor negotiating with the bank.

What this means for investors is that you can buy a contract from someone who's in foreclosure, or even, in some cases, get the deed, go to the bank, and persuade the bank to sell the property to you on a short sale. For example, you might say something like, "Is there something I can work out with you, the bank, in order to acquire this property at a discount, because we both already know this person's in foreclosure?"

If you're considering buying foreclosure property, you need to know that you're buying property "as is."

Here are the benefits you want to cite to the bank, in order to persuade it to sell you a property on a short sale:

- The bank won't have to go to the additional expense of foreclosing.
- The bank won't have to take the real estate back as REO.
- The bank won't have to incur the expense of trying to remarket the property.
- The bank will get this property off its books, which will thrill the bank's regulators and auditors.

That's the basic negotiation strategy you want to use if you're interested in investing in short sales.

Up until recently, I would have sided with some real estate "gurus" who believed that short sales are not a good strategy because what incentive would the banks have when there aren't a lot of foreclosures? However, now that the real estate market is so volatile, this is a strategy you could try. You're being up front with the bank. It already knows that the person to whom the bank has lent money is in foreclosure or about to go into foreclosure.

There are three stages where an investor can capitalize in foreclosures:

1. *Preforeclosure*, where the owner is in distress and is behind on his or her mortgage payments, and the bank sends a demand letter to the owner. The bank demands that the owner make up any back payments or the bank will start foreclosure proceedings.

2. *On the courthouse steps.* This is when the foreclosure has reached the point of no return, and the bank is auctioning the property for sale. The bank is trying to recoup what's left of its investment—i.e., the balance on its loan and all the payments associated with the loan. The bank would be delighted to just break even on its investment.
3. *REO (real estate owned).* In this case, the bank has already taken back the property and is trying to resell it so that it can get the property off its books.

The government—specifically, the Veterans Administration (VA), the Department of Housing and Urban Development (HUD), Fannie Mae, the FDIC, and other government entities—also has foreclosures on its books. The best way for real estate investors to find those foreclosures is through the Web. Each government agency has its own Web site that you can research. In some cases, you can get on the agency's mailing list by area. You can buy foreclosure property through these government agencies, but you must have researched the value of the property to know what it is really worth before bidding on the property.

In most cases, when HUD and the VA have an auction, if an investor and an owner-occupant bid the same price, the government agency will go with the owner-occupant because it wants to give the owner-occupant the ability to own a home. But if the agency can't get an owner-occupant, it will go with the highest bidder.

Also, in some cases in the past, the government agency has financed investors with a significant down payment. This is a great opportunity for investors to buy a property at a discount through a bidding system, either through the bank or through government agencies, getting you into the property at an affordable price, and possibly, with financing.

Make sure you do your homework, know what you are buying, and buy it at the right price. Do your research!

Buying Foreclosure Property

Over the last year or so, foreclosures have become more common. They are on the rise. Moreover, I think we're going to see even more foreclosures in the future. Experienced investors are hoping to capitalize on foreclosures.

If you're considering buying foreclosure property, you need to know that you're buying property "as is," what the benefits are and what to watch out for, what you'll need in financial terms, how to prepare for buying foreclosures at auction (which is the way they are typically sold), and how to buy foreclosed property from banks (i.e., REOs, or real estate owned properties).

Foreclosed Property Is Sold "As Is"

When you are looking at foreclosures, since you will be buying the property "as is," you *won't* be in a position to be able to negotiate the price because of a particular structural problem, or floor plan or anything else that under a conventional sale you might have had the opportunity to bargain. The whole idea behind a foreclosure is that the investor is picking up a property at a discount.

Is the price always wholesale? Absolutely not. The truth is that real estate investors are always trying to get the best price. When you buy a property as is, you don't know exactly what you're getting yourself into. Therefore, you need to take the worst-case scenario into consideration. For example, there are certain hazards in real estate that you need to know about and look for when you're getting a property inspected, such as mold, radon, lead paint (if you're buying a property that was built prior to 1978), asbestos (on a very old property), water quality, and carbon monoxide. In some parts of the Rockies, you also have to look out for bentonite in the soil. You should have an inspection to look for all of these items because they are things you cannot see.

When you buy a property normally—i.e., one that's not in foreclosure— you can have that property inspected and buy it "subject to" the inspection, so that you can get out of the contract should there be a major problem with the property. In a foreclosure situation, you're not going to have that same ability because you're buying the property "as is."

You Need to Make All Back Payments on the Property

Here are some other things you should know when you're considering investing in foreclosures. You need to know exactly what the cash costs (out of pocket) are going to be. Nine times out of ten, the mortgage is several months in arrears. The homeowner probably owes taxes, homeowners' association dues (which means that the homeowners' association has probably put a lien on the property), insurance payments, and other such liabilities. Therefore, when you're trying to figure out the best price, you need to factor in those amounts that the previous owner is in arrears, especially if you are bidding at the courthouse steps or trying to buy this property from the bank.

If you're buying a preforeclosure, you are also going to need some cash to bring the payments current. For example, suppose the owners are in distress, and they're three months behind on their payments. The number one negotiating strategy that investors use with a property owner who is behind in payments is to say, "If you sell the property to me, you'll avoid going through foreclosure and avoid ruining your credit." Even if the borrower were to deed the property to the lender in lieu of foreclosure (which people will often do), the borrower's credit is still ruined because the deed in lieu is included on his or her credit report. On the other hand, if the borrower sells the property to you, the borrower is out of a bad situation and won't have to worry that his or her credit is ruined. The investor makes up the arrearage and pays any fees the bank requires.

There are many benefits for investors who buy preforeclosures:

- First, of course, you're buying property at a discount.
- You can acquire a property in an area you desire, because you found this property in your targeted community.
- You're profiting by selling or renting out the house. You're buying the house at a favorable price, probably to make an immediate profit by generating cash flow from rent or by selling it at some point.
- You are helping the borrower move on and close a bad chapter financially.

The benefit to the seller is that he or she is avoiding the foreclosure. It stops the bleeding, and you're helping the sellers get out from a disastrous financial burden.

Clearly, there are benefits to doing foreclosures. However, I want to caution readers again that there are laws coming down the pike right now that, if you're not careful, could get you into major trouble. For example, Colorado just passed a law on foreclosures that says that if you don't do them a certain way, you can go to jail. Foreclosures are not a get-rich-quick scheme; they are a way to buy property wholesale, and they're a great way to resell property in a short period of time because you can fix them up and then resell them. But foreclosures may be a problem if you don't know what you're doing.

You Need Cash for Foreclosure Auctions

Your first step should be to make sure that you have the money in place. This is critical because when you buy foreclosure property in a preforeclosure situation, where somebody's in distress, if you can't get financing from the person's lender or another lender that you select, you'd better have the cash to follow through with your offer.

Furthermore, if you're buying property at the auction, or on the courthouse steps, you must have certified funds. What usually happens at the courthouse is that the property is auctioned to the highest bidder. The winner puts a deposit down on the property with the court. In most states, there is a redemption period, during which the borrower can still try to make up the payments and thereby keep his or her property. Once this redemption period expires, then you, the investor, need to fund the transaction, and the property will be deeded to you. Remember, the original property owner has *redemption rights*.

Depending on the county, redemption periods can run from nonexistent to more than one year. Check with the county where you are buying the real estate so that you know what the time period is in the area where you're buying property. Once that time period expires, you need to have the cash to take over the property. Therefore, you need to have your resources in place. The property is not yours until after the redemption period.

You Need to Be Organized to Find Properties in Foreclosure

You have to be organized if you are to be successful in the foreclosure arena. A quick way to do research is to check out the online service at www.dataquick.com which collects listings of individuals who are in default on properties around the country. There is a fee to use this service, but once you pay the fee, it allows you 250 searches a month.

Some investors who are interested in buying foreclosures mail out post-cards to property owners who are facing possible foreclosure. The postcard simply says something like this: "Behind in your payments? Let us help you. We buy properties for cash. Save your credit and call us now for a free consultation." An owner might call up, and the investor might then go over and look at the property, talk to the owner, and see what the situation is. Try to find out what the owner needs in order to get out.

Homeowners in a preforeclosure situation know they're in trouble when they get a notice from the bank. They know they're eventually going to be thrown out. Therefore, most investors find that the best time to negotiate is in a preforeclosure situation. Remember that these people are in trouble. You need to realize that they will not be thrilled to see you.

You may not make an offer the first time you find a possible foreclosure property. However, you should keep mailing out those letters and postcards. You will have some expenses—for postage and, of course, your time. You should also send thank-you notes to stay in contact with property owners and so that they'll remember you. All of this takes time and preparation, and does require some small amount of funds, although not a lot. You will need to spend time scoping out foreclosures. Therefore, finding foreclosures is a more time-intensive process than some of the other strategies for buying real estate. However, once you find the right property, you have a chance to get a good deal.

Do not get emotionally wrapped up in a foreclosure.
After you've done your research and have a price in mind,
you should stick to that price.

Preparing for the Foreclosure Auction

If you're going to go to an auction, you need to be prepared. Here's what you need to know:

- You should know what the comps in the area are in order to put in the right bid. You do not want to pay more than the property is worth. Know the prices of the last three sales within a one-mile radius of the foreclosure property (I think even one mile is too much, but that's a generally accepted rule of thumb).

- Know the rental market if you plan on holding the property for the long term.
- Before the auction, call the trustee's office, the Land Recorder's Office, the Register of Deeds office, or whatever the appropriate office is in your area to confirm that the auction is on and specific date and time that has been set. There have been many, many times when an auction has been advertised and then cancelled.

One important warning: *do not get emotionally wrapped up in a fore-closure.* After you've done your research and have a price in mind, you should *stick to that price.* Don't get caught up in the excitement of an auction, which is easy to do: for example, you might offer $55,000, and then the person next to you offers $60,000. You might think that you really want this property and bid $65,000, which is over your budget. If you do that, you're going to end up losing money on the deal.

Here are some other points to be very careful about at an auction:

- Don't pay too much.
- Make sure you're getting a house that has a clear title. You don't want to find out that the IRS has a major lien on this property and nobody did the research to discover that.
- Watch out for negative or unprofitable cash flow—i.e., make sure you're not buying a property that's going to cost you so much to rehab or renovate that even with a low purchase cost, you'll never be able to resell it for what you put into it, or you'll have to charge such a high rent to cover your costs that it will be difficult to attract tenants.

Before you make an official bid, you should have your financing in place, your insurance in place, and any rehab materials and labor on call. You want to make sure that you have the right people doing inspections to see what the costs of the fix-up will be. If you're going to keep the property and rent it out, you should also have a property manager lined up, if you decide you don't want to rent it out yourself.

If you are considering buying properties on the courthouse steps, I strongly suggest that *before you buy*, you go to at least three auctions and watch the process. See how people purchase foreclosure property. Also, if you can, follow up after the sale and see how the property is fixed up and what it sells for later. Follow the property, because you'll get to see the pitfalls before you yourself get involved.

Make sure you're getting a house that has a clear title.
You don't want to find out that the IRS has a
major lien on this property.

Buying REO (Real Estate Owned) Foreclosures from Banks

Now that foreclosures are becoming increasingly common, I think there will be more investors looking to buy REOs (real estate owned properties), from banks, because banks may be more flexible and willing to negotiate to get the property off their books. If a borrower has leveraged herself 100 percent with an adjustable-rate mortgage, she may not be able to afford those higher payments, and if she gets behind on the payments, the bank will foreclose and take back her property. If the bank cannot get its money back at the courthouse, it will try to relist the property for sale as an REO. Many investors prefer to buy property at this stage because they do not want to negotiate with the borrower, and they figure that if no one bid what the bank needed, the bank may be more flexible just to unload the property.

Second-Lien Holders

There are also situations where borrowers have more than one mortgage on the property. For example, suppose the first mortgage was with Washington Mutual for $1 million, and the property owner then got a second mortgage with American General Finance Company for $10,000. If the property goes into foreclosure, be assured that Washington Mutual will get paid back faster than American General. Therefore, you need to be careful when looking at small second mortgages behind large first mortgages.

Certainly, when you know a property is about to be foreclosed, you could go to the company holding the second mortgage and try to negotiate a buyout of that loan if it's more relevant in the loan-to-value equation—in other words, if the second mortgage and the first mortgage are relatively close in dollar amount. If you are able to buy out the second, you have a qualified interest in the property. If a property owner is getting ready to go into foreclosure, the process is moving right along, and the auction is scheduled to be held on the courthouse steps, if there's more than one mortgage on the property, you can negotiate with the second mortgage holder, buy that mortgage, and then go in and take over the first because you now have a vested interest in the property. You have a legal interest in the property, and you are protecting your legal interest. But you do not want to do this when you're in a situation where the first mortgage is much higher than the second mortgage.

For example, suppose you're interested in buying property in San Antonio, Texas, which was the number one real estate market in 2006: the average median price of a home was $148,000. Suppose you find a $148,000 house that is getting ready to go into foreclosure, and there's going to be an auction on the courthouse steps. Suppose there's a first mortgage for $115,000 and a second mortgage for $25,000. In this case, you might contact the holder of the second mortgage, whether it be a bank, a finance company, or a private individual and say, "How much are you willing to take for your second mortgage to walk away from this property? What is it worth to not be in a position to have to bid over the first position?" If the holder of the second mortgage does not want to be in the property business, then it will be worth something; in other words, the holder will negotiate.

Here's a real-life example of this from North Carolina. Carla bought the second mortgage on a property right before it was going to foreclosure on the courthouse steps. The $20,000 second loan was behind a $68,000 first. She bought the $20,000 loan for $4,000. Carla was able to get the bank to allow her to assume the first mortgage and take over the property. She purchased the property, which generated positive cash flow and made a great investment for her. By buying the second mortgage, she got the property at a discount.

Unfortunately, the original property owner, who was behind in his payments and was being foreclosed on, refused to deal with any investors. The poor soul could have gotten $5,000 in moving expenses, for example, or he could have broken even in getting out of the property, but he refused to sell. He couldn't believe that the bank was actually going to throw him out. It was really sad.

Carla was able to negotiate the second mortgage down to where it made financial sense. This is a great way to try to tie up property at a discount, and your competition may not necessarily think to go to a second mortgage holder and negotiate the loan.

Conclusion

Wise women focus on foreclosures when they

- Know the market.
- Are prepared, financially.
- Are organized and keep in touch with what's happening with the property.
- Follow up with the borrower, lender, or whoever they are trying to negotiate with to get a deal that is fair.
- Never pay more than what a property is worth.

It all comes down to being able to buy a property right.

12

For Realtors Only: You Can Be Both an Agent and an Investor

If you are already a real estate agent, the chapter offers suggestions for growing your business so that you're not just *selling* real estate and earning a commission on those sales, but also *investing* in your own properties, which can be far more lucrative. You can be both an agent and an investor.

Why More Realtors *Don't* Become Investors

Most real estate agents are accustomed to doing deals where the buyer puts 20 percent down and gets 80 percent bank financing, and the Realtor gets a commission. That's the strategy they know. Many Realtors *think* that they cannot afford to be investors. They don't have the mentality to be investors; they think of real estate only as a commission-based job. What they're used to doing is generating deals with 20 percent down and 80 percent bank financing, and getting their commissions from sellers. Their mentality is, "I'm not an investor; this is my job; I make my living selling real estate; I have no flexibility to look at any creative financing, nor do I have any flexibility to create my own deal." They can't see beyond simply making commissions.

Anna Mills is one Realtor who did see the potential. She told me, "30 years ago, I was a Realtor for only about a year before I became an investor. I realized that if I kept telling people, 'housing is the most important purchase of your life,' I should be doing it myself. I manage dozens of single-family [homes] that I rent and have not sold any."

If you're a Realtor and you're considering investing, there are techniques you can use to increase your investment experience and become an investor more quickly. For instance, you can work with an investor in an equity-share arrangement, or you can go into a partnership with an investor so that you can learn the ropes and become comfortable with using real estate as an investment. For example, Barbara O'Connell does this:

> I also use partnerships to put deals together. If the deal is large or I am running out of my ability to qualify for additional credit, then partnerships in the form of LLCs work great. People like doctors and dentists usually have lots of money and no time or expertise to invest in real estate. They usually need tax deductions as well. They make excellent real estate partners because they are usually investing for their retirement and don't particularly need their funds during the investment period.

Magi Bird also sees the benefits in Realtors becoming investors:

> I often tell my agents that by virtue of the fact they are in this business 24 hours a day, 7 days a week, twice a year a deal will drop on their desk that an investor is not supposed to get. These two deals a year are their retirement. If a client were to receive those deals, those would become the standard by which the investor would measure all investments and, as a consequence, most likely would never make another investment. The Realtor knows that investment for what it is, one of a kind and not easily duplicated.
>
> This is not to say that I teach my agents to "hog" all the good deals. Giving one of those deals to a client would destroy the client's investment future. Successful investing is doing more right things than wrong things over a long period of time.

Nevertheless, I go to the National Association of Realtors convention every November, and it shocks me that most of the real estate agents I talk to do not have any experience as investors. Second to this is the lack of education and understanding the mindset of an investor. It is my hope that if you the Realtor have read through this book I have helped to start you on the right road to understanding the investor mentality, which will also help you increase your commission in a tough, downward market. By having the ability to work with investors, your business will continue to flourish, no matter what your local market conditions are. Investors always buy. In other words, the realtor who has the *mindset* to be able to do both, be a realtor and an investor will most likely be successful. But, indeed, you can: learn how to partner with people, work the markets correctly, and develop strategic alliances with the right attorneys, CPAs, and financial planners. You are in a unique position, to be able to tap into properties before they hit MLS. For example, you can tap into an estate property more easily because when someone passes away, the attorneys handling the estate have a very strong need to sell that property, and the Realtor can buy properties out of probate and capitalize on such opportunities faster than individual, private investors.

Realtors can also find opportunities to work with corporations that are trying to sell relocation properties (which I'll cover in the next section of this chapter) before they list those properties, because the corporations just want to get those properties off their hands (and off their books!). Realtors also get opportunities to work with builders and land developers to acquire land that they can turn around and sell or hold for the long term, depending on their strategy. So a Realtor is in the best position to be able to capitalize on these opportunities as an investor. So unless someone is a full-time investor, out on the market, pounding the streets, and farming the chosen communities regularly, Realtors are going to be the first to find a deal and capitalize on it.

Finding Investment Opportunities through Relocation Companies

One strategy that very few real estate agent/investors use is investing in property that relocation companies make available to them to sell. Instead of *selling* the property, however, a Realtor could *buy* it as an investment. Major companies like Hewlett-Packard and IBM often transfer and relocate middle- and upper-level managers, and they not only pay for those executives' relocation costs, but also buy the homes they're moving out of. If you're the real estate agent handling that sale, you have an inside track on investing in the property yourself.

For example, the company I do consulting for here in California has just hired a chief operating officer. Larry is based in San Francisco right now, but he will be moving to another state, in the middle of November. In order to move, Larry needs to sell his house.

So, the first question Larry asked when he was negotiating his contract with the corporation was, "Are you willing to pay my Realtor fees in selling my house?" Of course, the company said, "No; we will put you up in a hotel where you will relocate for a determined period of time until you're able to sell your home and buy another one, but we need to set a finite timeline." The company gave him six months, during which time he will be living in the new area, on the company, which was a very generous offer for a small company. Larry has a major opportunity to sell his property in San Diego, for which he originally paid about $500,000, for $1.2 million. That's a huge profit that he can realize.

He feels very strongly that the best way to sell his San Diego property quickly is by working with a Realtor. Now, if the property is priced right, it should sell quickly. San Diego is one of the hotter U.S. real estate markets. If the price is below market value, this could be an opportunity for a Realtor to buy this property. If Larry can't sell his property by the end of November, the Realtor can offer to option the property and lease it out until he or she can sell it, and then the Realtor can make money on both the option and the sale of the property.

Realtors are in the best place to find the most investment opportunities because they are the first to see properties that are for sale.

The Realtor has a great opportunity here for the following reasons:

For Realtors Only: You Can Be Both an Agent and an Investor

- Larry has a lot of equity in his property.
- He needs to relocate.
- He doesn't want to leave his wife in San Diego when he moves.
- He's cannot afford to sit on his San Diego property forever or he will have that payment and either another mortgage or rental payment since he committed to relocate.

And the Realtor is right there, able to capitalize on an investment that has a lot of equity built into it. So although the seller is asking $1.2 million, if he doesn't have to pay the 6 percent real estate agent's commission, look what's shaved off the top: $72,000! If you were the Realtor/investor for that property, you would get the benefit of being able to invest in a property that meets your objectives—and you'd get it at a discount. That's the key thing for real estate agents to keep in mind if they're considering investing as well as being a Realtor.

So why aren't more Realtors taking the initiative and buying investment properties to increase their own portfolios, to compound their own wealth using rental property, or to turn around and hold a property for a short time and then resell it? As mentioned in Chapter 6, Realtors are in the best place to find the most investment opportunities because they are the first to see properties that are for sale—whether they're starter homes or, as in this case, higher-income executive homes.

Look at the possibilities that you, the Realtor, have to make money from a situation like Larry's:

- You could represent him: *sell* his house and earn a commission.
- You could *buy* the house as an investment at a discount because the guy needs to move. There's *motivation* there, and you, the Realtor, can capitalize on it before the property gets listed on an MLS and before any major commissions need to be paid.
- You could option the property from him and he could agree that you could sublease the property for a period of time until you either sell the option or find a tenant buyer.

These are three different ways to profit from a transaction. Realtors can easily be both agents and investors

As real estate agents, you also have other perks:

1. You can capitalize on a brand-new listing opportunity that is a good value before anyone else because you can get into the property today, before it hits the MLS computer system.
2. Caravan to view new property (a caravan is when Realtors working in a real estate office drive from one house to another to view new properties that have just been listed).
3. Nine out of ten corporate moves (i.e., corporate relocation properties) are sold through real estate companies. Get first dibs.

In 1998, I bought a property in an exclusive area that was for sale through a relocation company. From an investor's standpoint, I made a significant profit five years later. A successful real estate agent/investor could have also capitalized on this property because she was at the right place at the right time: she would have been able to buy it at a discount before it was available to the general public. Realtors know about properties that are on the marketplace very, very quickly by hearing about them through their network.

Most larger corporations go through a relocation (relo) firm, which is usually a real estate firm. For instance, HP works through Coldwell Banker (actually through Cendant, the parent company of Coldwell Banker/Century 21 and ERA realty company, although as of this writing, Cendant is breaking up; the relocation part of the business will be called Cartus).

Because most large companies work through relo firms, Realtors (or individual investors) who are looking for these investing opportunities should contact the relo company rather than contacting the client company directly. For example, you could call Hewlett-Packard to find out what relo company it uses and then tell the relo company what you're looking for. Contacting HP or IBM directly, however, would be a waste of time because large companies like these will not deal directly with Realtors; they most likely already have a contract with a relo company like Cendant.

If you are an investor who is trying to relocate to a new area or invest outside an area where you currently live, you should protect yourself from making poor investments in an area you're not familiar with by getting to know the area. One way to do this is to subscribe to the local newspaper or go on the paper's Web site to learn about local issues, read the real estate ads, and learn who the players are in that area.

Finding Investments by Working with Builders

Another way real estate agents can become investors is by working with builders. If a builder is putting up a condo complex and you get in on phase 1, you're already buying the condo as a *Realtor* working through the builders, but you're really an *investor* buying the condo with the intent of capitalizing on the opportunity and selling that project before phase 2 commences.

For example, Sheri is a Realtor in Nevada who does this, and it's all she does: that's her strategy. She has a real estate license only because she wants to be an investor. Sheri works with builders. When builders are just breaking ground and starting, there's a period of about a year to 18 months before the building is completed. Sheri comes in on phase 1, she puts a contract in on a property, and before that property is even completed, she has turned around and sold it to someone else, so she's making a profit. That profit is somewhere in the neighborhood of 10 to 20 percent of her down payment or her initial investment in that property. And that's Sheri's strategy: she's using her license to be able to work with a builder so that she can get that property at a discount because the builder is not yet ready to sell it to the general public. That's another strategy that Realtors can use to be investors.

Many Realtors **think** *that they cannot afford to be investors.*
They don't have the mentality to be investors;
they think of real estate as a commission-based job.
They are in the best postion.

Preconstruction is a big, big deal right now. Investors are pouring millions and millions of dollars into the preconstruction industry, and they're getting burned. Realtors who work as investors in this industry have the opportunity to see what the marketplace is going to do, and the ability to get statistical information that will help assess whether the opportunity is a good deal or not. And they can often (but not always) get first dibs: since they are getting the first introduction to the complex, they can get into a pre-construction deal at a lower price than the general public.

Realtors who are investing in preconstruction are banking on the fact that the property is going to increase in value over the long term, and that they can assign or sell the contract before the building is completed and therefore still make money from the deal. That's key, because if Realtors see that the market is turning, they're not going to want to invest their own money in it. Again, Realtors have the benefit of knowing what's happening in the market before the average individual investor does.

Improve the Way You Market Yourself to Expand Your Business

The real estate market has slowed. How do you stay alive and continue to build a successful real estate business? First, are you running your existing business like a business? Ask yourself these questions:

1. Why am I in real estate?
2. What is my goal, in dollars, over the next 90 days?
3. What will I need to do to accomplish that goal, starting now?
4. How much time can I realistically spend on promotion?

Checklist 12-1 lists some additional questions you should ask yourself in order to jump-start your brain on how to increase your business. The sections that follow explore the items in Checklist 12-1 in more detail.

E-blast your database with local news and tidbits about real estate that are relevant to your readers and are noteworthy.

Do Your Marketing

Having a marketing plan is like having a map. You have a starting point, and then you have the route that you need to take to reach your final destination outlined. The same is true of a marketing plan.

To hone your marketing plan, ask yourself questions like these:

For Realtors Only: You Can Be Both an Agent and an Investor

Checklist 12-1   Questions to Ask Yourself
So That You Can Increase Your Business

(*Hint:* The answer to all of the following questions should be a resounding yes! If the answer is not yes, that's where you need to focus your attention when the real estate market slows down.)

❏   Do you do marketing?

❏   Are you organized so that you can jump-start your business?

❏   Do you keep in touch with customers whom you have sold property to in the past?

❏   Do you have a marketing budget?

❏   Do you have a fresh Web page, with testimonials from past satisfied customers?

❏   Do you have a personal brochure that shows potential customers why they should use your services?

❏   Do you continually fill your pipeline by attending networking events such as Chamber of Commerce meetings or other professional women's organizations?

❏   Do you *stand out*? Does the community know who you are?

- Who is your customer? (Commercial, residential, land, investor, wholesaler? Be specific.)
- Are you a specialist, such as a CCIM (Certified Commercial Investment Member)? If so, put that down in your plan and focus on how you can market your specialty.
- What niche would you feel comfortable promoting? (The investor market, the rehabber, the first-time home buyer?)
- How much money do you think you can spend to market your business? (I'll discuss this in more detail in the discussion of your marketing budget.) How much did you earn in commissions in each of the past three years? Have your earnings increased or decreased?
- What are three things you can do right now to increase your business?

Checklist 12-2 offers some suggestions for things you can do now to start filling your pipeline with new customers and new business. Remember, you need to be different from everyone else, so no calendars with your name on them or football schedules, please! Be seen!

Checklist 12-2 New Marketing Ideas for Promoting Your Business

❏ E-blast your database with local news and tidbits about real estate that are relevant to your readers and are noteworthy. *Note:* Make sure that you have an "opt out" on the e-mail so that you are not spamming. Or, if you are a writer, create your own e-zine or blog, which is free.

❏ Update your photo, get new business cards made, add a byline or slogan that ties in with your personality to help you get remembered, and *be seen*. Talk to local radio stations and see if you can become the local real estate expert. Get on the air. Consider hosting your own radio talk show.

❏ Develop a "white paper" or special report, or go to your city or county and get statistics on the local economy, community, taxes, or other areas of interest. Attach a handwritten note to the materials with a "compliments of" card.

❏ Go to a local homeowners' association meeting in a neighborhood where people know you. Reintroduce yourself and find out what's new. Get to be the "Realtor of the Neighborhood."

Here's an example of someone who markets herself successfully. Katherine Munson has been a Realtor and owner of Lucas Valley Properties (LVP) in Marin County, California, for many years. This is a distinctive neighborhood where the homes were custom-designed and built in the 1960s. These are three or four-bedroom, two-bath houses with approximately 1,700 to 2,200 square feet—and they sell even in a slower market, for more than $1 million, in "as-is" condition. They are a hot commodity because of their unique architecture. Katherine is identified as the Realtor of Lucas Valley. She lives in Lucas Valley, and her daughter (who is also a Realtor) also lives in the neighborhood. Whenever people think about selling their homes, the Munsons are the first people they think of.

Sure, there are other Realtors who have sold property in Lucas Valley, a community of about 500 homes, but nine times out of ten, it is "Lucas Valley Properties" signage that you will see on a house for sale.

Put your Web site and e-mail address on all correspondence, and check your e-mail every day.

Get Organized

Even if you have an assistant, it pays to be organized. Consider hiring a professional organizer to arrange your office in a way that will save you time and help you offer outstanding customer service by having information at your fingertips. When you know where everything is, you can solve problems. Solving problems is what this job is all about.

What are some of the most common activities we all engage in in our personal lives? Go to the gym to work out? Go grocery shopping? Pay bills? Don't we make to-do lists so that we don't forget these things? Develop a checklist of task items and set aside a small percentage of your time each day to complete those to-dos.

Put your Web site and e-mail address on all correspondence, and check your e-mail every day. This will save you time because you will never miss a lead or follow-up opportunity. Even if your e-mail reply says, "I will get back to you tomorrow," that is better then not responding at all.

I once e-mailed and then called a Realtor in Reno, Nevada, to assist me with finding some commercial space. His name had been given to me by a professional referral source I knew in the area. I called him three times, and he never called back. I ended up e-mailing Magi Bird with Remcor Realty, who called me back the same day, set up a time for us to meet, and put me with the best agent she had (for the property type I was looking at). Magi got my business because of follow-up. It is a simple thing to do, but for some reason, most of us don't.

Keep in Touch with Past Customers

Tami Spaulding, of The Group Real Estate in Fort Collins, Colorado, is terrific at staying in touch. In addition to sending the usual birthday and anniversary cards (which include "happy anniversary of your home purchase"), she also sends mailings around different holidays—for example, she'll send a card with her dressed as a witch for Halloween or a turkey for Thanksgiving with a calendar of school closings and holiday gatherings on the same page. She loves to *be seen*. Good Realtors stay in touch. They're very good at making sure that you're not going to forget who they are. And those are key factors in making real estate agents successful.

What are some other ways of staying in touch?

Ask Your Previous Customers If They Would Take Part in a Short Survey. The information they give you could help increase your business. There is an excellent online survey from Zoomerang that is inexpensive to purchase. I have done several surveys using this online program, which is easy to use. The key is the questions you ask. You could also make this survey anonymous, so that people can be open and honest in their feedback.

In the real estate business, the majority of your business comes from referrals from your existing and previous clients.

I know two top Realtors who are partners that hold a New Year event every year. They invite 10 or 12 of their top clients to dinner and conduct a focus group to help them develop a plan for the next year. They asks clients questions and are open to honest feedback. They use the information to help them assess their strengths and weaknesses, build a better brand (them and their team) come up with new marketing and advertising ideas, improve retention and referral business, and look for ways to increase their business and how do a better job.

So, if you're a Realtor and you want to know how to offer better customer service, how to increase your listings, how to increase your closes, and how to make more commissions, doing a survey of your existing clients is a great way to find out. After all, in the real estate business, the majority of your business comes from referrals from your existing and previous clients. So, surveys, dinners, or some sort of focus group where you're able to assess what you've done right and what you could work on to be the best in the business gives you the information that will help you improve.

Use Phone Messaging Software.   There are software programs you can purchase that give you the ability to record a friendly message on a client's answering machine. The system can tell when the answering machine or voice mail picks up and automatically leaves a message. One successful ReMax agent I know in Kansas City uses this, along with e-letters, as his top marketing tool. One caution: research the "do not call" laws before doing this.

Use Direct Mail, Postcards, Fliers, Door Hangers, and Even Door-to-Door Sales, Bus Benches, Billboards...anything that gets your name out to the masses.   These are all part of building your business. Assess your past returns on the different types of marketing you have done. What I am encouraging you to do is promote your business.

The Web is a necessary tool in any business.
Recent studies show that more than two-thirds of potential buyers will do some research on the Net.

Set Your Marketing Budget

Develop a pro forma statement of all your expenses and income on a spreadsheet and include it in your plan so that you can view your financial picture and see if the numbers are realistic. You have to spend a little money to make money. You already have expenses associated with being in business. This marketing budget should pertain to new ideas to help you generate leads. Checklist 12-3 offers some suggestions.

Checklist 12-3   Ideas and Costs to Consider in Marketing Your Business

Idea:	Cost: (you need to research this)
❏ Buy a Web address (URL) that includes the community where you live in your address as an opportunity for new business. For example, mailto:lisa@marin.com or www.isellmarin.com.	
❏ Develop your own banner ad that you can use to hyperlink with others.	
❏ Have one marketing piece that you continually update to get people accustomed to receiving mail from you, reading about you, and seeing you. A simple postcard is sufficient. Postcards have a higher response rate than other marketing pieces if you do direct mail.	

Make your own unique list! Include mailmen in your list of possible referral sources!

Create a Web Site

The Web is a necessary tool in any business. Recent studies show that more than two-thirds of potential buyers will do some research on the Net. This is an excellent place to *be seen.*

If you have not developed a Web site as yet, and you want something unique and affordable, log onto www.elance.com or www.guru.com; here you will find contractors who specialize in ad copy, Web design, graphics, and other such areas. You can post the job you are looking for, and the respondent will come back with a price.

I just did this myself for a company I consult with that needed *fast* ad copy. The ideas my client received for graphics alone were worth the price we paid to get the copy that the company needed for a test project.

Don't forget to get a couple of testimonials. They need to be real and signed, or at least include the person's initials. Testimonials are gold.

Develop Your Personal Brochure

What do you leave with a prospect who has just met you at an open house or at the real estate office? What does this person know about you? Everyone has business cards. A personal brochure is like a letter from you to me (the prospect). It should include:

- A menu (and description) of your services
- Information on how you can help me
- Answers to frequently asked questions on real estate

The prospect needs to see the benefits of doing business with you. Checklist 12-4 offers a few suggestions for your brochure. You can make your brochure a mailer as well as a promotional piece. Again, make it unique.

Checklist 12-4   Suggestions for Developing Your Marketing Brochure

❏   Open with a question.

❏   Deliver a credibility statement.

❏   Spell out the benefits you can offer and reasons why your customers might need you.

❏   Tell the prospect what you do—and be specific.

❏   Include two commonly asked questions that you are an expert at answering.

❏   Include a "call to action" or next step.

❏   Offer a one-on-one consultation to help customers assess their needs.

❏   Make sure your Web address, e-mail address, cell phone number, picture, and other contact information are included on your brochure.

Network

Most women are excellent networkers. We can either talk or listen. When you are meeting people for the first time at a networking event or conference, you need to be aware of your goal for the event. It is to meet as many people who could be potential referral sources in the time period available. That said, if you meet exciting people, get their cards and arrange to follow up with them. Their goals are the same as yours, or else they would not be at the event.

Spend no longer than five minutes speaking with any new person. Maintain eye contact, and offer a firm handshake. Be careful to come across as being approachable, but not overly friendly. Also watch out for being perceived as a snob. Let me give you an example. As a marketing consultant, I have worked with CEOs of financial services companies. I was with a CEO at a national conference for his industry. He was looking to develop a relationship with a law firm that specialized in his business. There were several attorneys present. He got a name from another attendee and attempted to introduce himself to this attorney.

This woman could not be bothered. She said hello, but then she turned around and started talking to one of her other friends. He felt snubbed and ended up going with another firm—and so far, that firm has done work costing in excess of six figures. Imagine what might have happened if she had just taken a few minutes to introduce herself and find out what my CEO friend does and what his needs were. She might be six figures richer today.

When we are at meetings, we all get caught up with people we know. If we try to remain aware that the objective is more business, we can limit our socializing or do it outside of the networking event.

You never know whom you will meet at networking-type meetings. When I was new to California, I wanted to find two things: a good real estate agent who knew her stuff and a good mortgage broker or lender. I went to a local Chamber of Commerce meeting as a guest of another business owner. There I met Nancy, who works for Wells Fargo Bank. We exchanged pleasantries and cards. I moved on.

A few months later, I was attending the NAR convention in Orlando and stopped by the Wells Fargo booth. I started chatting with the person who was running the booth and asked if he knew Nancy. Not only did he know Nancy, but it turned out that she was among the top 10 loan originators in the Wells Fargo system.

Stay up to date on any changes in the real estate market, and be the first to report them. Contact your local newspaper and ask if you can write a column.

I called Nancy the week after I returned and arranged to meet her for lunch. I have worked with her ever since. She is a dynamo leader and a good person. In addition, she can move the lending process along faster than any broker I know. If I hadn't gone to that Chamber of Commerce meeting, I would never have met her.

Stand Out and Be Seen

Finally, Checklist 12-5 offers some suggestions for increasing your visibility in your community.

Checklist 12-5   Suggestions on How to Stand Out and Be Seen: Increasing Your Visibility in the Community

❏   Sponsor a walk for a charitable cause.

❏   Develop relationships with community leaders who have a large sphere of influence and can help your referral business.

❏   Attend investor club meetings, and offer to be speaker to this audience. A presentation on trends in the local marketplace would be useful.

❏   Do cooperative advertising with others, such as a title company or mortgage broker.

❏   Cosponsor a presentation being given by someone who is in a related industry to yours—for example, property management.

❏   Stay up to date on any changes in the real estate market, and be the first to report them.

- ❏ Contact your local newspaper and ask if you can write a column.

- ❏ Consider expanding your horizons by offering additional services.

- ❏ Reward a referral. The best gift I ever received on a referral was a day spa package. I never forgot it and have referred more business to this Realtor because "this was the only time I ever got a spa day as a referral gift." Find unique ways to reward your referrals.

Lindsey was new to real estate. Last year, she decided to give up her corporate job and get her real estate license. Now that the market in the areas where she lives has slowed down, Lindsey has decided to become a "design consultant," advising customers on home improvements both inside and out. She put an ad in her local paper and put up a Web site, and she has made a enough money over the last few months to cover all the costs of this new business, plus she just got a listing on a piece of property. Lindsey is a Realtor with a sideline that gets her referrals. She is also smart.

Conclusion

In this chapter, I have tried to outline creative solutions to help Realtors grow their business in a changing market. If you were in business when the market was down in the 1990s (or even earlier), you know that "only the strong survive." Take a chance, have some fun, and *be seen*.

13

Final Words of Wisdom: How to Be a *Successful* Real Estate Investor

This chapter wraps up the book by first reminding you that real estate is not the only way to invest and that you should diversify. I also recommend that you find a qualified team of professional advisors—and I provide you with the questions you should ask before hiring anyone for that team. Once you have those advisors, you should discuss with them whether you should buy property in your own name or through some type of business entity, and I'll describe the pros and cons of each. If you're serious about investing in real estate as a full-time business, I offer some suggestions on where to find additional information that will help you get started, what skills you should have before you start, and how to manage your risk. The chapter concludes with some final tips on how to be successful.

What I've tried to do in this book is provide a plan that any woman who's interested in investing in real estate as part of her portfolio can use. Obviously, you shouldn't invest *only* in real estate. Don't put all your eggs in one basket. As any financial professional will tell you, you should diversify, so real estate shouldn't be the only thing you do. You should also consider stocks, bonds, mutual funds, and CDs. If you're risk-averse and you want to get the highest rate on your CD, go to www.bankrate.com , which lists all the banks that give the best interest rates on checking accounts, money market accounts, and CDs.

There's a wonderful book I'd like to recommend called *The Richest Man in Babylon* by George Clason. I reread it every January. It's written like an Aesop's fable, so it's very easy reading, but there's a real message—and if you understand the book's message, you'll be successful not only in real estate but with your overall financial future.

To assume that you will become a multimillionaire as a real estate investor with no experience and no assistance is not reasonable.

Build a Team of Professional Advisors

Successful real estate investors have a team of professionals that they rely on. After all, you can't expect to know everything, so you should find the right advisors to help you. Yes, you'll have to pay them for their help—but the cost is worthwhile. Checklist 13-1 lists the advisors you should have on your team. My point is that you cannot do everything yourself. To assume that you will become a multimillionaire as a real estate investor with no experience and no assistance is not reasonable. You will need the help, so find the right professionals to guide you.

To find the best professionals who will be able to help you, ask each one a few key questions. These questions will help you determine whether you feel comfortable with each person, whether that person is sufficiently knowledgeable, and whether that person is going to be a good fit for you and your needs.

Questions to Ask before You Hire an Attorney

The following questions address the things you need to know about your attorney.

Final Words of Wisdom

Checklist 13-1   Professional Advisors
You Should Have on Your Team

❏ *A good attorney* who can review your leases and purchase contracts, provide you with solid contracts that you'll be safe with, and keep you up to date on any changes in the laws of your state.

❏ *A CPA or an accounting firm,* or at least a bookkeeper to manage your books for you. As mentioned in Chapter 9, there are a lot of tax shelters in real estate, such as depreciation, and good accountants know how to do the work necessary to take advantage of these. Many people think they can just buy Turbo Tax or some other tax software program and handle their accounting themselves; there are also many rent-specific software programs that you can use. But in the end, it's actually less expensive to have an accounting professional review your books once a year to make sure that you're straight.

❏ *A property manager,* if you decide to buy property and keep it for the long term and don't want the hassles of managing the properties yourself. Please reread Chapter 8 before you make this decision.

❏ *Real estate agents,* if you decide to work with them to help you find property and provide you with analysis that will help you buy property at a decent price.

❏ *A good contractor,* if you're going to get involved in rehabbing (see Chapter 5 for more information on how to find, interview, and hire good contractors).

"What Is Your Specialty?"   Obviously, you would ideally like to deal with an attorney who specializes in real estate. However, if you decide to buy property through a business entity (e.g., an LLC, which I'll describe in more detail in the next section), you may want to deal with a *business* attorney. Therefore, you need to base that decision on how you're going to conduct your real estate operations. Is real estate a business for you, or is it an investment? That will help you determine which type of attorney to go with.

"Do You Yourself Invest in Real Estate?"   If the attorney does, he or she will probably have a lot of empathy and a good understanding of what you're trying to do, and may even be able to give you some suggestions on how to protect yourself and your investments down the road. However, personal experience investing in real estate is a "nice-to-have" rather than a "need-to-have" requirement. It just helps to work with somebody who understands real estate investing.

"How Many of Your Clients Currently Invest in Real Estate?" If your attorney already has clients who invest in real estate, he or she will be familiar with the issues involved. For example, that attorney will know what kind of clauses to use in contracts to protect you, and you'll feel more comfortable with an attorney who understands what you're trying to do.

The accountant you hire should know the current rules regarding income tax in your particular state . . . and be up to date on any proposed tax law changes.

When I first moved to California, I wanted to buy property. I went to an attorney because I was interested in buying the property through an LLC. Unfortunately, this attorney was not at all knowledgeable about real estate. It turned out that he was an estate attorney, which would have been helpful if I had wanted to create an estate plan to protect my assets, but he was not confident in real estate law. I needed to learn about legal issues pertaining to: buying property through an LLC or a land trust. (I'll describe these later in this chapter.) Therefore, I had to find *another* attorney who had real estate law experience before I could purchase the property. It is important to have knowledgeable professionals in place before you buy.

From an investor perspective, you need to know how to protect yourself during the transaction. Could the seller of the property change her mind, and if so, what happens? In other words, ask the attorney what he or she would recommend that you look out for. Therefore, if the laws change in the state, the attorney should be up to date on the laws that apply to real estate investors.

Questions to Ask before You Hire an Accountant

First, you should ask questions similar to the ones that you asked your attorney. In addition, the following are other questions that you should ask an accountant before you include him or her on your team of advisors.

"Are You Aware of the Tax Incentives That Are Available for Investors?"

A related question is, "What do I need to do to get the maximum tax benefit from the real estate that I currently own?" These are important questions—in fact, you're almost testing the accountant to see how sophisticated he or she really is. The accountant you hire should know the current rules regarding income tax in your particular state, as well as other types of taxes, and be up to date on any proposed tax law changes. For example, Hawaii has an excise tax, so that when you buy anything—whether it's a service or a product, from getting your hair done to having a home built—you need to pay a 4 percent excise tax. Your accountant must know about such taxes, as he or she should be helping to protect you in situations that you may not have been aware could arise. You need to know that you are doing the proper accounting from a tax-sheltering/depreciation standpoint.

"How Can I Create Tax Credits in Addition to Tax Deductions?"

The CPA or accountant you are working with should be able to answer this question easily.

Questions You Should Ask Property Managers

Chapter 8 covered this topic in detail, but let's review the essentials here. If you're going to hire a property manager so that you don't have to be an active landlord to your tenants, you want to ask the following:

- "What is your property management fee?" Also (again, as described in Chapter 8), you want to make sure that the property manager doesn't add any type of lease-renewal fee on top of his or her property management fee.

- "How will you find potential tenants, and how will you find the right qualified tenant?"
- "What kind of lease do you use?"
- "Are you willing to use my lease?"
- "Do you increase rents every year?"
- "How many properties do you manage?"

Answers to these questions should give you a good overall assessment of your property manager.

Questions You Should Ask a Real Estate Agent

If you decide to work with a real estate agent to help you find properties to invest in, you want to first make sure that the Realtor's license is in good standing. Call the Department of Real Estate for the state you are buying property in or the state licensing agency; they have different names in different states. Make sure that the Realtor doesn't have any complaints against him or her through the Better Business Bureau. You want to make sure that the Realtor is reputable.

Besides asking typical questions such as whether or not the real estate agent invests in real estate for him- or herself, you should also ask:

1. "How do you spot a good deal?"
2. "What are the top three suggestions you would recommend in order to get the top sales price?"

Before you work with any contractor, you should get a formal bid in writing from that contractor. Don't agree to start work without a written agreement.

Information You Should Get about Contractors before You Hire Them

As with Realtors, you should check a contractor's licenses, whether any complaints have been lodged against him or her, and his or her reputation in the community. In addition, before you work with any contractor, you should get a formal bid in writing from that contractor. Don't agree to start work without a written agreement.

Here's a recent example—which fortunately was fairly minor, but there are many examples I could cite that were much more serious (refer back to Chapter 5, as well). One of my rental properties had a problem with its sprinkler, so I called somebody who was well recommended. One Friday, I stayed home waiting for this person to come because he would not come unless there was somebody there. He showed up, but he couldn't stay more than 10 minutes and said he'd be back on Monday. I was out of town on Monday, so I didn't know that he didn't show up. He did call me on Thursday—I was still out of town—and promised to come again on the next Wednesday. Clearly, he is not reliable—if I have a major problem, there's no way I'm going to hire this person.

Renee Falgout offers simple but good advice on how to ensure that you're working with a good contractor:

Ask friends and family for referrals. Check contractors' licenses with local regulatory agencies for longevity and authenticity and also with the Better Business Bureau for complaints. Most of this can be done online. Plumbers, electricians, carpenters, and tradesmen are often rated by local consumer organizations. Always, always ask for and check references. Women can be very shrewd when interviewing potential contractors.

Working with Women Only

If you're more comfortable working with other women, there are women's chapters within most professional associations or unions and there are agencies specifically for women, but they may not be active or they may not be well marketed. The National Association of Realtors has a separate association, the Women's Council of Realtors (WCR). The same applies in the financial planning industry and the accounting profession. To find them when you are building your network, start by calling your local Chamber of Commerce, and see whom it can recommend.

Talk to Your Advisors about Investing via an LLC or a Land Trust

One of the first topics you'll probably want to discuss with your attorney and your accountant is, "What is the best *entity* to use when buying real estate?" You have several options:

- You can buy real estate in *your name personally*.
- You can buy real estate via a *corporation*, whether that's an incorporated business or a limited liability company (LLC).
- You can buy property through what's called a land trust. In some states, buying through a land trust is very popular; people use it to minimize litigation by hiding their true ownership. In other words, the actual owner or beneficiary of the trust is not recorded; instead, what is recorded in the courthouse is only the name of the trust itself.

If you're going to buy real estate through a business entity, you should consult with your financial advisors before you set it up, because the benefits may vary in different states.

Most investors who buy property through a land trust do so to preserve their anonymity and privacy, because only the name of the trust is recorded in the public record, not your personal name. People generally will use land trusts when they don't want their name revealed in the courthouse records.

However, I want to caution readers: *land trusts are not the only tool, and in some states, land trusts may not be the best entity for you to use.* You really do need to check with your attorney before setting up a trust.

If you're going to buy real estate through a business entity, you should consult with your financial advisors before you set it up.

For example, in California, a land trust is a popular vehicle for protection, but in some states (including Colorado, for instance), it's not because the trust can be pierced, which means that even though the name of the buyer of a property is the name of the trust, anyone can go through the courthouse records and find out who actually owns the trust. Thus, it doesn't make any sense to buy through a land trust in Colorado (or any other state with similar laws), but only an attorney would know this.

The other very popular structure is an LLC, a corporation that you set up; you are a managing member of that corporation, and you use that corporation to buy real estate. Therefore, from the time you put the purchase contract in the LLC, the real estate is in the name of your corporation, which (like the land trust) protects your privacy and gives you anonymity. People who are trying to find out who owns your property won't find *your* name; instead, they'll find only the name of the LLC. Even though you're a managing director of the LLC, that information is generally not recorded in courthouse records.

The LLC and the land trust are two very popular structures that real estate investors use. They try to avoid using their personal names to avoid any potential liability.

To protect yourself further, you could also carry umbrella insurance, over and above the limits that you have on your homeowner's insurance as the landlord or the owner. Umbrella insurance is a cheap way to protect yourself should you have a trip and fall (i.e., a person getting hurt on your property): the umbrella kicks in over and above your basic insurance plan. You might want to do this in case there's a problem where somebody gets hurt on your property and that person sues you as a result, even if it wasn't your fault. Such insurance can also protect you in your dealings with contractors (which is another reason why you want to make sure that contractors you deal with are currently licensed and are in good standing): if something happens on your property and the contractor takes some sort of action against you, you definitely want to be protected.

One final word of caution on this topic: there are people who teach about and offer to structure LLCs and land trusts. Be very careful about considering these offers instead of working with your team of professional advisors. Yes, you can go online and get an LLC for $99 instead of paying your attorney to set it up. I also know of one person who teaches a course and sets up land trusts for $150. But if you decide to go this route, keep in mind that *you get what you pay for*. Who would you talk to if there were a problem with a property that you purchased in a land trust? The company that sold you the trust documents for $150? Will it be there to support you if you needed it? The answer is no.

And you'll find out what these methods truly cost you when the IRS reviews your books. If you don't file your income tax returns properly or you don't disclose everything that needs to be disclosed on your income tax return, and the IRS thinks you are trying to get away with something, you can count on an audit. I knew this couple who listed their Rolex watches as company timepieces on their tax return and took a business deduction; not a good idea. I strongly recommend that you get proper legal advice before you start structuring deals on your own so that you're titling your properties correctly. My own personal opinion is that it's worth paying for good legal advice. I certainly don't encourage readers to go out and just start buying without knowing what they're doing.

If You Decide to Invest in Real Estate as a Business

If you decide you want to look at real estate as a business, there are several really good Web sites that can help you set up your business, get loans, and do your taxes:

1. www.sbs.gov. This is the Small Business Administration's Web site. If you need a loan for a business, need information on how to structure your business, or you want good, thorough ideas on writing a business plan, this is a helpful site.
2. www.quickbooks.com. This site can help you get started in your accounting, recordkeeping, and bookkeeping if you want to do your own accounting.
3. www.smallbusiness.com.

These sites are primarily used by real estate investors who want to rehab property, flip property, or get ordinary income and make a living out of doing real estate as a business.

Don't just go gung-ho and start buying property if you have no money saved; you should have at least enough saved to cover all of your immediate expenses.

In this particular real estate marketplace, you need to make that decision for yourself. If you're just getting started, I recommend that you not go into real estate as a business until you really understand what you're doing, and you feel that you really have a good grasp of how to buy property and make a profit on it.

If you do decide to invest in real estate as a business, you've got to have financial reserves. There are different recommendations about this, but I believe you need to have saved a year's worth of living expenses if you're going to try to do this on a full-time basis. Some people say six months' worth; much more conservative people say two years' worth. If you can't start making a profit within a year and you keep getting yourself in a negative situation, then the handwriting is on the wall and this type of investing is not for you. If, however, you have some financial reserves, a little bit of a cushion, then your living expenses will be covered and you'll be able to sleep at night. Don't just go gung-ho and start buying property if you have no money saved; you should have at least enough saved to cover all of your immediate expenses.

Also, this goes back to what I discussed in Chapter 2 concerning your financial goals and investment objectives. As mentioned, in my experience, I've found that the key personality trait of people who are successful in real estate—especially women who are successful investors—is the orderly and well-organized way that they conduct their business on a daily basis. Successful real estate investors are disciplined, and they follow up; these are the key values.

Try not to think of real estate in an emotional way; instead, try to think of it only in financial terms. Walk away from a property if the deal makes no sense on paper.

Here's what you need to do to be successful at investing in real estate as a business:

- Make sure, at the completion of the transaction, that you've crossed all the Ts and that you are confident that everything was done correctly and that you legally own the property.

- Be decisive and be able to react quickly. You need to be able to make decisions when you have to, even if the decision's a mistake. That type of decisive behavior is very important. It will keep you focused on your objectives. Also, because you have an outcome for the property in mind, you will easily be able to handle unexpected issues.
- Have strong managerial skills. You need to make sure you feel comfortable about managing a process—which could be anything from overseeing the transaction to overseeing a contractor.
- Have good communication skills. These are important in real estate investing because you're going to be constantly talking with different people: sellers, bankers, contractors, buyers. You need to ask questions, have good communication and face-to-face dealings, and feel that you're contributing to the process, because when you do, other people feel that you're competent.
- Finally, be a little thick-skinned. You need to realize that sometimes deals will not go your way, so you mustn't take rejection personally. Try not to think of real estate in an emotional way; instead, try to think of it only in financial terms. Walk away from a property if the deal makes no sense on paper from the get-go. Do not make any exceptions to that rule.

How to Manage Your Risk

To manage—and hopefully reduce—the financial risk when you invest in real estate, follow these suggestions.

Buy at the Lowest Price You Can.   Obviously, you should try to buy property at below market value, if at all possible. For example, do not buy a property at its asking price; remember, the asking price is the seller's first offer. Practice negotiations skills.

Buy Properties That You Can Improve.   Make the largest profit you can through your own sweat equity. Simple cosmetic fix-ups can bring you a great return (as described in detail in Chapter 10). The simpler, the better; the less money you spend, the better.

Final Words of Wisdom

Buy Rental Properties Where the Seller Has Charged Below-Market Rents.

If you decide to buy property for the long term, and you're going to lease that property, try to buy properties with rents that are below market now so that you can raise the rent in a short period of time—e.g., within 6 to 12 months—and therefore start making more money on that rental.

Buy Properties with the Lowest-Interest Fixed-Rate Loan Financing That You Can Get.

I *strongly* recommend that you get a fixed-rate loan. *Don't* do adjustable-rate mortgages (ARMs) in this environment: they're too risky, because the rate is more likely to adjust *upward*, and you may find that you can no longer afford the interest on your loans.

Look for Properties in Up-and-Coming Neighborhoods.

Look for neighborhoods that at one time you wouldn't have set foot in—perhaps it was a high-traffic area, or a high-crime area, or an industrial area—but that are now being gentrified. Look for communities where older properties are being torn down and new properties are being built. If you can buy in those areas *at the right time*—because timing is everything—you can do very well.

Ellie, an investor from Kansas City, got involved with the local government and bought blocks of real estate with single-family homes that had problems. The city was threatening to have these buildings condemned: they were dilapidated and uninhabitable, and they were in neighborhoods that at one point nobody would have set foot in. The local government sold the properties to Ellie for pennies on the dollar, because no one else wanted them.

Ellie loves doing rehabs; she has a small firm to do them. She obtained financing from investor funds, which she used to fix up these properties. It took her about six months to complete the rehab. She then turned around and resold the properties to owner-occupants for a nice profit. Her investors put their money into these deals but got paid back only when she sold the property. Therefore, Ellie herself didn't have to make any payments, which helped her cash flow. Most of her investors not only got their money back but also received a piece of the profit for putting up their investment dollars. Ellie's risk was minimal. She bought only in areas that she knew, and she had worked with investors in the past and expected to use her expertise to make a very nice profit for herself and her investors.

**Don't *do adjustable rate mortgages (ARMs)
in this environment: they're too risky.***

Ellie has just moved to St. Louis, and she's been so successful at this type of rehab that she's already made arrangements with the local government there to do the same thing. She has a proven track record. Gentrifying neighborhoods can be a really good investment opportunity if you're comfortable with that situation.

Consider Investing in Section 8 Properties.   If you want guaranteed income from the federal government, then you should consider government-type rentals, such as Section 8 (see Chapter 8 for details). The rental income is guaranteed by the government (which subsidizes the tenants living in those rentals), though not necessarily by the tenants themselves. This is a real estate investing strategy to keep in mind if you're risk-averse (as many people are). You want to make sure you're comfortable with this type of investment *before* you get involved with government housing.

Don't Drown in Mortgage Payments.   If you have large mortgage payments and you're breaking even on the rent from your tenants, you need to sell that property, bring in a money partner, or do something else to lower your mortgage payment. Don't stay in a situation where you're "upside down," or negative, especially if this is causing you to have sleepless nights worrying about your finances. There are almost always solutions to real estate woes. You've just got to think through your problem, seek advice from a good mentor, join a local real estate investors' association, and learn how to solve the problem.

Final Tips on How to Be Successful

What makes a property a great investment is obviously a good return on that investment, but your due diligence and *what you do* as an investor is also critical to your success in real estate investing. I believe that many women are very sophisticated about real estate. We can pick it up very easily. I've described dozens of examples in this book, and there are countless more—but you have to create your own story. You have to be able to do what's necessary to make *you* successful, because your goals and objectives are different from somebody else's.

In this book, I have tried to give you the essential smarts that you need in order to at least look at a situation and assess each opportunity. Also, as mentioned, keep in mind that there are other ways to invest (e.g., stocks, bonds, mutual funds, and CDs) if you decide that real estate isn't right for you after all. It's better to find that out now, after reading this book, than to invest your hard-earned money in a property that doesn't bring you a good return—or that you lose money on. You need to do your due diligence to search out the best investment for you. I strongly believe that many women can do this successfully. So here are a few final words of advice.

Get your feet wet, do a couple of deals. . . .
Don't quit your day job.

Trust Your Instincts When Evaluating a Property

You need to trust yourself and your instincts when you're looking at a property as a potential investment. Consider your own financial picture and your own goals, and trust your gut. If real estate investing in general, or some property in particular, is not for you, *don't do it*. Many books written by experts will say, "Anybody can do this, and you're going to make $20 million in one year doing ABC." However, real estate investing—whatever type you're doing, whether you're considering buying actual property, buying cash flows, buying notes, making loans, or buying leases—is not for everybody. *You really need to take your time to assess if this is really right for you.*

It's better to read this book, do some research, and investigate the opportunity; then if you don't like it, if you decide you don't want to pursue real estate investing, or if you realize that it's something that you don't have the time, commitment, or energy for, then don't do it. You can always invest in a real estate investment trust (REIT), which will still give you better returns and dividends than the typical money market account or CD. A REIT is a portfolio of real estate, like a mutual fund of properties, and you receive an overall dividend from investing in the REIT. In other words, you can still be actively involved in real estate but not actually physically own any property, if you elect not to. Real estate is a great investment, it's a great way to diversify your financial portfolio, but *it's not necessarily for everyone*.

Make Sure You're Financially Secure before You Invest in Anything

Take it one step at a time. As mentioned earlier in this chapter, you need to have a reserve of living expenses for emergencies. Do not just decide, "I'm going to do this, and real estate investing is going to become my life's mission." Instead, get your feet wet, do a couple of deals, and see how much money or capital you end up earning and whether you were able to achieve your desired outcome. *Don't quit your day job*. I can't emphasize that enough. I've met too many people who have quit their jobs so that they could devote themselves full-time to real estate investing, and who have ended up getting stuck.

Get started slowly, take your time, and take the conservative approach. By doing your real estate business while you're still employed, you'll have a guaranteed income and the stability of your career or other business to fall back on.

Keep the "Rule of 72" in Mind When Planning Your Investments

Ideally, everybody wants to buy low and sell high; this is the basic law of investing. There's another law of finance, however, that most investors do not take into consideration but all of us should. It's the rule of 72, which is how to calculate and compound your wealth. The rule of 72 says that 72 divided by your rate of return is the number of years it will take for your money to double. For example:

- If you're currently earning 4 percent on a CD, you have to wait 18 years to double your investment. If you buy a $10,000 CD at 4 percent interest, in 18 years, that CD will be worth $20,000, because 72 divided by 4 (percent interest) is 18 (years).
- If you invest in something at 6 percent interest, you'll double your investment in 12 years (72 divided by 6 = 12).
- And if you invest at 8 percent interest, your investment will double in 9 years (72 divided by 8 = 9).

The rule of 72 is a very valuable guideline that every investor should know, no matter what you're investing in (real estate, the stock market, or something else).

To apply the rule of 72 to real estate investments, you need to know the rate of return you're earning on your investment properties, and admittedly, that's not always easy to calculate. In general, real estate gives you a higher return than other investments: The highest interest rate that you can get, at the time of this writing, on a money market account or a CD is 5 to 5.5 percent. Compare this to real estate: even in today's market, if you buy property right and hold it for the long term, you should make more than a 5 percent return.

My point in describing the rule of 72 is that you should keep in mind that compounding is *money making money*. For example, suppose your tenants' rent payments are helping you make the mortgage payments on your property. If that money sat in an account and accumulated over time, it would compound and make money on money. In addition, that return is going to compound faster, and your equity in the property will grow, through appreciation of the property itself. There will be more money in the long run.

That's the beauty of real estate: . . . it offers
appreciation, income, . . .cash flow, and . . .
the opportunity to make a profit.

Of course, if the market turns and goes south, just like the stock market, you lose that money, at least on paper. Many investors tend to forget that part; they say, "Oh, the rules don't apply to me. I can double my money in eight years," but they forget that if the market drops, then they won't be making what they thought they were going to make. It's just like Enron and WorldCom: most of their employees had invested all their money in those companies, and when both companies went out of business, those employees lost their entire pensions and their entire retirement savings. Therefore, you need to be aware that nothing's etched in stone. There are no guarantees in life, financially or otherwise.

Also, most people know that the earlier you begin investing, the more money you can accumulate. Financial publications are always encouraging people to start saving and investing when they're in their twenties because of *the time value of money*. A dollar today is more valuable than a dollar 30 years from now, but if you allow that dollar to compound, you're going to make a lot more money 30 years down the road.

---

*Buying and selling properties is a wonderful,
exciting, interesting (and sometimes dismaying)
business and investing opportunity.*

And that's the beauty of real estate: your investment is not totally liquid if you're going to buy and hold. That investment can be liquidated, of course, but it's not like having cash in the bank today. Instead, your money is being "forced" into a "savings plan" of sorts (i.e., the property you're investing in). So if you are not a good saver and you invest in real estate, you can accumulate wealth in an asset that, sometime down the road, you can sell for a profit. You have a built-in savings plan. That's the beauty of real estate: it offers appreciation, income, the opportunity to generate cash flow, and obviously the opportunity to make a profit.

Be Fair in All Your Real Estate Deals;
Look for Win-Win Situations with Sellers

Don't be greedy. Be fair. Try to create a win-win situation when you're negotiating, so that the property owners you buy from will feel that you've brought value to them and are going to feel good about doing business with you.

And Have Fun!

Finally, whether you invest in real estate as a business or as just another investment vehicle—i.e., whether you decide to do it part-time or full-time or even just occasionally—have fun with it. Buying and selling properties is a wonderful, exciting, interesting (and sometimes dismaying) business and investing opportunity. Personally, I don't look at my real estate investing as a business; instead, I look at it as my ticket to retirement. I can accumulate enough property, with my tenants paying off the mortgage so it is free and clear, so that I'll have monthly income when I retire. I'm not counting on social security or my children to take care of me. I've got to be able to have monthly income at some point, so that when I am no longer working, I can count on living off the income my properties generate and being able to have the lifestyle I want in my retirement.

Conclusion: Control Your Own Financial Destiny

Many women take their talents and skills for granted. Older women especially get to a point where they don't think they have the ability to be successful at either running a business or being an investor. That's absolutely not true. But because many women believe that, they tend to put their money in somebody else's hands, much more so than a younger woman or a man would.

Never let somebody else control your money. Assume that *you* are responsible for you. Take control and start managing your future today, and make yourself proud. You cannot depend on even your spouse to be successful. Your spouse could die tomorrow; then what would you do? Take the chance on you. Look at investments as opportunities to grow your own wealth, and also to have something that you can fall back on.

You can become a real estate "butterfly" by believing in yourself and doing what is necessary to set yourself free, whatever that term means to you. Many women today are succeeding in investing and in business: there are countless newspaper and magazine articles that describe various women's successes. The key is to *take control of your financial future* and to not only manage it, but grow it with investments that you know, understand, and can manage, so that you are in the driver's seat. Also, consider joining a women's professional organization, where members support one another in owning and running businesses and in investing.

I strongly encourage *you* to get started. Don't let this book become just another volume on the bookshelf. Exercise caution when getting started, but don't become paralyzed. Continue to educate yourself further so that you'll feel comfortable, but at some stage, you gotta get out there and get moving.

Don't borrow, borrow, borrow and leverage when you're just getting started. Instead, go slowly; form a pattern or a pace that you feel comfortable with. You will either fall in love with this type of investment choice or not. If you take it slowly, you won't get in too deep in the beginning. Again, *don't* just jump in if you don't know what you're doing. I don't recommend that you start out by doing preconstruction deals, because they can be complicated and risky. Instead, grow your investment portfolio slowly, just as you would anything else.

Take advantage of what's being given to you in this book. Reread it. Think about all the different examples from different women who have started with nothing and have made successes of themselves by investing in real estate. Then go for it—but do it right, manage your risk, and feel comfortable within yourself. Investing in real estate can help you realize your dreams and live the lifestyle you want to live.

Appendix A

Recommended Resources

Professional Real Estate Associations

- Department of Real Estate in your state capital
- National Association of Realtors: www.realtor.com
- National Association of Residential Property Managers: www.narpm.org
- National Real Estate Investors Association (NREIA): www.nreia.org
- State chapters of the NREIA
- Women's Council of Realtors

Useful Web Sites

For general information when you're looking to buy a home, whether it's an investment property or an owner-occupied home, check out the following sites:

- www.realtor.com. This is the National Association of Realtors Web site, which is considered the number one site for Realtors.

- www.nreia.org. The National Real Estate Investors Association Web site has a map of the United States; if you click on where you live, you'll find the name of your local real estate investors association. Some areas have multiple real estate investors associations. Join *today*; you can get a lot of knowledge from these associations, for free.
- www.homebuyingabout.com. This site can give you a little more educational information on the ins and outs of home buying. It is especially useful for someone who wants to buy a property as an owner-occupant; it does not go into depth about buying property as an investor.
- www.creonline.com. The Web site of Creative Real Estate online provides articles that people have written about real estate.
- www.realestatelink.net. This site also provides articles about real estate. Both this and www.creonline.com allow you to ask questions on discussion forums pertaining to the specific area in which you're interested in investing, and people will answer your questions.

To get a copy of your credit report, which will include your FICO score, you can contact any or all of the three largest credit-reporting agencies:

- Equifax: www.eqifax.com.
- TransUnion: www.transunion.com.
- Experian: www.experian.com.

To help you research your target market, the following Web sites will show you what has sold in the last 90 days in the area that you're looking to farm:

- www.HomeRadar.com
- www.domaina.com

To find discount "for sale by owner" properties, check out the following sites:

- buyerowner.com
- propertysites.com

To find property by placing your own ad on the Internet, check out

- www.craigslist.org. This site has branches throughout the United States (and internationally), and it's a great online advertising mechanism that many people use to advertise for everything from cars to furniture to real estate.

To learn more about managing rental property yourself, check out

- www.narpn.org. This is the National Association of Rental Property Managers Web site; it offers professional courses and seminars and a community of people who are owners of single-family homes or small residential properties.

To get good recommendations for property managers, contact the following Web sites:

- www.naahq.org. This is the Web site of the National Apartment Association, which has chapters in just about every local area.
- www.azama.org/iroc. This is the site of the Arizona Multihousing Authority's Independent Rental Owners Council; see if the area you are interested in has its own independent rental owners' council similar to this one in Arizona.

For help in developing a Web site to market your real estate business, log onto

- www.elance.com.
- www.guru.com. At both these sites, you will find contractors who specialize in ad copy, Web design, graphics, and other such areas. You can post the job you are looking for, and the respondent will come back with a price.

For help in setting up a real estate business, getting loans, and answering questions about taxes, go to

- www.sba.gov. The Small Business Administration's Web site; it is helpful if you need a loan for a business, information on how to structure your business, or good, thorough ideas on writing a business plan.

- www.quickbooks.com. This site can help you set up your record-keeping and bookkeeping, if you want to do your own accounting.
- www.smallbusiness.com.

For information on foreclosure properties, go to

- www.dataquick.com. This Web site collects listings of individuals who are in default on properties around the country. There is a fee to use this service, but once you pay the fee, you are allowed 250 searches a month.

For information on buying property through your IRA or 401(k), go to

- www.theentrustgroup.com. This is the Web site of The Entrust Group, which is the nation's largest administrator of truly self-directed individual retirement accounts.

Books on Real Estate and Success in General

How to Invest in Real Estate and Pay Little or No Taxes: Use Tax-Smart Loopholes to Boost Your Profits by 40%, by Hubert Bromma. McGraw-Hill, paperback, 2004.

Dare to Win, by Jack Canfield and Mark Victor Hansen. Berkeley, paperback, 1996.

The Richest Man in Babylon, by George Clason. Signet, paperback, 2002.

Grow Rich! with Peace of Mind, by Napoleon Hill. Ballantine, paperback, 1996.

Think and Grow Rich, by Napoleon Hill. Aventine Press, paperback, 2004.

Buying Real Estate Foreclosures, by Melissa S. Kollen-Rice. McGraw-Hill, paperback, 2003. A good book that includes updated sample forms and documents.

Investing in Real Estate with Lease Options and Subject To Deals: Powerful Strategies for Getting More when You Sell and Paying Less when You Buy, by Wendy Patton. John Wiley & Sons, paperback, 2005. Wendy Patton has been a real estate broker and investor since 1985; she has bought and sold more than 600 properties.

Deals on Wheels: How to Buy, Sell, and Finance Used Mobile Homes for Big Profits and Cash Flow, by Lonnie Scruggs. Dow Enterprises, 2002.

The Wisdom of Florence Scovel Shinn, by Florence Scovel Shinn. Fireside, paperback, 1989.

Newsletters on Discounted Notes

Noteworthy

The Paper Source

Both of these newsletters provide an enormous amount of information about the cash flow industry and buying notes at a discount. They are investor-based newsletters. In the back of each, there are ads for institutional buyers of paper, which you can contact if you're interested in buying and selling notes.

Appendix B

Background on the Women Interviewed for This Book

Magi Bird is the president of Remcor Real Estate, where she is also a broker. She is the founder of Remcor Educational Systems, an instructor for the National Council of Exchangors (a group of people who do 1031 exchanges), and a life member of *Who's Who in Creative Real Estate*. Her training programs teach new Realtors the sophisticated art of exchanges and equity conversions; she also teaches portfolio development and aggressive capital growth techniques to experienced Realtors, investment counselors, and financial planners. She is a member of Toastmasters International and ATM Gold, a frequent public speaker, and the author of the "Creative Corner" column.

Jennifer Dizmang has been a real estate investor since 1992. She has invested in many types of real estate, including buying water rights on land. She has worked for several elite firms in the financial services industry for 12 years, serving as financial advisor to more than 1,000 clients. She is also an entrepreneur who consults in many arenas and a professional speaker on investing in real estate within retirement plans, such as self-directed 401(k)s and IRAs. She is a former vice president of equity funds for a New York City–based venture capital firm, and she served as a director on the advisory board for a Boston-based start-up company.

Renee A. Falgout is the president of Windsor Capital Mortgage Corp. in Palm Harbor, Florida. She has seven years' experience in real estate, mostly as operations manager of a central Florida mortgage company. She is an expert on investor loans and works with builders and private investors nationwide.

Rebecca McLean is the executive director of the National Real Estate Investors Association. She has been in the rental business for her entire career: her family owned rental property along with their other businesses to provide long-term security. She is also the executive director of the National Apartment Association.

Anna Mills has been a Realtor with Century 21 in Ohio and Michigan for more than 30 years. She is past president of the Ohio Real Estate Investors Association (OREIA) and the National Real Estate Investors Association (NREIA), and she is currently serving her tenth term as local president of the Toledo REIA. Early in her career, Anna became a builder and an investor and started acquiring properties with no money down. She currently holds seven professional real estate and contractor's licenses, including the skilled trades of plumbing, heating, and electrical contractor. She coauthored the *Landlord Tenant Handbook*, teaches landlord workshops, and cohosts two radio call-in shows: *House Calls and DIY: Do-It-Yourself Real Estate Investing*. In 2003, Century 21 gave Anna awards for pure volume in number of listings, sales, and satisfied customers, and in 2005, the company gave her an award her for achieving more than $1.7 million in listings and sales.

Barbara O'Connell has had extensive experience as an investor, developer, real estate agent, project manager, property manager, and consultant and seminar leader in many aspects of both commercial and residential real es-

Background on the Women Interviewed for This Book

tate since the mid 1980s. She has been president of Wise Investments Inc., a real estate development and investment company, since 1990. She is also the managing member of Pueblo Home Development Co., LLC, a local real estate developer in Pueblo, Colorado, that develops raw land into residential subdivisions, builds high-end custom homes, and invests in strategic commercial and residential real estate holdings. Barbara also owns and manages an extensive portfolio of individual homes throughout the United States and in other countries. She has taught seminars on equity sharing and lease options as well as been a consultant to individual clients on these topics and many others.

Jaime Raskulinecz is a CPM and a New Jersey–licensed real estate broker. Since 1994, she has been a principal and founder of a third-party property management firm that manages subsidized rentals, market rentals, community associations, cooperatives, and small commercial properties. She has been a real estate investor for 20 years. She is also a principal of Entrust Northeast, LLC, an independently owned and operated office and part of the Entrust Group, an administrator of self-directed retirement plans.

Tracy Z. Rewey runs and co-owns Diversified Investment Services, Inc., a successful note investment company, and has handled millions of dollars in real estate and note investments since 1985. She is one of the nation's top 10 note buyers. Tracy specializes in the use of tax-deferred retirement funds to purchase both notes and real estate, and she is an approved instructor for continuing-education classes on the subject. She is also a frequent speaker at investment groups, and she has written a series of hands-on manuals on buying and brokering real estate notes.

Tami Spaulding has been a Realtor for 26 years. For 18 of those years, she has sold real estate; during the 8 years before that, she worked for Stewart Title as bookkeeper, closer, sales rep, and branch manager.

Dorrliss Cisy Ware is a broker/associate and a residential property manager who has been working in real estate since 1997; she received her broker's license in 1999, and has been in property management since 2001. She serves on several committees on the local and state level for the NAR, the Women's Council of Realtors, and the National Association of Residential Property Managers.

Index

Accountant, 305
Acknowledgments, vii. *See also* individual interviewees
Adjustable-rate mortgage (ARM), 208–211
Administrator, 235
Advisors. *See* Professional advisors
Air fresheners, 253
Appraisal fee, 65
Appreciation rates, 78
ARM, 208–211
Assignability clause, 160
Attack dogs, 181
Attention to detail, 4–5
Attorney, 161, 182, 302–305, 310
Author's contact information, vii

Bank
    best loans, 216
    due diligence, 219
    fees, 220, 221
    mortgage. *See* Mortgage
    questions to ask, 217–218
    REOs, 280
    what they want from you, 218–220
Bank fees, 220, 221
Basement, 257–258
Bathrooms, 98, 257
Bird, Magi, 16, 54, 86, 118, 119, 124, 154, 263, 284, 327
Bird dog, 129
Body language, 145
Borrowing. *See* Financing
Borrowing from relatives, 40–41
Bromma, Hubert, vii
Bromma's contact information, vii
Buying right, 69–70, 241

Caravan, 288
Carpet, 245

Index

Cartus, 288
Cell phone, 145
Cendant, 288
Charges/fees, 65
    bank fees, 220, 221
    home inspection, 99–100
    property manager, 37, 191–192
    rehabbing, 99
City planner's office, 79
Clason, George, 302
Cleanliness of property, 246
Closing costs, 99
Closing time, 153–154
Coldwell Banker, 288
Commercial property, 62
Compounding (money), 316–318
Condition of home, 147–148
Conforming loan, 208–209
Contingency clauses, 158–163
Contract, 158–163
Contractor, 108–112, 306–307
Conventional financing, 215–217
Corporate relocation properties,
    285–289
Cosmetic improvements, 105
Costs. *See* Charges/fees
Countrywide, 216
Courage, 23
Credit card, 33, 34
Credit rating/credit history, 30–36
Credit reporting agencies, 31
Current listings, 77
Custodian, 235–236

Deals On Wheels (Scruggs), 53
Deck addition, 98
Deferred payments, 212
Discount FSBO sites, 83
Discounted notes, 227–231, 325
Discounted rent, 173, 181
Diversification, 12
Dizmang, Jennifer, 14, 86, 125,
    327–328
Do-it-yourself renovation, 107–108

Do-it-yourself staging, 247–248
Down market, 259–282
    cautionary note, 261–264
    foreclosure. *See* Foreclosure
    lease option. *See* Lease option
    second-lien holders, 280–282
    short sales, 272–274. *See also*
        Foreclosure
    "subject to" sales, 271–272
Due diligence, 129. *See also*
    Research
    bank, 219
    before closing, 153–155
    foreclosure, 66
    importance, 76
    interviewees' comments, 57
    property manager, 191
Due-on-sale clause, 271

E-mail agreement, 111
Economic outlook, 81
Enron, 318
Entrust Group, 235, 236
Escrow account, 155, 158, 206
Eviction, 186, 187–188
Expired listings of properties, 77
Eye contact, 144

Fairness, 139–140, 318–319
Falgout, Renee, 15, 30, 34, 96, 154,
    178, 205, 206, 210, 214,
    216–217, 220, 307, 328
Farming an area, 46, 73, 84, 89–90
Fax agreement, 111
Fear, 13
FICO score, 31–32, 35
Financial comfort level, 29
Financial considerations, 25–46
    credit rating/credit history, 30–36
    FICO score, 31–32, 35
    financial comfort level, 29
    financial goals and objectives,
        27–29
    financing. *See* Financing

Index

goals for prospective property, 36–37, 38

questions to ask, 26

Financial goals and objectives, 27–29

Financial planner, 18–20

Financial Planning Association, 19

Financing, 37–44

    1031 exchange, 231–233

    assemble financial documentation, 43–44

    bank. *See* Bank

    borrowing from relatives, 40–41

    control your own financial destiny, 319–320

    conventional, 215–217

    custodian, 235–236

    discounted notes, 227–231

    hard-money lenders, 41–43

    line of credit, 220–221

    mortgage. *See* Mortgage

    owner, 69–71, 142, 222–223, 224–227

    owner *vs*. non-owner-occupied property, 221

    pension/IRA funds, 39–40, 233–236

    private invvestors, 41–43, 224–227

    schools of thought, 204

    tax benefits, 231–236

Finding investing opportunities. *See* Identifying investing opportunities

First impression, 146–147

Fixed-income tenants, 194

Fixer-upper. *See* Rehabbing

Flexibility, 137

Fliers, 248–251

Flipping, 95–96

Floor registeres, 244–245

Following up, 127, 145–146

For sale by owner companies, 248

For sale by owner (FSBO) sites, 82–83

Foreclosure, 65–66

    auction, 278–280

    back payments, 275–277

    cash requirement, 277

    cautionary note, 261–264

    due diligence, 66

    emotional attachment, 279

    government-owned, 274

    guidelines, 282

    Internet, 274, 277

    pending legislation, 276–277

    preparation, 277–280

    property sold "as is," 275

    redemption rights, 277

    REOs, 280

    when to act, 273–274

Foreclosure auction, 278–280

401(k) plan, 233–236

FSBO sites, 82–83

Full-time realtor, 126

Full-time realtors, 126

Fun, 319

Gentrifying neighborhood, 102–104, 313–314

Getting started, 311

Handshaking, 144

Hard-money lenders, 41–43, 107

Hard-money loan, 214

Heat grate, 244–245

HELOC, 212

Hewlett-Packard, 286

Home equity line of credit (HELOC), 212

Home inspection, 99–100

    clause in contract, as, 158

    fee, 99–100

    lead paint, 155

    mold, 155–156

    small, minor problems, 163

    types, 148

Homeowner's insurance, 207

Index

IBM, 286
Identifying investing opportunities
  foreclosure, 65–66. *See also*
    Foreclosure
  looking for properties, 82–84
  open house, 67–68. *See also* Open
    house
  probate, 66–67
  relocation companies, 67
  tips (checklist), 68–69
  when to look, 85–89
Imagination, 22
Individual retirement account (IRA),
  233–236
Information sources. *See* Resources
Initial rent payment, 181
Inspection. *See* Home inspection
Instincts, 315
Insurance, 200, 207, 309
Interest, 206
Interest-only mortgage, 211–212
International markets, 63
Internet. *See also* Web sites/Web page
  cautionary note, 69
  foreclosure, 274, 277
  looking for property, 82–83
  mortgage notes, 229
  motivated sellers, 141
  research target market, 82
Interruptions, 145
Interviewees, 327–330
*Investing in Real Estate with Lease
  Options and Subject-To Deals:
  Powerful Strategies for Getting
  More When You Sell and
  Paying Less When You Buy*
  (Patton), 264
Investing strategy, 48–49. *See also*
  Type of property
IRA, 233–236

Jumbo loan, 208

Kitchens, 98, 257

Land, 58
Land trust, 308–309
Landlord and tenant. *See* Rental
  property
Lawyer, 161, 182, 302–305, 310
Lead paint, 155
Leading indicators, 75
Lease, 182–183, 201. *See also* Term
  of lease
Lease option, 35–36, 264–271
  assign, 268–269
  benefits of, 266–269
  cautionary note, 261–264
  where to find them, 269–271
Leverage, 71, 204
LIBOR, 211
Light switches, 245
Limited liability company (LLC),
  308–310
Line of credit, 220–221
Listening, 1–4
Loan-to-value (LTV), 221
Loans. *See* Financing
Location, 104–105. *See also*
  Neighborhood
Long-term investing. *See* Rental
  property
Looking for properties, 82–84
Lots (subdivision), 57–62
LTV, 221

Male domination, 9–10
Marginal neighborhood, 52
Marketing flier, 250–251
Master bedrooms, 98
McLean, Rebecca, 15, 57, 117, 262,
  328
Mills, Anna, 11, 18, 86, 117, 119, 120,
  153, 262, 284, 328
MLS, 116
Mobile home, 52–53, 64
Mold, 155–156
Moren Bromma's contact information,
  vii

Index

Mortgage, 203–214
  ARM, 208–211
  broker, 213–214
  cautionary note, 314
  fixed-rate, 209, 210
  HELOC, 212
  interest-only, 211–212
  neg-am, 212
  PITI, 205–207
  prepayment penalty, 207–208
  second, 280–282
  tax benefits, 203, 231–236
  terminology, 207–209
  wrap-around, 223–224
Mortgage broker, 213–214
Mortgage insurance, 220
Mortgage loan default rates, 81
Mortgage notes, 227–231
Motivated seller, 131–133, 137–138
Multiple listing service (MLS), 116
Multiple residential properties, 29–30
Munson, Katherine, 292–293
Mystery shoppers, 168

NAFA, 19
Napier, Jim, 20
NAR, 116
National Association of Fee-Only
    Planners (NAFA), 19
National Association of Realtors
    (NAR), 116
Negative-amortization (neg-am)
    mortgage, 212
Negotiation, 131–162
  basic principles, 151
  body language, 145
  build rapport with seller, 133–137
  cell phone, 145
  condition of home, 147–148
  defensive, hostile sellers, 148–149
  eye contact, 144
  fairness, 139–140
  finding motivated sellers, 140–142
  first impression, 146–147

  flexibility, 137
  follow up, 145–146
  get seller to talk, 133–137, 143
  handshaking, 144
  have financing in place, 215
  interruptions, 145
  making other comfortable,
      144–152
  motivated seller, 131–133,
      137–138
  open-ended questions, 133, 134,
      136, 149
  personal attire, 146
  positive note, 162
  preapproval letter, 161
  professionalism, 146
  questions to ask, 143
  real estate agents, 126–127
  seller objections, 149–151
  smokers, 148
  tone of voice, 145
  when things don't work out, 162
  when to walk away, 151–152
Neighborhood. *See also* Farming an
    area
  gentrifying, 102–104, 313–314
  marginal, 52
  undervalued, 103
Network
  finding motivated sellers, 142
  real estate agents, 127
  realtors, 294–295, 298–299
New-home construction, 7, 80
New neighborhoods, 78–79
New subdivision, 57–62
Newspapers
  looking for property, 82
  motivated sellers, 141, 142
  placing an ad, 83–84
  read local paper, 89
Non-owner-occupied property, 221
Nonconforming loan, 208
Nonportfolio lenders, 216, 218
Nonrecourse loan, 235

Index

Note business, 227–231
Noteworthy, 230, 325

O'Connell, Barbara, 17, 58–62, 85, 87, 161, 204, 284, 328–329
On-the-spot financial decisions, 23
One-age fliers, 248–249, 251
One-on-one financial guidance, 19
1 percent rule, 72
Online activities. *See* Internet; Web sites/Web page
Open-ended questions, 133, 134, 136, 149
Open house, 67–68
    finding tenants, 174
    selling the property, 250–253
    source of information, as, 90–91
    tenants, 251–253
    why go?, 84
Option agreement. *See* Lease option
Oral agreement, 111
Organization
    buying, 70
    foreclosure, 277–278
    real estate agent, 293
    trait of successful investor, as, 22–23
Origination fee, 65, 221
Out-of-state owners, 101, 141–142
Over-55/fixed-income tenants, 194
Owner financing, 69–71, 142, 222–223, 224–227

Paneling, 245
Paper Source, The, 230, 325
Patton, Wendy, 264
Pay attention, 89–91
Persistence, 22, 68
Personal attire, 146
Pets, 173–174, 180–181
PITI, 205–207
Planned developments, 78–79
Portfolio lenders, 218
Positive note, 162

Potpourri, 253
Preapproval letter, 161
Preconstruction property, 53–57, 64, 289–290
Preforeclosure, 66, 273, 276
Prepayment penalty, 207–208
Presentation to seller, 128
Prices of existing homes, 76–80
Principal, 206
Principal, interest, taxes, and insurance (PITI), 205–207
Principal residence, 230
Private financing/investors, 41–43, 224–227
Probate, 66–67
Professional advisors, 302–307
    accountant, 305
    contractor, 108–112, 306–307
    financial planner, 18–20
    lawyer, 161, 182, 302–305, 310
    property managers. *See* Property managers
    real estate agents. *See* Real estate agents
Professional real estate associations, 321
Professionalism, 146
Property management. *See* Rental property
Property management fee, 37, 191–192
Property managers, 189–198
    fee, 191–192
    finding one, 192–193
    lease option, 270–271
    over-55/fixed-income tenants, 194
    questions to ask, 189–192, 305–306
    should you hire a manager?, 196–198
    source of information, as, 90, 141, 270–271
    student tenants, 193–194
    what they do, 194–196

Index

Property taxes, 199–200, 206
Property types. *See* Type of property
Purchase agreement (contract),
 158–163

Qualified intermediary (QI), 232

Raskulinecz, Jaime, 14, 54, 86, 117,
 119, 120, 154, 165, 329
Raw land, 58
Reader. *See* Women
Real estate agents, 115–130, 283–300
 bird dog, 129
 buyers, as, 283–290
 commission, 118–120
 complaints, 121–123
 different properties, different
  realtors, 130
 evaluating, 120–129
 full-time realtor, 126
 growing their business, 290–300
 ideal sequence of events, 127–128
 interviewees' comments, 116–118,
  124–125
 keeps you up-to-date, 127–128
 marketing, 290–296
 negotiation skills, 126–127
 network, 127
 networking, 294–295, 298–299
 past experience, 120–121
 personal marketing brochure, 297
 presentation to seller, 128
 questions to ask, 306
 real estate investors, as, 283–290
 reference checks, 121
 selling your property, 239–240
 stand out and be *see*n, 299–300
 understands your goals, 124–125
 Web page, 296–297
 women, 10–11
Real estate golden rule. *See* Due
 diligence
Real estate investment trust (REIT),
 316

Real estate notes, 227–231
Real estate owned (REO) foreclosures,
 280
Recording fee, 65
Redemption period, 277
Redemption rights, 277
Rehabbing, 96–113
 best types of renovations, 98
 budget, 105
 cash flow, 105
 contractor, 108–112
 cosmetic improvements, 105
 costs, 98, 99
 do-it-yourself renovation,
  107–108
 finding properties, 100–102, 108
 gentrifying neighborhood,
  102–104
 objective for each type of property,
  112–113
REIT, 316
Relocation companies, 67, 285–289
Relocations, 132
Renovation. *See* Rehabbing
Rental property, 163–202
 advantages/disadvantages,
  170–172
 after renting, infom rejected
  applicants, 179–180
 applicant's credit history, 177–179
 application fee, 176
 application for rental, 176, 177
 assessing whether to buy,
  169–170
 database of interested prospective
  tenants, 180
 discounted rent, 173, 181
 do-it-yourself landlord, 188–189
 do little extras for tenant, 186
 eviction, 186, 187–188
 finding properties, 169
 finding tenants, 172–186
 friends as tenants, 200–201
 how long to rent, 174

Index

Rental property *(continued)*
  improving property to maximize
    rents, 198–199
  initial rental payment, 181
  inspect property with new tenant,
    184–185
  key to property, 184
  know the law, 201
  late fee (rental payment late), 181
  lease, 182–183, 201
  maintain the property, 186–187
  meet with new tenant, 180–181
  minor repairs, 183
  non-payment of rent, 188
  open houses, 174
  over-55/fixed-income tenants, 194
  partial rental payments, 201–202
  pets, 173–174, 180–181
  property managers. *See* Property
    managers
  property taxes, 199–200
  rent for less, 173, 181, 202
  section 8 properties, 167–168
  security deposit, 174, 181
  selling the property, 251–253
  student tenants, 193–194
  tenant's suitability to property in
    question, 179
  term of lease, 174–175, 183
  utility bills, 171
  variety of rental areas, 202
  verify who's going to live there,
    182–183
  why people rent, 164, 166–167
  you as agent for property, 183
Rental survey, 36
REOs, 280
Reputation, 37
Research, 5–7, 75–91
  appreciation rates, 78
  current listings, 77
  due diligence. *See* Due diligence
  economic outlook, 81
  expired listings of properties, 77

  Internet, 82
  leading indicators, 75
  lease, 79–80
  new-home construction, 80
  new/planned developments, 78–79
  prices of existing homes, 76–80
  rate of foreclosure/mortgage
    defaults, 80–81
  sold property data, 77
  vacancy rates on rentals, 79
Resourcefulness, 22
Resources
  books, 324–325
  newsletters on discounted notes,
    325
  professional real estate associa-
    tions, 321
  Web sites, 321–324
Retirement communities, 50–52
Rewey, Tracy, 16, 48, 118, 120, 153,
  262, 329
Richest Man in Babylon, The
  (Clason), 302
Risk taking, 23
Roth IRA, 234, 235
Rule of 72, 316–317

Scruggs, Lonnie, 53
Second-lien holders, 280–282
Second mortgage, 280–282
Section 8 properties, 167–168
Secured loan, 217
Security deposit, 174, 181
Self-confidence, 22
Self-directed retirement funds,
  233–236
Seller-financed notes, 227–231
Seller financing, 224–227
Seller objections, 149–151
Selling, 239–258
  advertising the property, 248–249
  cleanliness of property, 246
  do-it-yourself staging, 247–248
  marketing flier, 250–251

Index

one-age fliers, 248–249, 251
open house, 250–253
realtors, 240–241
staging the property, 242–248, 253–258
tenants, 251–253
Web page, 249
what do buyers want, 241–242
when to sell, 239–240
SERVPRO, 148
Shaking hands, 144
Short sales, 272–274. *See also* Foreclosure
Short-term investment strategies, 93–114
conclusion/checklist, 113–114
flipping, 95–96
rehabbing, 96–113. *See also* Rehabbing
Single-family homes, 49
Sinkhole, 100
Smokers, 148
Sold property data, 77
Sources of information. *See* Resources
Spaulding, Tami, 14, 48, 117, 119, 124, 127, 129, 153, 165, 294, 329
Staging the property, 242–248, 253–258
Starting up the business, 311
Straight loan, 207
Student tenants, 193–194
Subdivision, 57–62
"Subject to" clauses, 158–163
"Subject to" sales, 271–272
Subprime lending, 214
Successful business, what to do, 311–320
Successful investors, traits, 22–23

Tax returns, 44
Taxes
1031 exchange, 71–72, 231–233

financing, 231–236
mortgage, 203, 231–236
property, 199–200, 206
1031 exchange, 71–72, 231–233
Tenancy in common (TIC), 19
Term loan, 207
Term of lease, 174–175, 183
Third-party administrator, 235
TIC, 19
Time commitment, 44–45
Time for closing, 153–154
Time value of money, 227, 318
Title insurance, 156–158
To do list, 4
Tone of voice, 145
Type of property, 47–73
commercial property, 62
international markets, 63
marginal neighborhood, 52
mobile home, 52–53, 64
objective viewpoint, 64
preconstruction property, 53–57, 64
retirement communities, 50–52
single-family homes, 49
subdivision, 57–62
urban real estate, 49–50

Umbrella insurance, 309
Undervalued neighborhood., 103. *See also* Gentrifying neighborhood
Unsecured loan, 217
Urban real estate, 49–50
Usury laws, 230
Utility bills, 171

Vacant properties, 141
Volatile market. *See* Down market

Ware, Dorrliss Cisy, 15, 174, 194, 202, 329–330
WCR, 116
Web sites/Web page. *See also* Internet; individual Web sites

Index

Web sites/Web page *(continued)*
 realtors, 296–297
 reference list, 321–324
 selling the property, 249
 setting up businesses, 310
When to look for investment properties, 85–89
Win-win situation, 318–319
Window blinds, 244
Women
 attention to detail, 4–5
 listening, 1–4
 nonthreatening, as, 8–9
 real estate agents, as, 10–11
 real estate license, 130
 researchers, as, 5–6
 special chapters in professional
 associations, 307
 start-up businesses, 12
 why so few investors, 13–18
Women Council of Realtors (WCR),
 116
WorldCom, 318
Wrap-around mortgage, 223–224
Written contract, 111–112
www.azama.org/iroc, 323
www.bankrate.com, 302

www.buyerowner.com, 83, 322
www.craigslist.org, 83, 323
www.creonline.com, 322
www.dataquick.com, 277, 324
www.domain.com, 82, 322
www.elance.com, 296, 323
www.guru.com, 296, 323
www.homebuyingabout.com, 83,
 322
www.HomeRadar.com, 82, 322
www.naahq.org, 323
www.narpn.org, 323
www.nreia.org, 322
www.propertysites.com, 83, 322
www.quickbooks.com, 310, 324
www.realestatelink.net, 322
www.realtor.com, 83, 321
www.sba.gov, 323
www.sbs.gov, 310
www.smallbusiness.com, 310, 324
www.theentrustgroup.com, 324

You. *See* Women
You make money when you buy,
 69–70, 241

Zoomerang, 294

About the Author

LISA MOREN BROMMA is a successful real estate consultant with an investment portfolio worth millions of dollars. She has taught more than 1,000 real estate, private mortgage, and marketing workshops and is also a board member of the National Real Estate Investors Association.